THE NA

THE NABOB AT HOME

[*Frontispiece*

THE NABOBS

A Study of the Social Life of the English in Eighteenth Century India

PERCIVAL SPEAR

DELHI
OXFORD UNIVERSITY PRESS
CALCUTTA CHENNAI MUMBAI
1998

Oxford University Press, Great Clarendon Street, Oxford OX2 6DP

Oxford New York
Athens Auckland Bangkok Calcutta
Cape Town Chennai Dar es Salaam Delhi
Florence Hong Kong Istanbul Karachi
Kuala Lumpur Madrid Melbourne Mexico City
Mumbai Nairobi Paris Singapore
Taipei Tokyo Toronto

and associates in

Berlin Ibadan

First published in Oxford India Paperbacks 1998

ISBN 0 19 564381 X

Printed at Pauls Press, New Delhi 100 020
and published by Manzar Khan, Oxford University Press
YMCA Library Building, Jai Singh Road, New Delhi 110 001

PREFACE

The object of this essay is to treat the social life of the English in eighteenth century India as a connected whole, to trace and account for the various phases of its development. While several studies of various localities and different portions of the period exist, no attempt, so far as I am aware, has yet been made to treat the subject as a whole.

In thus taking a broad survey of the whole century I have tried to lay comparatively less stress on the picturesque and eccentric sides of Anglo-Indian life, a side which has already been sufficiently exploited and which will long continue to provide a fund of diverting anecdote to any writer who will read a few contemporary travel books. Instead I have tried to distinguish the different phases of the settlement life, and to trace a logical connexion between them. So I have sought to describe, not a series of brilliant and fantastic episodes, but everyday life as lived by everyday men. If this should result in a loss of dramatic quality it should also bring a more real understanding of the period.

Apart from these general considerations, the special interest of the period is that it witnesses the transition from isolated commercial factory life to a vigorous settlement life, when each station was a small English city in itself. This period of social transition has a further importance in that many of the problems of racial relations in India had their rise at this time.

The sources for this subject are large and widely spread. The difficulty has lain, not in the paucity of material, but in the lack of any certain source of information. Nearly all the information provided by records, travellers' reports and diarists, is given only incidentally to some larger subject, with the consequence that the investigator finds himself often vainly tapping the most apparently obvious authorities, and occasionally stumbling upon rich mines of information in quite unexpected places.

The first and most obvious source has been the published records or selections from records of the India Office, like C. R. Wilson's *Early Annals of the English in Bengal*, and H. D. Love's

Vestiges of Old Madras. These are chiefly based on the Public Consultations, the Letters to and Despatches from the Directors.

Next come the Company's Records themselves. The Despatches and Letters Received, proved to be mines of occasional information. From about 1730 the general records become more and more purely commercial and political, and the subsidiary records are more useful. The series of Wills, which begins in Calcutta about 1730, has some interesting information. The Series of Bengal Inventories, which extends from 1755 to 1780 throws much valuable light on European customs and ways of living, and the ' Europeans in India ' series is invaluable for the criminal section of the later settlement population. Most valuable and uncertain of all, perhaps, are the various Miscellaneous series, the Home and the Factory Miscellaneous Series in London, and the Home Miscellaneous Series in Calcutta.

After the records themselves come letters and diaries. Many of these, like Mrs. Fay's *Letters from India* and William Hickey's *Memoirs* have been published, and many others exist in manuscript in libraries and private collections. Finally come books of travel. They vary a great deal in authority, and have always to be treated with caution. Some, however, like those of Thomas Ovington and Charles Lockyer, are of outstanding merit. A list of works consulted will be found at the end of the volume.

With regard to Indian names, the modern spelling has been used everywhere except in the case of quotations when the original spelling has been retained, and in the case of such words as ' Moghul ', ' Lucknow ', or ' Cawnpore ', which may now be regarded as having been naturalised into the language.

The word ' Anglo-Indian ' has been used in the sense of an Englishman resident in India, and the word ' Eurasian ' has been retained for those who are now officially known as Anglo-Indians. In the first case the current eighteenth century usage is followed to save possible confusion in the case of quotations ; while the second word is adopted as comprehending the Indo-French and Indo-Portuguese or ' Luso-Indians ' as well as the Anglo-Indians proper.

For the general reader, who may desire some historical background to the period, a sketch of the political history of 18th century India has been added. It will be found as Appendix A on p. 175.

In conclusion I would express my deep debt of gratitude to Mr. W. A. J. Archbold, whose constant interest, kindly counsel and friendly encouragement made this book possible, and the preparation of it a pleasure. I also owe grateful thanks to Professor H. H. Dodwell for his interest and his advice on a number of difficult points, to Mr. C. B. Young, of St. Stephen's College, Delhi, who not only read over the whole in manuscript, but also spent many hours in de-orientalising its grammar, to my colleagues of the History department of St. Stephen's, Mr. R. S. Capron, Mr. K. M. Sarkar, and Mr. I. H. Qureshi, whose cheerful and ungrudging acceptance of extra burdens rendered the completion of the work possible, and to many other friends whose sympathy, advice and forbearance have lightened and sweetened my task.

T.G.P.S.

CONTENTS

ILLUSTRATIONS

(Reproduced by kind permission of the Librarian of the India Office and of the British Museum Authorities)

Facing page

CHAPTER I

THE EARLY SETTLEMENTS TO 1750

THE study of English life in India in the eighteenth century is of interest from two points of view. First the settlements themselves underwent during the century a striking transformation. From small collections of traders and seamen they developed into large settlements, each with a vigorous corporate life and a subsidiary life of isolation and adventure in the provinces; from communities based entirely on trade, a sort of exiled union of commercial travellers, they became imperial cities largely made up of soldiers, and completely imbued with a military and imperial spirit. At the beginning the soldiers wished their swords were pens, that they might make money more easily; at the end, as is well known, the clerks turned their pens into swords, while merchants converted their bank balances into coronets. During the century, the transformation was steadily going on, which, aided by the large influx of short term royal soldiers in the middle of the period, and by mature politicians, scholars and traders in the latter half, wrought before its close a complete revolution in the habits, numbers and outlook of the settlements. Governor Thomas Pitt and Lord Wellesley, men of a similar masterful temper, well sum up this difference. The climax of the former's career was the acquisition of the Pitt diamond, which laid the foundation of the Pitt family's fortunes in the eighteenth century; of Wellesley's the virtual establishment of British supremacy by the defeat of the Marathas.

The second point of interest is the effect on the English settlers of a distant and alien environment, of a complicated civilization with few points of contact with their own. Traditionally endowed with national pride from the time of the Venetian ambassador who reported that 'whenever they see a handsome foreigner they say that he looks like an Englishman', how would they react to the pride of the Moghuls, or be later affected by the heady wine of political and military power? Would there be absorption, as in the case of the Portuguese, or real intermixture, or a rigidly oil and water relation? The position, at first simple owing to the isolation of both settlers and Indians from outside influence, became later complicated by two factors—the increasing contact of England with India and the influx from Europe of many purely temporary residents, and the discovery of the superiority of European military science over Indian methods of warfare. All problems of cultural contacts, racial relationships and political adjustments, which have since puzzled Indians and English alike, had their rise during this period and had taken recognizable shape by the year 1800.

At the opening of the century English society was confined to the four main settlements of Madras (Fort St. George), Calcutta (Fort William), Surat and Bombay. In only one of these, Bombay, did they enjoy full political sovereignty, and that settlement, ravaged as it was by disease, by war and internal dissension, showed no sign of its future greatness. Of the others, Calcutta had recently been founded (1690) by Job Charnock in the midst of a disastrous war with the Moghuls ; Surat was suffering from the ravages of the interminable Maratha war ; and Madras, under the wary guidance of the ex-interloper Thomas Pitt, was embarrassed equally by the Marathas, who had just been dislodged from the fortress of Gingi after a siege of eight years, and by the mingled threats and civilities of the Moghul general Da'ud Khan. Nor were the English the only Europeans in the field. They were only one of many rivals, all competing for the India trade, all equally ready to over-reach each other, all equally dependent on Indian governmental favour. Madras was balanced by Pondicherry, Negapatam and Tranquebar,[1] and Calcutta by French Chandernagore, Dutch Chinsura and Danish Serampore ;[2] the Dutch held Ceylon and the Portuguese Goa, and the Imperial Ostend Company also appeared on the scene for a time.[3] In the older centres of trade like Masulipatam, Murshidabad and Surat the chief nations of Europe outwitted and intrigued against each other as if they had never left Europe. The merchants still lived in collegiate settlements, desiring only peace in their time, very respectful to the aged autocrat Aurungzeb, and continually apprehensive of the provincial Moghul governors. They were intensely jealous of outside interference and regarded interloping as the deadly sin ; but they had not escaped dissension amongst themselves, and to the seizure of Bombay by Keigwin and the troubles of the Child régime were now added the rivalry of the old and new companies.[4] The actual conditions of the settlements are fortunately described for us by three singularly accurate and intelligent travellers, who all visited India about the beginning of the century—the interloper Alexander Hamilton,[5] the chaplain Ovington and the trader Lockyer. Captain Hamilton, the first of these, combined a nautical love of a story and a not unnatural indignation against the East India Company's distaste for ' interloping '—' though the conscript fathers of the Colony disagree in many points among themselves, yet they all agree in oppressing strangers ',[6] he ruefully remarks,—with a faculty of accurate observation and clear description. He thus describes the new-founded settlement of Calcutta.

> The English settled there about the year 1690, and after the Moghul had pardoned all the Robberies and Murders committed on his Subjects, Mr. Job Charnock, being then the Company's agent in Bengal, he had liberty to settle an Emporium in any part of the River's side below Hughly, and for the sake of a large shady tree chose that place, tho' he could not have chosen a more unhealthful place on all the River; for three miles to the North Eastward is a saltwater lake that overflows in September and October and then prodigious numbers of fish resort thither, but in November and December, when the floods are dissipated these fishes are left dry and with their putrefaction affect the air with thick stinking vapours, which the North-East Winds bring with them to Fort William, that they cause a yearly Mortality. Fort William was built an irregular Tetraon [*sic*] of brick and mortar called *Puckah,* which is a composition of Brick-dust, Lime Molasses and cut Hemp and is as hard as and tougher than firm Stone or Brick, and the Town was built without Order as the Builders thought most convenient for their own Affairs, everyone taking in what Ground most pleased them for Gardening so that in most houses you must pass through a Garden into the House, the English building near the River's Side and the Natives within Land . . . About fifty yards from Fort William stands the Church built by the pious Charity of Merchants residing there . . .
>
> The Governor's house in the Fort is the most regular Piece of architecture that I ever saw in India. And there are many convenient Lodgings for Factors and Writers within the Fort and some storehouses for the Company's Goods and the Magazines for their Ammunition. The Company has a pretty good Hospital at Calcutta, where many go in to undergo the Penance of Physick but few come out to give account of its Operation. The Company has also a pretty good garden that furnishes the Governor's Table with Herbage and Fruits; and some Fish-ponds to serve his kitchen with good Carp, Calkrop and Mullet. . . . In Calcutta all religions are freely tolerated but the Presbyterian, and that they browbeat. The Pagans carry their Idols in Procession thro' the Town, the Roman Catholics have their Church to lodge their Idols in and the Mohamedan is not discountenanced; but there are no Polemicks, except what

are between our High-Church Men and our Low or between the Governor's party and other private Merchants on Points of Trade.

Madras was a more developed and flourishing settlement than Calcutta ; it had enjoyed a longer history and under Governor Pitt experienced greater prosperity in spite of the anxiety caused by the movements of the Moghul armies engaged in the Maratha wars. Charles Lockyer about 1710 was enthusiastic.

> The prospect it gives (he says) is most delightful ; nor appears it less magnificent by Land ; the great Variety of fine Buildings that gracefully overlook its Walls, affording an inexpressible Satisfaction to a curious Eye. Towards the Land it is washed by a fruitful River that every November, half a Mile distant, discharges itself into the Sea, the Bar being first cut for its passage, which proceeding from the wet Monsoon, would otherwise occasion great Damage, by overflowing the adjacent Country. . . . The Streets are straight and wide, pav'd with Brick on each Side, but the Middle is deep Sand for carts to pass in : Where are no Houses are Causeways with trees on each side to supply the Defect. These being always green render it pleasant to those who otherwise must walk in the Sun. There are five Gates—the Sea, St. Thomas, Water, Choultry and Middle Gate. The Second and the Fourth may be opened for Passengers at any time of Night, if unsuspected, but neither of the other three after Six. The Publick Buildings are the Town Hall, St. Mary's Church, The College, New House and Hospital, with the Governor's Lodgings in the inner Fort. . . . The inhabitants enjoy perfect Health as they would do in England, which is plainly discovered by their ruddy Complexions ; a good few of our other Settlements can boast. The Heats in Summer are the greatest Inconveniency they suffer under ; yet I never heard of any ill effect from them. The delicious Fruits which the Country abounds with are a great Help in their Extremity ; nor are they wanting to themselves in other Respects ; Bathings and Wet Cloths being often apply'd with Success to the Relief of the Panting. It seldom lasts above four or five Hours in a day ; when the Sea-breeze comes on, the Town seems to be new born. The Governor, during the Hot Winds, retires to the Company's new Garden for Refreshment, which he has made a very delightful Place of a barren one. The costly Gates, lovely Bowling Green, spacious Walks, Teal-pond and Curiosities preserved in

> several Divisions are worthy to be admired. Lemons and Grapes grow there, but five shillings worth of Water and Attendance will scarcely mature them.[8]

Bombay, the only other settlement under English control of any size, is thus described by Ovington.

> The island lies in about Nineteen Degrees North, in which is a Fort, which is the Defence of it, flanked and Lined according to the Rules of Art, and secured with many Pieces of Ordinance, which command the Harbours and the parts adjoining. In this one of the Company's Factors always resides, who is appointed Governor to inspect and manage the Affairs of the Island; and who is vested with an authority in civil as well as Military Matters, to see that the several Companies of Soldiers who are here, as well as the Factors and Merchants, attend their various Stations and their respective Charge.
>
> The Island is likewise beautified with several elegant Dwellings of the English and neat Apartments of the Portuguese to whom is permitted the free exercise of their Religion.[9]

Hamilton is less enthusiastic:

> The ground is sterile and not to be improved. It has but little good Water on it and the Air is somewhat unhealthful, which is chiefly imputed to their dunging their Cocoanut Trees with Buckshoe, a Sort of small Fishes which their Sea abounds in. These being laid to the Roots of the Trees, putrefy, and cause a most unsavoury Smell; in the Mornings there is generally seen a thick Fog among those Trees that affects both the Brains and Lungs of Europeans and breeds Consumptions, Fevers and Fluxes.[10]

Mortality was heavy and gave rise to the proverb: 'Two Monsoons are the Age of a Man.'[11] In addition both writers testified to the devastation caused by Sir J. Child's war with the Moghul. Bombay was but a shadow of its former self under Gerald Aungier. 'Of the seven or eight Hundred English that inhabited before the War, there were not above sixty left by the Sword and Plague and Bombay, that was one of the pleasantest Places in India, was brought to one of the most dismal Deserts.'[12]

This is the picture of the English Settlements at the opening of the century—a deserted Bombay, a rising Calcutta, and a flourishing Madras already divided into three distinct parts, the Fort for the English, Maqua Town to the south for the boatmen and Black

Town where the Indian merchants lived.[13] The societies which these settlements contained had trade for their sole reason for existence, and were severely paternal in character. At their head was their President or Governor, a being poised midway, so to speak, between heaven and earth, to the settlement a sort of tutelary deity, to Indian ambassadors and durbars the representative of the Britannic Majesty, and to the Directors an inveterate object of suspicion, liable to supersession and dismissal with each despatch from England. In the settlement itself he kept up considerable state; he never went abroad, says Lockyer, without being attended by eighty armed peons as well as English guards, with two Union flags carried before him and 'country musick enough to frighten a stranger into belief the men were mad'.[14] At Surat he did much the same. In India he was as a prince, to the Directors a chief merchant, to be all the more narrowly watched because the opportunities of abusing his power were great. Every Governor was liable to have his character blackened by the Members of his Council in private letters to the Directors, and though such informing was strongly reprobated when discovered as in the case of Robert Orme,[15] few of the early Governors' consciences can have been clear enough to enable them to greet the arrival of a company's ship from England with unaffected pleasure or to open their private despatches without a tremor. The Governor was usually no exceptional man. He was the senior member of Council, the eldest of the few who had survived the strain of English habits in a tropical climate, and owed his position more to longevity and a tough constitution than to anything else. The appointment of an outsider like the interloper Thomas Pitt was most exceptional, and in his case was only due to the fact that it was the only way to get rid of his interloping. The Governor's duties were as much commercial as political; he was the chairman of a board rather than a proconsul. As such, he had no power of over-riding his colleagues and only a casting vote in the event of a tie. He spent most of his time, when not in the consultation room, in the sorting godowns, inspecting and checking the country goods, preparing the annual cargoes, and receiving goods from Europe, and only as a secondary duty maintained order in the factory and negotiated with the country powers.[16] He was not yet intoxicated by military success nor dazzled by dreams of empire. His first duty was the profit of 'his Honourable masters', his second good order, and his third good relations with the country powers. His judicial power over Europeans was very limited, and the position about capital punishment was not finally cleared up until the Charter of 1726.[17]

Apart from his Council the Governor was little more than a

dignified figure-head, chiefly distinguished by his larger salary and allowances, his private garden for the hot weather and his rather more obvious personal pomp. This lack of real power in his commercial capacity which the Company's jealousy and the merchants' independence combined to effect, contrasted with the splendour the Governor assumed as head of the settlement, a splendour adopted partly by reaction from his practical impotence, partly as a salve to the wounds which letters from his 'honourable masters' periodically inflicted on him, and partly in order to impress the Indian mind.[18]

Next to the Governor came the Councillors, consisting of senior merchants arranged in order of seniority. Together with the Governor they formed the governing body and with the other senior merchants the aristocracy of the settlement. In style they were a little below the Governor but, like him, their chief concern was trade, and like him, they were deeply committed to private commerce, in addition to the Company's trade. As each man had risen through the grades of Writer, Factor, Junior and Senior Merchant to his place in the Council by seniority, and owed his promotion to the Directors and not to the Governor, and as each hoped in due course to succeed to the Governor's chair, ambition and self-esteem united with their natural independence to make them assertive, sometimes obstructive, and often quarrelsome. The Council was often more a ring for verbal fencing than a place of sober discussion, each member suspecting all the others as possible competitors and being always ready to go behind the President in appeals to the Directors. Thus in turbulent Bombay, we find John Lock being suspended from Council in 1701 for striking Sir Nicholas Waite and refusing to apologize, and the absence of another Member, Benjamin Morse, from Council, was explained on the ground that his intellect was disordered by liquor and that he was 'unfit for virtuous conversation'.[19] Later this same reverend senior caused further scandal by getting drunk in another senior's room and finally breaking his head with a bottle. But vanity and self-assertion, equally with the weakness of the flesh, were fruitful of incidents. In the *Bengal Public Consultations* we find Benjamin Walker being fined Rs.20 for 'abusing Mr. Hedges by using bad language to him'.[20] In 1706 a 'long and stormy debate' took place on receiving the news of the allocation of seats on the Council between the old and new Company's servants in Calcutta.[21] In 1708 it is reported that 'in spite of much stormy discussion they cannot come to a decision', whereupon they agreed 'to cast lots as our masters have bidden us in times of disagreement'.[22] A few years earlier Mr. Hedges had put the following questions to his Council :—

1. Is either of the Chairmen obliged to answer the challenge of every bully that pretends to be affronted and challenges him to a fight ?
2. Are any other of the Council obliged to fight on a like challenge ?
3. If one of the Chairmen be challenged without offering abuse for the Council, is the party challenged only affronted or the whole Council ?[23]

The occasion for this questionnaire was the challenge of a certain Captain Smith to Mr. Hedges to combat because the Captain considered himself insulted by not having the Fort guns fired in his honour on his arrival. This condition of morbid sensitiveness lingered on throughout the century, and a somewhat similar incident was one of Sir P. Francis's first grounds of complaint against Hastings.

Below the Council came the Senior and Junior Merchants, the Factors and the Writers, and outside the ranks of the Company's servants would come a sprinkling of free merchants. In Madras these were sufficiently numerous to justify the appointment of twelve Aldermen for life or residence in Madras with a Mayor chosen annually by them.[24] The Mayor, whose office lasted throughout the century, presided at the Mayor's Court, which tried all cases civil and criminal with a right of appeal to the Council in civil cases where the value of the award exceeded three pagodas, or in Indian criminal cases where the offender was condemned to lose life or limb.[25] The Mayor and Aldermen had their own sense of dignity. They were allowed ' to enjoy the Honour and Priveledge of wearing *Rundellos* and *Kettysols* born over them, and . . . may ride on Horseback in the same Order as is used by the Lord Mayor and Aldermen of London, having their Horses decently furnished with Saddles, Bridles and other Trimmings after one form and manner '.

The President and Council acted as a Court of Appeal, but the presence of two authorities in so small a community did not make for harmony, and it is hardly surprising to hear of disputes between the two. During a quarrel in 1702, the Mayor on receiving the Governor's messenger, snatched the Governor's letter from his hand before he had time to read it, with the remark that it might contain ' that which was not fit to be read ' or for him ' to hear ', which expression, says the Council, ' we can't but condemn as impudent and saucy '.[26]

At Madras two or three Councillors, if bachelors, resided in the Governor's house, or otherwise, like the Senior Merchants, had houses inside the Fort.[27] In the early days Armenian and Jewish merchants and Capuchin Fathers also had houses within the Fort, but as the numbers of the English grew they were from 1743 gradually eliminated by the process of refusing any further entrants.[28] There remained the Factors, the young writers and the soldiers. The former were housed in a College, the residence, says Lockyer, of 'seven or eight hopeful young gentlemen'. The building, he says, was 'very ancient, two Storeys high and has a paved Court, two large Verandas or Piazzas and about sixteen small rooms in it';[29] and according to Hamilton was in 'ill repair'.[30] They had long been strictly forbidden to be out of the Fort after the gates were shut, and the resulting use of windows for doors and of walls for ladders was so general as to cause Sir William Langhorne to threaten every offender with transhipment to England, 'there to receive condign punishment.'[31] In 1712 a new college was built, because factors lodging out were considered 'less likely to mind our affairs and more subject to temptation'. The writers were a constant source of trouble both now and later. Their attention to their work is thus described by Davenport in a letter from Bombay to the Secretary of the Directors.

> In the Generall Letter by the Heathcote I observe the complaints against not margening the Consultations and the ill transcribing of the Letters, to which I answer that the young Gentlemen that are sent out writes [*sic*] those Letters, and generally the best of their writing, and when they have learned [*sic*] one to write but tollerable well, and begin to understand business, they grow dissatisfyed and uneasy as being where nothing is to be got, so make an Interest to be removed to some other Employ more advantageous.[32]

In 1726 there were complaints of the number of writers in debt, and a suggestion was made to send them in rotation to the sub-stations so that they might learn business and the language, and avoid the temptations of Calcutta;[33] and in 1752 the Directors were still complaining of bad writing and faulty accounts, and insisting that writers must live within their income and have neither palanquin, horse or chaise.[34]

The garrison of Madras, according to Lockyer, consisted of two hundred and fifty Europeans, two hundred Topasses[35] or 'black Mungrel Portuguese', and two hundred armed peons.[36] They lodged in the 'New House', the scene of many a drunken frolic, where 'each soldier kept his Boy, who tho' not more than ten years old, is Procurer and Valet de Chambre, for seven or eight fanhams a month'.[37] Their main duty was to mount guard and particularly 'to see no disturbance is made in the streets thro' which they pass;

to suppress gaming houses, to stop all people suspected to be running of goods '.[38]

Apart from the Company's servants, and the free merchants, the only representatives of the professions were the Company's Chaplains and Surgeons. The Chaplains were the more important of the two. They enjoyed a salary and a precedence, in true Puritan style, next to the Governor himself, while the Surgeon had to wait long before he could obtain regular fees from his patients or even commissioned rank. Indeed he was not even always left alone to do his own work ; at Surat his duties were shared with an Indian physician.[39] In consequence the early surgeons frequently abandoned their profession for trade, and their places were filled by men with no knowledge of medicine. The Chaplain's duty was to read public prayers thrice on Sundays, to take morning and evening prayers at 6 a.m. and 8 p.m.—in Calcutta it was changed from 10 a.m. to 8 p.m. as the former hour interfered with business[40]—' to catechize all the youth ' and to visit the sub-stations.[41] In practice a large part of his duties must have consisted of funerals, particularly in the hot season, in one of which Hamilton says there were 460 funerals in Calcutta out of 1,200 English in four months.[42] There were churches at both Madras and Calcutta, one half-built at Bombay at the beginning of the century, and at Surat a chapel 'decently embellish't ' without images in order to avoid offence to the Mohammedans. The early chaplains were influenced to some extent by Puritanism, but the strain of the climate caused frequent vacancies, when prayers were said by the President or some Factor who received a special allowance.[43] The spirit of the amateur was supreme in the early settlements ; as the doctors drifted off into trade, so laymen like Manucci and Voulton became doctors.[44] We find one chaplain being dismissed for his commercial proclivities,[45] and the Rev. G. Lewis being appointed to the proposed embassy to the Moghul in 1709 as being ' a very worthy, sober, ingeneous man, and understands the Persian language very well '.[46] In 1713 he secured the surrender of Fort St. David by the recalcitrant Raworth.

The Hospital and the Punch-houses (in the early days closely related), frequented by soldiers, sailors and the lower Company's servants, complete the picture of the early settlements. The Madras hospital had a good reputation, but the Calcutta one, according to Hamilton, had not ; they depended entirely on a far from certain supply of conscientious surgeons.

At the opening of the century the English settlements were still microscopically small, but they were already becoming nuclei of Indian towns, where Indian merchants, attracted by trade, were encouraged by the good order and security to settle. In this feature the English settlements contrasted with the Dutch, whose East Indian factories never grew into great cities, and with the Portuguese, whose inquisitorial and proselytizing zeal left their cities in the eighteenth century to be inhabited by monks and nuns and to be crowded by nothing but churches and monasteries. The confidence reposed in the government is shown by the 'joy' with which the merchants returned to Madras after the French occupation from 1746-49. Of the principal factories, only that of Surat was in a large Indian city, the others being established on new sites like Fort St. David and Bombay, or being transferred from an old city, as Madras was from Masulipatam and Calcutta from Hughli. Madras as the oldest established settlement with a history of more than half-a-century was the largest; its population was reckoned at about 300,000,[47] at which figure it remained about stationary throughout the century; Calcutta, more recently founded, was smaller and reckoned by Hamilton to have 10,000 to 12,000 inhabitants.[48] Bombay, still overshadowed commercially by Surat, was still in the stage of Moghul and Maratha alarms, pirates and mortality bills. The English civilian population of Madras was estimated about 1700 as 114, twenty-seven being company's servants, twenty-nine freemen, thirty-nine sailors, eleven widows and eight 'maidens'.[49] The addition of a company of soldiers would bring the total up to nearly 400. On the whole Coromandel coast in 1699 there were estimated to be 119 men and seventy-one women, only forty-seven of whom were married, and many of whom were not English.[50] In Calcutta Hamilton speaks of 1,200 English, of whom 460 were buried in one hot season.[51] Reckoning this figure to include wives and children and allowing for seamen waiting for their ships, it would give a permanent population not much greater than that of Madras. Bombay on the other hand seemed on the point of extinction. Hamilton reckoned that there were seven to eight hundred English there before Sir John Child's governorship, and only sixty afterwards, and this statement is confirmed by Sir John Gayer in 1699 who wrote that only seventy-six Europeans were left on the Island and that they had only one horse and two oxen between them.[52]

With such small numbers a strong corporate life was still possible. At the opening of the century the English merchants still lived within the fort, the gates of which were shut every night, and they still met for dinner and supper at the common table, at which the Governor presided.[53] The factors sat in order of seniority, with an ensign at the bottom to act as taster, officer, carver and chaplain.[54] The exuberance of the young writers and factors imported an undergraduate air into the lower part of the room, and the jealousies of the elders often gave a certain liveliness to the senior table. Quarrels and brawls were always possible, and if the President was either weak or neglected his duty of presiding, the atmosphere seems often to have been that of a bump supper without the bumps. Sometimes the seniors were absent altogether, when the disorder naturally grew worse. What might happen is indicated in the despatch from the Directors in 1710, where they remark, ' We are sorry to hear that of late there has not been sufficient decorum kept up among our people, and particularly among the young writers and factors, and that there has been Files of Musqueteers sent for to keep the peace at dinner time.'[55] Two years later the absence of the seniors led to further disorders, and a steward was appointed to housekeep. The Company's servants believed in liberal fare washed down by copious draughts. At Surat, says Ovington, an English, a Portuguese and an Indian cook were maintained, the choicest meats were eaten and Persian and European wines, English beer and Arrack punch, were ' drunk with temperance and alacrity '.[56] He lovingly describes the various dishes—palau ; ' cabob '—beef and mutton cut small, and sprinkled with salt and pepper, dipped with oil and garlic, and roasted with herbs ; dumpoked fowl—boiled with butter in a small dish and stuffed with raisins and almonds ; mangoe achar and sony sauce. The feasts provided on Sundays and ' Publick days ' included ' Deer and Antelopes, Peacocks, hares and partridges, and all kinds of Persian Fruits, Pistachoes, Plums, Apricots, Cherries, etc.' With this we may compare Woolaston's list in 1717, which included ' Kishmishes, Bengall Goats, Sugar Candy, Almonds, Brahminy Bull, Soyce, Turkeys, Geese, Sheep, Rabbits and Lime '.[57] All these things, he complains, had greatly increased in price, but he had also to explain the increased expense of the general table at Calcutta by the fact that the Company's servants now had fifteen courses for both dinner and supper, instead of their former diet of milk, salt-fish and rice for supper and nine dishes for dinner.[58] The provision of wine was on the same liberal scale as the food. ' With the factors you have a great deal of punch and a little wine, with the Governor what wine you please and as little Punch.'[59] The difficulty of growing grapes in India early caused the importation of European and Persian wines which in 1717 already arrived in these varieties[60]—a specimen dietary of the settlements is given in the *Madras Dialogues*—' Mountain Wine, Rhenish, Syder, Galicia. Florence, Hock, Canary, Brandy, Claret, Ale, Beer, Shyrash Wine.'[61]

But the meals at the common table did not constitute the whole social life of the settlements. The collegiate factory life was based on the idea of celibacy, and it could not long survive the advent of women. At the beginning of the century they were already allowed by the Company to come out, partly in order to prevent illicit unions with country women and partly to lessen the temptation to marry Portuguese Roman Catholics.[62] But as yet there were few of them and in consequence husbands were easy prey. Ovington already remarks that an Englishwoman in India could be sure of a succession of wealthy and choleric husbands. The consequence of this shortage was twofold : some married French and Portuguese wives, but more remained single and established zenanas. In 1678-1679 there were seventy-four Company's servants in Madras ;[63] only six were married of which five had their wives with them. One of the wives was English, one Dutch, two English half-castes, and two Portuguese. In addition there were three widows and two unmarried ladies in the settlement and sixteen other Europeans in white or black town. In 1699,[64] of 119 recorded Englishmen on the Coromandel coast twenty-six had English wives, fourteen 'Castee'[65] wives, four ' Mustees ',[66] two French and one a Georgian wife. The remaining twenty-four women consisted of fourteen widows and ten ' single English young women '. There was no very lasting colour prejudice in the early eighteenth century, and marriage with coloured women was accepted as the normal course. During most of the century sons of domiciled families were considered to have a moral right to employment. Companies of Topasses[67] were employed extensively and we wait till the nineteenth century to hear the bitter complaints of Colonel Skinner at his gradual supersession on grounds of race, and his placation with the Order of the Bath.[68]

What the English women lost in numbers, however, they amply made up in vigour. Lockyer says that they were as active in trade as the men and their influence is traceable in not a few of the early quarrels. In 1706 the Calcutta Council received a letter from Mr. Arthur King, a factor in the Company's service, who considered himself insulted because the surgeon's wife had taken her place in church above his wife.[69] He asked the Council to order that his wife should be placed above the surgeon's wife in future. After an attempt to settle the matter privately, he wrote again to say that the surgeon's wife continued ' to squat down ' in his wife's place, and that if they would not see to it he would let them know that they as well as he ' had masters in England, and that they must hold themselves responsible for any disturbance or unseemly conduct that may happen in Church in consequence '.

The general life of the early settlement can already be divided into official, non-official and military. Each had his particular mode of life, though they were still united, as afterwards they ceased to be, by an underlying devotion to trade. There was separation without exclusiveness, there was class but no caste. The ideal of all was the same—the maximum of wealth in the minimum of time. And if opportunities were more limited than they later became, if the branches of the pagoda tree were tougher than subsequently and less heavily laden with fruit, so that the hands that shook it often tired before the fruit descended, the vision of a triumphant and affluent return to England nevertheless shone bright if distant before the adventurer's eyes. While wealth was then as a rule only acquired slowly and with effort, so that many died without ever attaining it, and many of those who did had lost through long absence or large establishments the desire or the power to return, there was always the chance of some unexpected windfall like Governor Pitt's diamond to whet men's appetites and sustain their hopes. So there were the commercial Governor and Councillor, the commercial factor and writer, the commercial soldier and surgeon and the commercial parson, just as later the dazzling prospect of empire directed everyone's secret ambition to the army and produced the military 'writer' in Clive and the imperialist Governor in Dupleix.

For the Company's servants the day opened with morning prayer at 6 a.m. The morning was devoted to business, the writer in his office, the Governor in the consultation room ('curiously adorned with fire-arms in several Figures imitating those in the armoury of the Tower of London ')[70] consulting with the councillors, or in the godowns examining arrivals of cloth from the interior or superintending the making up of cargoes for Europe. Dinner at noon was the grand meal of the day, after which came a period of rest.[71] In the afternoon the junior servants might return to office, but the seniors would repair to their own or the Company's garden, or in Calcutta take to the river in budgerows. The more energetic already drove their own chaises,[72] but the evening diversion *par excellence* at the beginning of the century was the taking of one's ease in 'gardens 'neath which rivers flow' with the help of arrack, punch and shiraz wine. In Surat, where the English were most influenced by this characteristically Moghul custom, the habit perhaps reached its climax. There, Ovington writes, evening and morning the factors go to gardens, 'and spend an hour or two with a bottle of wine and a cold collation which they carry with them.'[73] The evening was the time for paying calls and for social intercourse generally. The day was wound up by supper at the common table and prayers at 8 p.m.; the gates of the fort were shut at 10 or 11 p.m. after which none was allowed to go out.[74] Eleven p.m. saw a patrol marching through the streets of Black Town to close late punch houses and round up tardy revellers, and at midnight the settlement would be, at any rate in theory, at rest. This manner of living is well summed up by Hamilton in his description of Calcutta: 'Most gentlemen and ladies live both splendidly and pleasantly, the forenoons being dedicated to business and after dinner to rest and in the evenings they recreate themselves in chaises or palanquins in the fields or to the gardens; or by water in their budgerows which is a convenient boat that goes swiftly with the force of oars. On the river sometimes there is the diversion of fishing or fowling or both, and before night they make friendly visits to one another, when pride and contention do not spoil society, which too often they do among the ladies, as discord and faction do among the men.'[75]

The soldier's life in Madras was not very strenuous. Beginning with a beat of arms at 7 a.m. it was mainly confined to guard duty at the Main and Choultry Gates, occasional drill on the island and to patrolling the streets at night, going the rounds at 10 p.m. and finally shutting the gates at 11 p.m.[76] There was to be no man out of the factory after gun-fire 'except one sergeant, one corporal and twelve men, half black, half white, who are to go from the barracks with arms to the Governor's Garden house, from thence a sergeant and six men go at 11 o'clock round the suburbs to see if the boutiques are all shut and that no disturbance is made in the streets through which they pass, to suppress gaming houses, to stop all people suspected to be running of goods. And a corporal and six men go the same at two'.[77] Apart from these not very arduous duties the privates filled in their time at taverns and punch houses in the bazaars, and the officers in standing on their dignity or speculating in trading ventures. The regular Indian army did not begin its existence until 1746 during the first French war, and until then the garrisons of Madras and Calcutta were rather commercialized military police than serious soldiers.[78]

Such was the daily routine. But, as befitted a society still influenced by the almost spent force of Puritanism, Sunday was a day apart. The Directors frequently enjoined a strict observance of the Sabbath; the settlers observed it but not quite in a spirit which the Directors could have sympathized with or divines approved. At Surat[79] prayers were read thrice on Sundays and the rest of the day was occupied with a feast and a procession to the Company's garden, with as much magnificence as the factors could muster. 'The President goes thither in a palanquin with six peons, two large Flaggs or English Ensigns carried in front with Persian and Arab horses of state richly trapped.' He was accompanied by forty or fifty armed peons, then by the councillors in large coaches decorated with silver and by the other factors in coaches or on horseback as their means allowed. At Madras church-going seems to have been the most solemn event of the day, 'Betwixt Eight and Nine the Bell tells us that the Hour of Devotion draws near, a whole Company of above 200 soldiers is drawn out from the Inner Fort to the Church Door, for a Gard [*sic*] to the passing President, Ladies throng to their Pews, and Gentlemen take a serious Walk in the Yard if not too hot. On the Governor's Approach, the Organs strike up, and continue a Welcome till he is seated, when the Minister discharges the Duty of his Function, according to the Forms appointed by our prudent Ancestors of the Church of England.'[80]

Apart from the weekly event of Sunday, there were the occasional events of particular ceremonies which will be touched on later, and the seasonal arrival of ships. Then the Sea Gate was thronged with people, 'some laying wagers, others waiting for Masters and the rest to satisfy their Curiositys.'[81] On the first day supplies and passengers were landed and on the second goods which were sold at 'public outcry' after a week's notice.[82] To this sale every man would repair to replenish his stores or his stocks, so that in the season these sales were one of the centres round which the life of the settlement revolved.

With early rising and the mid-day siesta, which made two days out of one, and the absence, for the seniors at any rate, of any official occupation in the second, time must have lain heavy on the hands of most of the settlers. This ennui was not alleviated by any hope of a hill holiday or even of occasional leave, and it was accentuated both by the enervating effect of the climate and the lack of any intellectual interests to fall back upon. Clive, who was given the run of the Governor's library, was the exception who proved the rule.[83] In young writers who came out at the age of fifteen or a little over, the sudden and complete change of environment, the deprivation of all familiar and congenial occupations, produced the helplessness that often overtakes the English soldier in a modern Indian cantonment,[84] but with an added sense of solitude and interminable misery which only the shortsightedness of youth can experience.[85] But unlike the modern soldier he had not even fellows of his own kind with whom to mix; his little world was bounded by the Black Town in Madras and the Maratha ditch in Calcutta, his social life was regulated by the fashions of the punch house, his ideas borrowed from the gossip of the general table, and his activities curtailed by the pitiless sun or insidious attacks of fever. In nothing so much as in sport did he feel the restraints of his new situation. Most of the more vigorous sports were forbidden by the climate; for others like hunting there was at first neither space nor security, while for racing there were not as yet sufficient resources. So it was that in the realm of recreation and pleasure he was influenced by Indian customs more than in anything else, and became more Indianized in this respect than he ever did in his clothes, speech, habits or ideas. Shooting is the first sport which is mentioned,[86] and bowls were also of course played. Riding and coursing were the most vigorous sports ;[87] the driving of chaises had just begun to come in at Madras, but it was at first the luxury of a few.[88] A less exciting and more modern diversion was picnicking to Woolf Tope or St. Thomas's Mount. At the beginning of the century, there were no houses outside the fort at Madras, but the picnicking habit led to the building of the first garden houses at St. Thomas's Mount. Later they covered the Choultry plain to form an easy prey to Hyder Ali's flying squadrons in 1769 and 1780. In Calcutta the equivalent amusement was provided by trips on the river in budgerows and the equivalent retreats by the building of garden houses in the Garden Reach.

But most of these amusements required wealth and were beyond the means of the writers and junior factors. After work time hung heavy on their hands, and so they fell back on the one habit for which there was still ample scope, loafing in the open spaces and gossiping in taverns. ' Billiards and backgammon in a Punch House '[89] were common games, and they easily developed into the most ancient and characteristic vice of India, gaming. Gambling is a good index of boredom and of the craving for excitement in an unintellectual mind, and we can measure the dullness of the early factors' lives by the violence of the methods they adopted to relieve it. Throughout the early period as through the later, there are notices of the extent and laments of the evils of gaming. In 1720 the Directors wrote to Madras, ' It is of great Concern, we hear of the itch of gaming hath spread itself over Madras that even the Gentlewomen play for great Sumes and that Capt. Seton makes a trade of it to the stripping of several of the young men there.'[90] In 1728 they wrote in much the same terms to Calcutta, again mentioning the women. Gaming for sums of £10 and upwards was prohibited as in the Act against gaming in England, and any factor discovered was to be *ipso facto* dismissed and sent home.[91] But in 1750 the Council are still deploring the evil.[92]

The second solace of the bored Englishman was food and wine.

اي شكمِ خير (O unconscionable stomach !), the Englishman might well have sighed with the Persian poet, for it was at once his chief luxury and principal enemy. For long people did not suspect the connexion between drink and mortality bills, and when they did, many of them like Hickey continued to drink heavily in spite of it. The unhealthiness of a heavy meat diet and of gargantuan meals in the heat of the day seems never to have been suspected, or if so, was obstinately disregarded.[93] Europeans in India early acquired a reputation as wine-bibbers. Akbar is said by Manucci to have permitted the sale of wine to his English gunners because 'he said that as the European people must have been created at the same time as spirits and if deprived of them, were like fish out of their element, unless they had drink, they would not see plain '[94]

The staple drink at this time was arrack which took the place of the whisky of the nineteenth century.[95] There were two chief brands, from Bengal, which was the stronger, and from Goa, where it was of better quality and the staple commodity of the place.[96] The Goa arrack was made single, double or treble distilled, of which the double was most usually exported; it was drawn in earthen jars, and acquired therefrom a peculiarly mild character, and it was used by the English for yeast as well as for drink. Captain Symson, an authority on these matters, distinguished several sorts and uses of arrack.[97] It was distilled sometimes from rice, sometimes from toddy and sometimes from black sugar and water mixed with the bark of a tree called 'Baboul', when it was known as 'Jagre Arrack' and was as 'hot as brandy and drunk in Drams by Europeans'. Toddy was 'the liquor that runs from the Coco-nut tree without any other mixture', and sold at a quart for a pice or two. 'It affects the head as much as English Beer. In the morning it is laxative and in the evening astringent.' To arrack also were ascribed medicinal properties, all varieties being reckoned 'good for the gripes'. Symson also described a less well-known potion called neri.[98] This was drawn from the areca tree in a new earthen vessel and was 'as sweet and pleasant as milk but more spirituous'. 'Several Europeans,' he remarked, 'lose their lives by the immoderate use of these tempting liquors with which when once inflamed, they become so restless that no place is cool enough; and therefore they lie down on the ground all night which occasions their being snatched away in a very short time. The best remedy after hard drinking is to keep a close and convenient covering.'

Arrack formed the basis of punch. Punch is first mentioned by Albert de Mandelslo in 1638 as 'Pale-puntz', or 'Pale-punzen' in the original,[99] and was an established drink by 1700. It derived its name from the number of its ingredients,—arrack, rose water, citron juice, sugar and water. This was the universal drink in the first half of the century and gave its name to the Portuguese drinking taverns.

European wines as well as English beer,[100] as has already been noticed, were extensively imported from the beginning. Madeira was the favourite wine, as it was the only one said to improve in the Indian climate, and 100 pipes were shipped annually to Calcutta and Madras by the Company.[101] One ship was specially laden with the wine, and, if it failed to arrive, the year was a lean one indeed. In addition, Shiraz wine came in chests from Persia;[102] the English had an agent there and it was much drunk until Nadir Shah's invasion interrupted communication in 1738, and the troubles of the Kajar dynasty in Persia and the Durranis in Afghanistan made trade dangerous.[103] Even in 1750 it was still included in a list of current wines.[104] We will conclude this section with the list of wines given in the *Madras Dialogues*, which it should be remembered speaks for the poorer rather than the wealthier sort of settler.[105]

> JOHN: What liquor is there in the Cellar?
>
> PETER: There is Beer four Bottles, Claret wine twelve bottles, Sack nine Bottles and Madeira one hundred Bottles . . .
>
> JOHN: What sorts of wine are there?
>
> PETER: In the first place you must know that we have four and more sorts of French wine, likewise so many sorts of wine from the Cape of Good Hope. Further there is to be had White wine, red wine, claret wine, Rhenish wine, Moselle wine, Muscadel wine, Malmsey wine, Madeira wine, Palma-wine and Persia-wine.
>
> JOHN: I wonder at the large species of so many sorts of wines; but which is the best in this country?
>
> PETER: Dear brother John. They are all together very good but the Madeira wine gives the best taste when drunken with water.
>
> JOHN: What, good brother Peter, is this to say, Drink with Water? I don't understand what you mean.
>
> PETER: Very well, I'll tell you presently the meaning thereof. If anybody is dry and calls for Drink, he fills the glass up with three parts of water and one part of Madeira wine and then it is very savoury to quench the Thirst.[106]

However hard the lot of the Madras factors, they can hardly be said to have drunk of the water of affliction. There was inevitably much intemperance; the rule seems to have been that everyone drank a good deal and a good many of all classes drank too much, the income of the drinker determining only the *quality* and not the quantity of the drink. The soldiers and sailors were naturally the worst sufferers, since they drank the most fiery liquors. So drunkenness appears again and again in the records, from the complaint of

Chaplain Warner in 1676 of factors who continued in a garden 'a whole day and night drinking most excessively', so that the next day 'a person worthy of credit numbered by the heads 36 pottles';[107] through the case of Ensign Fullerton, who was dismissed for 'incorrigible sottishness' and being two nights successively drunk on duty;[108] the fight recorded by Ananda Ranga Pillai between two drunken councillors in Pondicherry;[109] down to the withdrawal of an arrack licence in Calcutta from Mr. Hundle in 1758 (which he had bought for Rs. 4,000) because the military 'were continually intoxicated with liquor in his tavern'.[110]

In addition to these drinks, tea was drunk in the north and coffee in the south. In Bombay and Surat both were drunk by all classes, both European and Indian. The factors must have acquired the habit in India, for Mandelslo in 1638 mentions 'thé' as being drunk at ordinary meetings every day.[111] The habit was perhaps taken by the English from the Dutch, who, says Ovington, 'used it as such a standing entertainment, that the tea-pot's seldom off the Fire or unimploy'd.'[112] It was generally drunk at this time with sugar candy or small conserved lemons, and mixed with hot spice was considered good for 'Headach, gravel and griping of the guts'. The *Madras Dialogues* speak of tin 'tea-dishes' and the use of sugar candy with them in 1750.[113] Macdonald in 1771 drank tea with citron leaves.[114] After spreading to England, the habit of tea drinking in its modern form returned again to the India of the later settlements; Lady Jones in 1790 wrote of returning from drinking tea in the interval created by the shifting of dinner from noon to evening.[115]

The habit of drinking coffee after a moderate quantity of wine was also introduced at that time.[116] Ovington did much to popularize tea-drinking in England by his *Essay on Tea*, published in 1699, which aroused a fierce controversy. Tea in India continued as an addition to more generous potations, and never became a substitute. The Company's efforts to recommend the latter view to their factors never found any response and was not very seriously maintained.[117]

If drinking after gaming was the most constant diversion of the factor, a diversion so continuous as almost to be an occupation, he had an occasional excitement in the form of elaborate ceremonies and processions, on the visit of some important personage or in celebration of some auspicious event. The visit of the Moghul general Nawab Da'ud Khan to Madras in 1701 is thus described:

'About twelve this noon the Nabob, the King's Duan and Buxie was conducted into town by Messrs. Marshall and Meverell, the streets being lined with soldiers from St. Thomas Gate up to the fort and the works mann'd with the Marrein Company handsomely

EUROPEANS WATCHING A NAUTCH GIRL DANCING

[*face p.* 21

clothed with red coats and caps and the curtains of the inner fort with our train hands, all which made a very handsome appearance. The Governor, attended with the Council, the Mayor, the Commander of the Europe ships and some of the principal freemen, received him a little way out of the gate of the fort, and after embracing each other the Governor presented him with a small ball of amber Greece cas'd with gold and a gold chain to it and thus conducted him into the fort and carried him up to his lodgings . . ' Dinner was in the consultation room, ' consisting of about 600 dishes small and great,' and after dinner they were entertained by dancing girls.[118]

Celebrations took place at the accession of Queen Anne, the accession of George I, the proclamation of peace with France in 1715, the inauguration of the New Charter in 1727, and regularly on the King's birthday. In fact any notable event was a good excuse for a feast, the firing of guns and processions through the streets. On the news of Farruksiyar's farman granting possession of five villages round Madras in 1717, two processions went round the town, one of all the civil authorities, a company of soldiers and ' all the English musick ' which toured the fort ; and the other led by the Peddanaik on horseback, and consisting of Talliars and native music, a company of British soldiers, two trumpeters, the chief Dubash[119] mounted, a palanquin with the farman, six sergeants and the company's merchants. A salute of 101 guns was fired for the King, fifty-one for the Royal family and thirty-one for the Company, and all the merchants of the town, English, Portuguese, Armenians and Mohammedans were entertained at dinner.[120] ' The day concluded with feasting of the soldiers with tubs of Punch, and a bonfire at night ; and the black merchants, to show their joy at the Hon. Company receiving so much favour from the Moghul, made abundance of fireworks on the Island.'[121]

One more example will suffice. It is the procession formed at the inauguration of the New Charter on 17 August 1727. The procession marched to the Company's garden in the following order:

Major John Roach on horseback at the head of a Company of Foot.
Soldiers, with Kettledrum, Trumpet and other music.
The Dancing Girls with the Country Music.
The Pedda Naik on horseback at the head of his Peons.
The Marshall with his staff on horseback.
The Court Attorney on horseback.
The Registrar carrying the old Charter on horseback.
The Sergeants with their maces on horseback.

The old Mayor on the right hand and the new on the left.
The Aldermen two and two, all on horseback.
Six halberdiers.
The Company's chief Peon on horseback with his Peons.
The Sheriff with a White Wand on horseback.
The Chief Gentry in the town on horseback.[122]

To what extent were the early settlers absorbed into the main stream of Indian life? It seems clear that generally speaking the early factors kept apart and aloof from Indian life, though they had developed no contempt for Indian social customs or political power. They were proud of being what they were, though they had no prejudice whatever against adopting any Indian fashion or custom which made life more comfortable or more luxurious. In a word this Indianization was only superficial, a thing of clothes and food and not a radical transformation of essential ideas. What they borrowed from India were the excrescences of Indian customs and not their essence. Thus they took the zenana from Musulman society but never became Musulmans; and they adopted various current Hindu superstitions without ever absorbing any Hindu philosophic ideas. They adapted Indian words to form numbers of 'Hobson-Jobsons', many of which have been adopted into the language, but they never learnt the local vernaculars themselves, conducting their business in the debased Portuguese current round the coast or by means of interpreters. The rest of their borrowing was concerned with the details of life—wearing of banian clothes in their houses, the eating of food in the Indian manner when away from their houses,[123] the chewing of 'pan' and 'betel'[124] and the smoking of hookahs. The love of processions, fireworks and salutes was only a common tendency expressed in an Indian form. The Englishman in the factory period of his life in India, remained at heart very much what he was in England. He learned how to deal with strange people and adapted his life to the climatic and social conditions, but he remained an Englishman still in his essential ideas. It was left for the later settlers and soldiers, as a result of their far greater contact with Indians of all ranks, to become much more aggressively English on the surface, while at the same time unconsciously imbibing some characteristically Indian ideas.

Chapter II

THE TRANSITION PERIOD

1750-85

Between 1750 and 1785 there occurred in India a radical change in the English life and outlook, a metamorphosis from the secluded if not always very elegant life of the early factories, to the fevered cosmopolitanism of later Calcutta, a brilliant if slightly tawdry imitation of the world of the 'First Gentleman of Europe'. To explain this change, it is not enough simply to cite the Anglo-French Wars and the conquest of Bengal, for if the factors had remained exactly the same these events could not have suddenly changed their whole outlook on life, and developed them from pettifogging traders quarrelling over their seats in church and overlooking each other's derelictions of duty, into imperialist swashbucklers and large scale extortionists. The fact is, of course, what anyone who describes a condition of affairs at any given moment, from Macaulay's description of England under James II downwards, is liable to forget, that conditions at that moment were not static at all, and that the people of the time were very far from being content with them. The flow of history is like a cinema reel rather than a series of detached lantern slides, and any description of any given moment is really, to continue the metaphor, the isolation of one exposure from the whole series of the film. The necessity of clarity involves the illusion of permanence. While these slow changes were continually taking place, however, there intervened a period of much more rapid development, occupying about twenty-five years, during which the speed of the film, to continue the metaphor, was greatly accelerated. This period of rapid development, as distinct from the continuous slow changes of normal times, commenced both in the case of Madras and Calcutta with a sudden blow to the Company's fortunes. In each case the disaster was followed by a confused period of quick change when new social forces appeared and intermingled with the old, haphazard and largely unrestrained by the older customs and traditions. These two crises also weakened the force of tradition so as to prevent the old settlers from greatly influencing the new. So the normal process of change was accentuated by political circumstance to such an extent that the settlements may in some ways be said almost to have commenced life anew.

These two catastrophes were the capture of Madras by the French in 1746 and of Calcutta by Siraja-daula in 1756. The first made a violent break with the past, and ushered in a period of opposition to the French and of participation in Indian politics. The second began that period of adventure and cosmopolitanism which only ended with Cornwallis.

The first result of the French wars was an influx of soldiers, both Company's and Royal troops. Royal troops were first sent at the close of the Austrian Succession war, and in addition the Company itself began to raise regular European regiments of its own in place of the early sepoy companies, after the loss of Madras in 1746. The subsequent Carnatic war confirmed both these developments, and in addition brought the factors into the orbits both of war and of Indian politics. The war with Dupleix, the fortune of which depended on the balance of a few hundred Europeans and the course of which could be changed by such incidents as the defence of Arcot and the siege of Trichinopoly, caused military entanglements ; and the alliance with Mohammad Ali, the Nawab of Arcot, who soon made Madras his virtual capital from prudential motives, effected an entry into politics. The Seven Years' War continued the process. It brought an influx of Royal regiments, a further increase in the Company's army ; and the overthrow of the French power, which was its result, involved the transfer of the Northern Circars to the Company's management (previously under French control and used to support the French General Bussy in Hyderabad) and diplomatic relations with all the chief Deccan powers—Hyderabad, the Marathas, Mysore and Travancore. The rise of Mysore under Hyder Ali followed so closely on the eclipse of the French that Madras had no opportunity, even had it had the inclination, to slip back again into its old position of a prosperous but provincial city. It now became the virtual capital of the Carnatic state, in practice controlled by the Company on behalf of the Nawab. The power and abilities of Hyder Ali were so formidable and constituted so serious a menace to Madras, that it remained a military arsenal rather than a commercial depot until Hyder's successor, Tipu Sultan, was finally defeated in the fourth Mysore war in 1798. Then Madras, no longer a military base for operations in the interior, became the capital of Southern India. The process was completed by the definite annexation of the Carnatic by Lord Wellesley in 1801.

In Bengal the period of rapid change began later and ended sooner. It began abruptly and disastrously with the capture of Calcutta in 1756, and it developed rapidly with the subsequent defeat of Siraja at Plassey and the establishment of a military supremacy in Bengal. These political changes brought to Bengal men from Madras who had already become accustomed to high politics and higher finance; there they found opportunities for wider and more lucrative corruption than any they had known in Madras. The pace became accordingly much hotter, and as the period of cosmopolitanism was shorter, so was its activity also more intense. The lack of any adequate military opposition made the Nawabs of Bengal little better than the tax-gatherers and concession contractors to the Company, and this state of things was confirmed by the break-up of Mir Kasim's army in 1763 and by the defeat of Shuja-ad-daula at Baksar in 1764. Bengal was virtually annexed when Clive obtained in 1765 from the Moghul Emperor the grant of the 'Dewanni' or civil administration, but a condition of power without responsibility remained until Warren Hastings by 'standing forth as Dewan' in 1772, abolished the Deputy Nawabship to which Clive had entrusted the Dewanni, and undertook the collection of revenue himself by means of English officials. The English in Bengal were in a sort of political vacuum; they had no very real menace like Hyder Ali in the south and the Marathas in the Deccan to sober them, and in consequence the period of corruption was more unrestrained while it lasted, than ever it was in Madras.[1] On the other hand, civilians more easily asserted control. The Bengal counterpart of the imprisonment of Governor Pigot in 1776, the civil opposition to Clive in Calcutta, was very quickly suppressed, and never afterwards repeated, and the mutiny of officers in 1766 took place far enough away from Calcutta to prevent a sudden seizure of power in Calcutta. Civilian administrators appear with the appointment of the supervisors in 1769, and as collectors they extended all over Bengal after 1772. Calcutta was never anything else but a commercial centre and steadily established its claim to the title of 'City of Palaces'.

So the social developments varied in the two cities in accordance with the differing political conditions. In Madras the period of transition covering the French war led on to the society of late eighteenth century Madras from about 1765 onwards, and the settlement remained as much military as commercial in character down to 1798. It was confined to one city and the military camps adjacent, and its corruption centred round the court of the Nawab Mohammad Ali and the Council; some reform was accomplished by Lord Macartney after 1780, but social conditions remained in essence the same until the close of the period. In Bengal on the other hand, the changes were both more rapid and more frequent; there was more than one transition, and more than one crystallization into a stable social system. The first period of transition lasted roughly from 1756-65, a period of unbridled corruption and abuse, and led to the first period of social crystallization achieved by Clive in his second Governorship and reinforced by Warren Hastings. A second transition was the reformation carried out by Lord Cornwallis and led to a second social equilibrium with well-marked features under him and Shore, until finally a third period of change began with Wellesley which left Calcutta with much the same arrangement of classes and much the same outlook as it retained through the nineteenth century.

Parallel to the changes in the European settlements went changes in the Indian political situation. The Moghul Empire retained most of its prestige and much of its power down to the sack of Delhi by Nadir Shah in 1739, and until that time a dominant personality at the centre might have still preserved the reality of an empire in Northern India at least. But the lack of a vigorous Emperor made the strong men at court rivals before that date, and founders of dynasties afterwards. Hyderabad became virtually independent in 1726 and was isolated from Delhi by the Maratha treaty of 1738. Bengal was virtually independent under Ali Verdi Khan in 1740, Oudh in 1744; Gujerat was lost in 1748; the Punjab after the Battle of Panipat in 1761 went to the Sikhs and the Afghans, and only Delhi remained as a sort of aristocratic city state. At last, after a last gleam of prosperity under Mirza Najaf Khan, like the dying flicker of a guttering candle, the imperial power was finally extinguished by the excesses of Ghulam Kadir Khan in 1788. By 1756, therefore, the Moghul Empire had ceased to be a political reality. But like the Roman Empire of the fifth century it retained its hold over the imagination even of those who were dismembering it, and remained the legal source of all authority until the Company's supremacy was finally established. Every fresh usurpation was legalized by the issue of a 'farman' from Delhi, as when Dupleix produced one to uphold his claim for supremacy in the Deccan against the English, and the Company in Bengal, after defeating the Emperor Shah Alam in the field, relied on another formally to legalize its position.

The chief operative facts in the first transitional period were the break of continuity caused by the early disasters of the French wars, the influx of professional soldiers (men of mature habits and fixed ideas before they came to India), the transformation of merchants into politicians and the mere mathematical increase of numbers. But besides these external features of the period which reacted on the outward circumstances of the settlers, there are also internal elements to reckon with—changes which took place in the mental attitude of the factors themselves.

A number of inhibitions, partly real, partly imaginary, were removed by the European successes in the Indian wars and politics. The first was the barrier which limited power and opportunity had erected against the ambitions of the merchants. The earlier merchants were no more solid merchants and dutiful agents in their hearts than the later adventurers, and when opportunity offered, their suppressed ambitions revealed themselves in the ease with which they changed their occupations and the frequency with which stray Englishmen took service with the country princes in the hope of acquiring a fortune.[2] In fact they were potentially as turbulent as any of the Benfields or Whitehills of later days ; all they lacked for their achievements to equal the most skilful of the Bengal ' nabobs ' was opportunity. But it must not be assumed that they were worse than their contemporaries in England ; rather their natural ambitions for wealth and power found no outlet in the circumstances of their exile in India and of factory life. Just as the dissolution of the monasteries and the industrial revolution gave the acquisitive instinct a hitherto undreamt-of scope and made it a new danger to mankind, so the expansion of the English power in India gave free play to the desire for self-expression in every direction which the earlier factory life had denied.

The second of these inhibitions was a great respect for authority both in India and England. The exaggerated rejoicings in Calcutta on the return of Surman from his successful embassy to Farruksiyar in 1717 show a respect for the imperial authority which was far greater than the English fear of the Moghul army.[3] For them the Emperor at Delhi was the source of law and the origin of their legal rights in India ; they considered him much as medieval Europe regarded the Holy Roman Emperor, as one who might be cajoled or wheedled or intimidated, but one whose authority must always be formally respected. Like the whole of India, they had come to regard the Moghul Empire as something indestructible and irremovable, as the incarnation of all authority as well as the materialization of the Mohammedan supremacy, and so strong was this belief that they failed to draw the obvious conclusion even from the sack of Delhi in 1739.[4] So they carefully obtained a sanad for their Bengal Government while they were defeating the Moghul troops at the battle of Baksar, and continued to govern in their name right into the nineteenth century.

But far greater than this was their respect and submission for the Company at home. A perusal of any of the Court's letters to Bengal or Madras shows the paternal tone the home authorities adopted and the detailed control they exercised. The visits of a Roman Catholic priest to an up-country factor's wife in Bengal were gravely forbidden 'if he is to remain in our service'.[5] Job Charnock was commended and given an increase of £20 a year in the style of a manager giving a rise to a junior clerk;[6] there were recommended and despatched individual books;[7] and it was not until 1759 that the Council during Clive's governorship ventured to protest against the bullying attitude of the Directors.[8] The whole tone is that of a rather overbearing and inquisitorial central office communicating with its country branches. The settlers for their part quite accepted the position; Wellesley's remark about 'the cheesemongers of Leadenhall Street' would have horrified them as much as it did the later Directors, for they accepted their position as the paid agents of the cheesemongers. In the early records we have frequent references to 'our Honourable Masters' in a tone which now smacks of servility, but to them seemed obviously right and natural. In a dispute they decided to cast lots 'as our Masters have bidden us to do in times of disagreement';[9] as late as 1754 the Council at Madras can write of 'our Honourable Masters, out of their indulgent care'[10] sending annually a ship to Madeira for wine. They did in actual fact consider themselves as a species of country managers for a multiple company, and though they may have been quite ready to become millionaires if opportunity offered, in practice such ideas were as yet no more than fantastic dreams.

The first external agent of change was the transformation of factors into soldiers and statesmen. It is true that the factors required no encouragement to effect such a transformation, but the actual metamorphosis had a very important effect on the character of the new settlements. It meant that soldiers and officials brought commercial minds to their new duties, in which, if they were not always over-careful of the Company's coffers, they never forgot their own. Practices like the taking of commissions for clothing and feeding of companies by captains,[11] which involved no great scandal in the day of small things, were inevitably magnified indefinitely until we reach the case of the regiment which on disbandment was discovered only to have existed on paper.[12] To the influence of natural acquisitiveness must be added the attitude of the Company which refused to increase salaries to a reasonable figure until the time of Cornwallis, and actually annulled Clive's scheme for augmenting salaries from the profits of the salt and tobacco monopolies.[13] The licence for private trade on which they continued to rely, and which before had only meant that the merchant looked after himself as best he could, now in the new conditions became a licence to private tyranny and the terrorization of the countryside. The merchant was now often an official (and the official a merchant) while the whole English community gained the status of a ruling race.[14] The merchant had behind him power and not persuasion, and in consequence some of the worst exactions were committed by his 'gomastahs' or commercial agents. The exactions of the English 'gomastahs' and their refusal to pay the proper river dues, was one of the principal causes of friction between Mir Kasim and the Company in 1763, an issue on which Hastings sided with Mir Kasim until he put himself out of court by his attack on Ellis at Patna. The eighteenth century was the classic period of placemen and corruption, and when the special circumstances of the East India Company are added to the general atmosphere, the period of corruption in India seems not only intelligible, but almost inevitable.

The coming of the soldiers first began in earnest after 1746.[15] The Company's European army then began its regular existence with the training of two battalions of Europeans for their service, and the Royal troops were constantly coming and going during the prolonged French and Indian wars from 1754 to the end of the century. These were men independent of commerce, unfettered by awe of suspicious superiors at home, possessed of a professional *esprit de corps*. Honour and fame were their ideals, efficiency, at any rate to a certain extent, was a principle of life. The old Company's officer had occupied a definitely inferior position in the social scheme ;[16] he was as much interested in trade as in his guard duty ; it was possible to be drunk and incapable on duty without incurring serious censure, and he could usually secure reinstatement on a profession of repentance.[17] The difference in quality between Company's Europeans and the King's troops continued right up to the time of Cornwallis, who frequently deplored the wretched quality of the Company's Europeans.[18] Further, the soldiers proved by demonstration what others had only talked of—the superiority of European methods of war to the Indian, and the possibility of using with success Indian troops drilled on European lines.[19] To the example of the English troops must be added the further stimulus of Dupleix's example, first by his defeat of Anwar-addin's troops at Ambur in 1749, and then by his and de Bussy's policy of alliances and subsidiary forces in the Deccan.

Next must be noted the effect of increased numbers on the character of the settlements. In 1740 a Fort St. George list gives 168 as the total official and non-official European population, to which we may add a Company of European soldiers.[20] This shows little change from the beginning of the century.[21] After 1746 the Company raised both European and Indian troops, and the regiments of both were soon officered by Englishmen.[22] The lower class of European became, therefore, predominantly military, and its number was continually augmented by time-expired soldiers who remained to keep punch houses, European shops, or act as coachmen to settlers. Similarly the influx of officers affected the merchant and official class. They were not segregated in barracks or in camps like the privates, and had long periods of leave which they inevitably spent in the Presidency towns. In 1746 in Fort St. David there were only 200 European troops of all ranks,[23] by 1748 there were 589,[24] in 1759 at the siege of Madras there were 1,758 troops[25] and in 1769, 2,590.[26] The civilian population, while it increased, multiplied in nothing like the same proportion. In 1777 the number of non-official Europeans, including women, is given as 253.[27]

In Calcutta the same condition of things is found. In 1756 S. C. Hill's list gives 671 certain and 133 uncertain names of Europeans in all the Bengal factories, and this included many Portuguese, French and Dutch names.[28] The total European garrison was then 200. In 1763 there were 1,118 men and seventy-two invalids on the rolls and in 1765, 1,598 men.[29]

By their military employment and their professional outlook the new soldier element on the one hand helped to drive the settlement from purely commercial into more imperialistic channels. Through their influence all the settlers became more race-conscious, more of an aggressive political group. But as the Company's officers, like the factors, came out for life or long periods and came out early, so, on the other hand, they imbibed more of the older mercantile spirit and Indianized social habits than their numbers would have seemed to make probable. The early soldiers were merchants in essence; the later soldiers were merchants and contractors without ceasing to be soldiers, just as the later factors were politicians without ceasing to be merchants. In things military their influence was purely English; but in civil life they conformed to their Anglo-Indian environment. Thus the sepoy army was rapidly Europeanized in its appearance and treatment as well as in its discipline; the old easy-going tolerance of Indian customs by the early merchants found no place there. The sepoys were given uniforms in 1759,[30] which consisted in 1780 of a red light infantry jacket, a blue turban with a tassel, a blue sash loosely wound round the loins, with the end passed underneath and fastened behind, tight white drawers half-way down the upper leg, sandals, white cross-belts, firelocks and bayonets.[31] In 1767 Indian tomtoms and trumpets were discontinued as soon as the men could learn the European beats,[32] being replaced by drum and fife bands; and the words of command were also English.[33]

On the other hand, there are many indications to show that they had quite adopted the Anglo-Indian attitude to trade. Apart from such profitable duties as the clothing and feeding of companies by their captains,[34] it was necessary to lay down in the first military regulations that no one should hire another to do duty for him, or keep a public house, or a retail shop, without leave, in which case he would be discharged on condition of serving in an emergency; and that no presents should be accepted on pain of dismissal.[35] A custom grew up of using soldiers as personal servants, and in 1778 we have a list of twenty-nine European soldiers and sepoys who were serving high officers and civilians in capacities ranging from groom, coachman, bagpiper and theatre attendant to huntsman and cockfeeder.[36]

More purely European in their outlook and more corrosive in their influence upon Anglo-Indian life were the Royal regiments, who were sent out during the French wars and returned after the peace. They were not only military, but English military men, and they arrived too mature to be influenced by existing Anglo-Indian manners. The first Royal troops to India were sent in 1662 to Bombay under Sir Abraham Shipman, but the influx did not begin in earnest until the French wars. In 1748 twelve 'independent companies' of hastily raised troops and eighty artillerymen were landed in Madras by Boscawen.[37] The first complete regiment to land was the 39th, commanded by Col. Adlercon, and conveyed by Admiral Watson's fleet in 1754 to Madras. During the Seven Years' War several regiments were sent to India.[38] After the Treaty of Paris in 1763 four of them returned but 545 men and twenty-five sergeants were left behind.[39] From 1767-80 there were no Royal troops in India when the 73rd regiment arrived.[40] In 1787 four regiments were specially raised for service in India,[41] who finally returned home in 1805 after nearly twenty years' service.[42] When the numbers of the settlement are remembered, it will easily be understood that the influx of so many mature and opinionated men was bound to have a marked effect. They inaugurated the conception of service in India as a temporary vocation undertaken with a view to retirement in England.

The next new element in Anglo-Indian society was the new civilian official class. This appeared in 1769 with the appointment of English 'supervisors' in Bengal and extended all over Bengal after the assumption of the Dewanni in 1772. As collectors though they increased the official as apart from the purely mercantile element in the Company's service, yet their social influence was of an Indianizing rather than a Westernizing character. There were many reasons for this. The collectors retained the privilege of private trade until 1787, and it was only then that Cornwallis separated the Revenue from the Commercial service. Until that time a Company's servant might indifferently hold commercial or administrative appointments ; the merchant and the administrator were interchangeable. Next these officials usually came to India as writers at the age of fifteen ; with habits and principles unformed they easily assimilated the customs and traditions of the society into which they had just entered. Further, the distribution of the collectors all over Bengal brought them into contact with the local country gentry, the nawabs and zamindars. In consequence, they not only failed to increase English social influence, but strengthened the already existing tendency to Indianize manners.

From these Indian gentry with their wealth and ostentation, their retainers, their despotic temper and their luxury, they acquired the tastes and habits which marked the ' Nabob ' of later eighteenth century England. Before 1750 the few Company's servants who acquired fortunes did so as merchants living in European settlements. On their return they invested their money in land as any successful London merchant might have done, and we hear no tales of extraordinary extravagance and pomp. It was the migration of the factor to the country districts after Plassey that changed their outlook from that of merchants desiring to get rich quickly to that of gentlemen desiring titles and deference, prestige and social distinction. ' Nabobs ' first appeared in England after Plassey. They entered Parliament in force at the election of 1768,[43] and they were first publicly exposed by Foote in his play ' The Nabob ' in 1771.[44] Rural collectors had not then become at all numerous it is true, but the process had already begun with the commercial and political residents who had previously spread over Bengal. The isolation of men in country stations also helped, perhaps, in the growth of the cosmopolitan spirit which marked the times of Hastings. In the ordinary official it produced oriental habits and establishments, in the more cultured like Shore, Hastings or Forbes an interest in Persian literature or Hindu mythology.[45]

One more class of Englishmen appeared at this time, the order of adventurers. The exemption obtained from river tolls for the Company's merchants by Clive from Mir Jafar, and the Bengal government's impotence to deal with English agents, opened the country to ' English, French, German and American ' adventurers,[46] who came in with forged ' dustucks ' or passes, employed ' gomastahs ' or agents dressed as English sepoys and using the English flag, and used their privileged position to compel merchants to buy goods at from 30 to 50 per cent above market price.[47] It was this behaviour that was largely responsible for the war with Mir Kasim in 1763.[48] They gave the English name its bad reputation in Bengal during the sixties, but their career was ended by the reforms of Hastings from 1772-4.[49] Henceforward adventurers in the interior were confined to indigo planters and hangers-on at local courts. The government was determined to have 'as few Europeans as possible dispersed about the country', and though it never rid itself of the embarrassment of their presence,[50] the reign of terror which they had established never revived.

In the towns another type of adventurer appeared concurrently with the changing times and the vague talk of boundless riches. Often highly connected, this class hoped to collect large fortunes quickly in the unsettled conditions, but their day of opportunity was also short. As early as 1765 it was passing away. 'The place [Calcutta]', wrote Topham to Burrington, 'swarms with people, who are some of them connected with the first People there, and who are well qualified for such Employments as the gentleman you mention seems to benefit from, and yet are starving for want of bread.' 'The Company's Civil Service,' he added, 'is the only certain Track to a Fortune or Preferment, and much more on the Bengal Establishment than any other.'[51]

In this transition period there is a parallel development of English and Indian influence, of the royal soldier and the 'nabob', of the cumulative effect of numbers in fostering a class spirit, and of the orientalizing effect of contact with Indian society. The result was the cosmopolitan society of Hastings' time,[52] which lasted until the next wave of European influence, encouraged by Cornwallis, upset the balance. For the moment, however, the two currents ran side by side.

On the English side began that turning away from India to Europe which later developments have tended continually to increase. The Europeanization of the army has already been noticed, and the same subtle change of outlook is to be found in other directions as well. From this time onwards, for instance, no European seems to have been able to appreciate Indian music. Bernier had found the Imperial Band at Delhi trying at first, but had grown to like it,[53] and the early factors, from the frequency with which the 'country musick' is mentioned in the records, must at least have tolerated it. They probably enjoyed the songs of the nautch girls in their entertainments.[54] From this time, however, the 'country musick' was banished from public functions as it was from the army; instead European musicians multiplied and concerts began to be given. The European's first impression of Indian music is almost bound to be unfavourable, owing to the great difference between their respective idioms, and now Europeans had no longer to wait for a second impression. So the Frenchman de Pagé found the Nawab of Surat's band 'remarkable only for its noise',[55] as Captain Campbell considered it 'inelegant, harsh and dissonant',[56] and the general verdict was summed up by Major Blakiston when he wrote of Indians: 'in fact they have no music in their souls.'[57] The fate of the band presented by Mohammad Ali to the Madras Government in 1754, which was disbanded in 1757, is a good illustration. In earlier years bands were regularly provided for on great occasions by the Company itself.[58]

Another sign of the times was the changing taste in wine. Arrack, either alone or in the form of punch, was the most popular drink of the early century, but now gave way to Madeira and later to claret and beer. Arrack became a poor man's drink, and it was perhaps because of this and of its resemblance to arrack that whisky was considered 'no gentleman's drink' down to 1810.[59]

Developments in the settlements' amusements were another sign of the changing times. As the number of English settlers grew the means of organizing English amusements grew with the desire for indulging in them. Dancing was one of the most prominent of these, either in private houses or 'routs and assemblies'; by 1775 it was, according to Shore, who arrived in 1769, one of the chief amusements along with riding, hunting and shooting.[60] In this it largely replaced, except among the military, the practice of doing one's dancing vicariously by engaging troops of dancing girls.[61] The military adopted both methods to the end of the century.[62] Other forms of distinctively English amusement also appeared: the Harmonic Hall was built in Calcutta in 1780[63] and the first theatre was opened in Hastings' time. The church, which had been destroyed in the siege of Calcutta, however, was evidently less essential as it was not rebuilt till 1787. The first newspaper was the notorious *Hickey's Journal*, suppressed in 1782 by Hastings.[64]

All these developments were symptomatic of the changing taste which larger numbers and closer contact with Europe were bringing about. The settlers were beginning to adopt English rather than Indian standards of living and amusement; the ideal of making every English settlement an exact replica, as far as possible, of an English town was just coming into fashion. Nowhere is this seen more clearly than in the architecture of the time. There was never any attempt to adopt the Indian style of a house opening inwards on a courtyard, which with the resources possessed by the Europeans of the time, could have been made cool and luxurious enough with verandahs, fountains and formal gardens. Instead the classical style was imported bodily, and the verandahs were not even lowered sufficiently by means of arches to keep out the sun.[65] The whole verandah was laid bare in order to exhibit the full grandeur of an Ionic portico or piazza, which had then to be filled up by immense

Venetian frames. Their gardens tell the same story. The Moghul style with its formal lay-out and its use of ornamental water never became fashionable, because the English wished their gardens to be as nearly like their English prototypes of the new landscape style of Bridgeman and Kent as possible.[66]

But this increased European influence was only one side of the picture. Parallel to it went the influence of the Indian environment, sometimes elaborating what already existed, sometimes taking new forms. Foremost among these Indian customs was the European addiction to the nautch. As soon as enough ladies arrived in India to make European dancing practicable, the whole community took to it with enthusiasm, but they retained their taste for the nautch as a spectacle. To see a nautch was something like attending the ballet in Europe, with the difference that the troop always came to a private house ; in the transition period it was the substitute for the theatre. The difference between the Indian and English ideas of pleasure as consisting respectively in repose and action is in nothing better illustrated. 'Villagers,' says Hunter in his *Journal*, 'were much surprised to see us dance, saying that it was very extraordinary that we, who could afford to have dancing girls, should wish to dance.'[67] The European taste for a nautch is further shown by the fact that it became the recognized form of entertainment for an Indian merchant to provide for his English guests. As so easily happens in India, it became traditional, and continued long after the European taste itself had disappeared.[68] 'When a black man has a mind to compliment a European, he treats him to a nautch,' wrote Mrs. Kindersley in 1754,[69] and the custom still existed at the time of Mrs. Fenton's visit to Calcutta in 1826.

During the transition period its popularity continued unchecked, and though some had doubts of its propriety, all acknowledged its charm. 'It is their languishing glances, wanton smiles, and attitudes not quite consistent with decency, which are so much admired,' wrote Mrs. Kindersley.[70] Hart in 1775 speaks of 'six or seven black girls being brought in after dinner' when 'they sang and danced well',[71] and in 1778 they were still 'much admired by the European gentlemen'.[72] Their later history may perhaps here be summarized. In the civil stations they became gradually of less importance, though in 1794 it was still customary for ladies and gentlemen to be given a view of the nautch by friends on their arrival.[73] After this time the English taste gradually changed from a slightly guilty appreciation or naïve enjoyment to frank incomprehension, boredom and finally disgust. The chaplain Tennant in 1803 thought little of them, but advised attendance at these nautches, as a matter of courtesy.[74] Lord Hastings in 1814 was contemptuous,[75] while in 1826 Mrs. Fenton described a dancing girl as ' an odious specimen of Hindustanee beauty ', who ' made frightful contortions of her arms and hands, head and eyes. This was her poetry of motion. I could not even laugh at it '.[76] De Jacquemmont summed up the matter when he appreciated the nautch, but said it was liked best by those who had forgotten European musical time.[77]

In the army enthusiasm for the nautch continued till the end of the century, perhaps because of the lack of facilities for European dancing. According to Sir J. D'Oyley ' the influx of officers from 1778 led to the best sets going to the cantonments ' until ' reason rode past on the wings of military retrenchment, and the Auditor General's red ink negatives dissolved the charm '.[78] The taste nevertheless continued, and at the different camping grounds the officers would be entertained by sets from the neighbouring village or pagoda.[79]

Hookah smoking was another Indian custom which increased at this period. Though hookahs had always been used by some—in Mr. Charles Bendysh's Inventory of 1675 appears : ' 1 Chamolet Hoake with a green baise '—yet pipes had been far commoner in earlier days.[80] In the inventories scattered through the early *Consultation Books* there are many entries of pipes, but few of hookahs. But as soon as the series of inventories opens in 1754 hookahs begin to appear. A hookah was more expensive than a pipe and required a hookahburdar, and it would therefore naturally come into fashion with increasing wealth and ostentation. To the new arrivals it was a luxury, and so, in spite of all their increasingly English tastes they were devoted to its charms. By 1778 it was ' universal ',[81] and Hickey's refusal to smoke was perhaps the first sign of that insular independence, which, combined with economic reasons, eventually caused its decline.[82]

To the Indian customs which increased their hold at this time must be added the zenana. This was again an extension of a custom which new resources had made possible. In the earlier times it had been limited by the larger number of marriages with Portuguese and other Christians, and its growth after 1760 was helped by the influx of officers and factors who considered such marriages beneath them and established zenanas instead. The small numbers of European women having made some such development inevitable, it was natural that it should have taken the line of contemporary Indian custom. The custom was too strongly rooted to be affected by new arrivals, and as a result increased ; wealth only meant larger establishments. As long as the institution of the zenana lasted it was in its turn a powerful Indianizing influence. In 1780 Asiaticus, speaking of the expenses of the hookah, considered it ' absolute parsimony compared to the expenses of the seraglio . . . for those whose rank in the service entitles them to a princely income '.[83] Williamson and D'Oyley, both of whose experience covered the last twenty years of the century, wrote of the zenana as a normal custom ; the former in his *Vade Mecum*, dedicated to the Directors, calculated the monthly expenses which the young recruit might expect it to cost him.[84] In this case also an existing Anglo-Indian custom was developed rather than superseded by the increase of wealth and numbers.

But perhaps the most characteristic of all these Indian influences was the ideal of a 'nabob'. The earlier merchant made his money by trade, and if he was fortunate enough to survive returned to England to settle down as a country gentleman. He had little to do with nabobs and regarded himself as a merchant until his return, when he followed the normal course of his successful London brethren. But the factor of the transition period, with his connexion with politics and intercourse with real nawabs, quickly acquired the taste for being an oriental prince. He became a 'nabob' in ideal, and commerce was only the method by which he obtained the necessary wealth. Indeed he often gave up trade for contracts because that promised speedier results.[85] So we get a rapid transformation from the purely commercial factor of the 'fifties to the merchant turned soldier or politician in the 'sixties, and finally proclaiming himself a 'gentleman'. It was a unique feature of Anglo-Indian society, and one which caused the returned nabobs much of their trouble, that commerce and trade should be compatible with gentility. In England it raised up a wall of prejudice on the part of the landowning gentry, and in India it prevented the formation of any strong middle class to which the merchants should naturally have belonged. It began the separation of Anglo-Indian society into officials and 'poor Europeans' with a great gulf fixed between, leaving the few who were unattached to either by ties of interest or occupation (who in England would have formed the liberal element of the middle class) in a void place between the two.

The spirit of change and the absence of all precedents were characteristic of the transition period, and produced an extraordinary mixture of magnificence and disorder. Any picture of these years is bound to be confused and blurred by contradictory details and it is possible only to give one or two random illustrations. After 1756 Calcutta spread with great rapidity, and the custom began of erecting garden houses outside the city in the Garden Reach at Baraset, Barrackpore, etc., as well as of having town houses along the Chowringhee. But there was no supervision ; all building was at random so that the magnificence of the new houses was often obscured by their haphazard arrangement and their mean surroundings. Calcutta was more a city of scaffolding than a city of palaces. The drains were open as late as 1769,[86] and troops had to be kept out of Calcutta owing to its unhealthiness.[87] In the administration as in the city there was confusion owing to the lack of experienced men, and to a carelessness which existed even before the violent break of continuity caused by the capture of Calcutta. In 1756 the Directors wrote indignantly, 'The original letter from the Chiefs and others at Patna and a Leaf torn out of the original Diary of Mr. Surman's Embassy to the Great Moghul (1717) were picked up in a Publick Necessary House which the Writers make use of and are now in our Hand, where we are informed many Fragments of Papers of great Importance have likewise been seen.'[88] Many of the writers had phenomenal rises, and owing to their ignorance both of the language and of business, their work fell into the hands of their banians. 'The business of the Secretary's department,' wrote Clive in his trenchant way in 1766, 'was committed to a youth of three years standing in your service; the employment of Accomptant is now discharged by a writer still lower in the list of your servants; the important trusts of Military Storekeeper, Naval Storekeeper and Storekeeper of the Works, were bestowed, when last vacant, upon Writers; and a Writer held the post of Paymaster to the Army, at a period when near twenty lacks of rupees had been deposited for months together in his hands. Banians became principals in the several departments; the affairs of the Company flowed through a new and unnatural channel, and your most secret concerns were publicly known in the bazaar.'[89] Amongst the highest officials the same laxity prevailed, so that just before the coming of Clive the Calcutta proceedings recorded six unsuccessful attempts to assemble the Court of Cutcherry in April and May, together with the various excuses of the members. These included, in addition to the usual 'gone to Baraset' or 'out of town', such surprising individual pleas as that of the man who did not know he was a member, of another who was 'busy', and finally of the gentleman who 'said he could come but came not'.[90] Socially there was much the same confusion. 'In proportion as the inhabitants of this Settlement have increased,' wrote Shore in 1775, 'we are become much less sociable than formerly. The demon of party and politics has now broken loose among us, and in the room of public and private confidence, has planted suspicion, envy and distrust.'[91]

Finally we have an account of an animal fight by Colonel Champion, which seems more like the after-breakfast entertainments of the Nawabs of Oudh, and cannot have occurred often in Calcutta except at this strange transitional period.

FIGHT BETWEEN A BUFFALO AND A TIGER

[*face p.* 38

'The whole town assembled at the new Fort to see a Fight between a Tygar and a Buffaloe, an Elephant and Rhinoceros and two Camels. A large square place with struts being made, six buffaloes with their riders were put in and afterwards a Tygar loose; who did not attempt once to seize one of the Buffaloes; one of the Buffaloes ran at him first, after which there was little or no sport. They then set loose a very large Royal Tygar but he being hurt in his hind quarters was rendered useless, however the Animal behaved with noble spirit, and did his utmost. The Buffaloe by being led on to the beast attacked furiously and would lift and gorge the Tygar and throw him over his head with the greatest ease. As there was no opposition it afforded but little sport or pleasure. The Tygar being at last killed and being late, the Company broke up. Camels were brought and fought; they seize chiefly each other's legs, but it affords no diversion. An Elephant which had been prepared for a Battle ran wild and endeavoured to force the square, as great numbers of people were about it—seven were killed; when he found he could not accomplish his design he then ran through a Garden Wall, and lifted a roof off a House and had not the Rider behaved well, he would have brought it to the ground. As the Rhinocerous could not be moved there was no battle.'[92]

The first period of consolidation which followed the first period of transition covered roughly the years 1765-73. It can conveniently be traced in the diary of Colonel Rennell, the first Surveyor-General of Bengal, a copy of which is amongst the India Office Records. Rennell was in Madras and Bengal throughout the transition period, and a gradual change of outlook can be accurately traced in his pages. In 1762 he wrote from Madras that the chairman was going home worth £300,000, adding, 'This is certainly a fine country for a young gentleman to improve a small fortune in.' 'The inhabitants affect a deal of ostentation in their manner of living. Few private gentlemen live at less expence than £5-6,000 a year and those married about £8,000-£10,000. The Governor lives at the rate of £20,000 per annum.'[93]

In 1764, on his appointment as Surveyor-General in Bengal, he hoped to return in a few years with £5,000 or £6,000 and wrote optimistically that, while he had an allowance of £900 and perquisites of £1,000, 'I can enjoy my Friends, my Bottle and all the Necessaries of Life for £400[94]—Besides when I get acquainted with the Trade of this part of India I shall make much greater advantages, as I shall always be able to command a Capital.'[95] But a year later, soon after the advent of Clive, his tone began to change. The Company's Civil Service was now the only certain road to fortune. Pure adventurers were already at a discount and these private letters form perhaps the best evidence of the efficacy of Clive's second governorship. Things grew worse (from Rennell's point of view) rather than better. By 1768 he only hoped to retire on £120 a year ;[96] in 1769 he was growing tired of service ;[97] and in 1771 he was 'fearing the worst' in the shape of government interference, in which case 'twill be high time for us to decamp'.[98] He thus summed up the altered conditions. 'Bengal is surprisingly altered within a few years. Happy now is he who can pick up a bare Competency instead of the overgrown Fortunes that were formerly amassed here. But what even have the Fortunes availed ? Many of the Proprietors of them are forced to come out again to get more ; but this I presume to be owing to their dissipated way of living, for I don't by any means want to quarrel with a large Fortune.'[99]

So the period of corruption, confusion and groping for precedents, of adventurers and nabobs, passed imperceptibly into the period of later Calcutta and Madras. The transition from factory to settlement life was complete. Henceforward there is a continuity in social development, marred by no great changes or sudden catastrophes. The further transitions were secondary to the one which we have just considered, they took place within the framework of a settled society and did not change the society itself. As such they are more fully dealt with in later chapters but their chief features may be briefly summarized here. The second transition, which is marked roughly by the arrival of Cornwallis, is really only a development of the first. Externally it was marked by further reform, and internally by a great increase of European ideas and influence, imported partly by Royal officers, partly by independent officials like Cornwallis himself and the judges and attorneys of the High Court, and partly by the increasing number of women in the settlements. The third transition was a further development and completion of tendencies already apparent in the second. The way in which the influx of Europeans in middle life with set ideas contributed to change the outlook of the Indian settlements, and their reaction upon those whose outlook they wished to change, is shown in an illuminating letter of Colonel Pearse in 1779, with which we will conclude this chapter.

> Ever since Europeans came to India until the introduction of this [Supreme] Court,[100] it was the custom for them to exercise over their immediate servants the power of inflicting slight punishments to compel the people they employed to do the duty they set about ; they found it the custom of the country and necessity and example made them adopt it ; no man ever thought it wrong till the introduction of this Court ;

but a set of men, bred up in the prejudices of our Courts were, in an advanced age, lifted out of the middle of London into the midst of a set of people who, having conquered a mighty kingdom and being very few in number, were under the necessity of adopting many of the manners and customs of those they had conquered. The clamours raised against the whole body, for the actions of a few individuals, had been used to support the party they wanted to partake of those riches which they saw with envy in the hands of the Company's servants (*sic*).[101]

CHAPTER III

THE LATER SETTLEMENTS

THE visitor to eighteenth century Calcutta was wont to ascend the Hughli in a very chastened frame of mind. From the time of leaving England he had been tossed in small and confined quarters for anything from three months to a year, with few sights of land and rare stops to lighten the monotony of the voyage. A stop at Madeira where passengers were expected to find their own quarters while the ship was taking aboard pipes of the Hon. East India Company's madeira, a week or two of the Cape in which to complain of the quality of the Dutch food and the sharp eyes of the 'meinheers' for profit, and perhaps one at Dutch Trincomalee in Ceylon for water—these were the total of his halts. On board ship, if he possessed influence or a deep enough purse, he probably dined at the Captain's table, who for the outward voyage at least, with an eye to the more lucrative homeward trade, was usually civil enough. The fare was reasonable, with fresh poultry unless a storm washed the hen coops overboard, fresh mutton and possibly fresh milk; but the captain kept his eye on the bottle, signalling the conclusion of dinner by a solemn corking, and no smoking was allowed. Moreover, the ladies, destined for the Calcutta marriage market, often monopolized the largest cabin or 'round house', and their quarrels and intrigues too often occupied the attention of the rest of the boat. It was on board ship that the highly respectable Hastings met the Baroness Imhoff, but there were often tales and allegations far more serious than an ordinary flirtation and elopement. Sometimes the ladies' wardrobes, stocked with the latest London fashions destined to dazzle Calcutta society, vanished in the heat of the disputes in the round house; one captain was accused of seducing a lady passenger, and in the subsequent inquiry the doubtful point was not the fact of the seduction, but who was the seducer; and Mrs. Fay has kept a vivid record of the difficulties of constricted but uncongenial society. For amusement, the traveller had exercise on the deck, occasional fishing, visiting from ship to ship, and indoors gaming.[1]

As the jaded passengers approached the Coromandel coast, stories would be told of Hyder and Tipu and their ways, of the Carnatic invasions of 1768 and 1780 when the Madras garden houses went up in smoke and a scared settlement had believed that the governor had decamped before the disaster by arrangement with Hyder, 'having shaken the Pagoda tree,' says one writer feelingly, 'so thoroughly that no more has since been found on it.' Stories were told of the fate of prisoners who fell into the hands of the Sultans or were handed over by de Suffren, and of the adventures of casual ships (like Mrs. Fay's) which touched at Mysore ports and were detained. Tipu Sultan and the Mysoreans were regarded in something of the same light as the Kaiser and the Prussians in the late war; there was the same catalogue of barbarities industriously circulated, the same feeling of civilization in danger, *and*, what is often forgotten to-day, very much the same feeling of respectful dread. The personal prestige of the two Indian monarchs was indeed greater, for Hyder was a Bismarck as well as a Moltke, and Tipu a Hindenburg-Wilhelm. The difference in the English attitude was that between modern and eighteenth century society; there were no cries for common vengeance and shouts of 'Hang Tipu'; to the Wellesley brothers they were first of all princes and thus necessarily gentlemen. Too many generals had been outwitted by Hyder and the Carnatic had been too frequently pillaged by his 'lootywallahs' for them to be regarded, as we are sometimes tempted to do to-day, as obscure adventurers who delayed for a moment the inevitable growth of the British Dominion. Finally, the passengers' impatience would be fed with descriptions of the Madras and Calcutta which awaited him—vague stories of untold wealth and oriental luxury, of wild extravagance and incredible vice, of pomp and power, and perhaps less pleasing rumours of disease and sudden death. 'Nabobs' had become a household word in England since the conquest of Bengal; the older travellers would very likely approach Madras with feelings of strong disapproval not unmixed with apprehension at their reception, the younger and more numerous cadets of fifteen and upwards, with repressed exaltation and secret delight at the prospect of 'seeing real life'. Disgruntled travellers after three months' discomfort would welcome any relief, and to them Madras would appear as a promised land indeed.

From Trincomalee the ship crept up the monotonous breaker-lined palm-strewn Coromandel coast, past a string of European settlements—Dutch Negapatam neatly laid out with squares and characteristic canals, Danish Tranquebar, French Pondicherry, an open town since the last French war, and English Fort St. David—until finally St. Thomas's Mount, the legendary Glastonbury of Indian Christianity, would come into view, and then the gleaming houses and offices of Fort St. George. The ship approached the triple line of breakers and anchored in the open roads. Immediately a crowd of small boats or ' catamarans ' put off from the shore, some bearing agents and merchants to treat with the captain concerning his cargo, but most to take the passengers ashore.[2] The new-comer was immediately impressed with several things. He noted the long flowing garments and the mild countenances of the Hindu merchants on deck, and at first mistook them for women. Soldiers, indeed, sometimes only discovered their mistake on beginning a flirtation.[3] Then he observed the practical nakedness of the boatmen, and was surprised to find himself without any feeling of disgust, for the colour of their skins,[4] says one writer, took the place of a covering, and next he marvelled at the skill of the boatmen who crossed the three lines of breakers with scarcely one accident a year.[5] On landing he immediately found himself in a crowd of all nations, peoples and languages, Europeans and Indians, some come to view the cargo, more to view the spectacle and perhaps most to seek their fortune from the securities of the newly arrived. Before he had time to analyse the cosmopolitanism of the crowd he was beset with a number of ' dubashes ' clamouring for appointment. Every Englishman was convinced of the knavery of the Madras dubash or steward and of the Calcutta banian, and every dubash was convinced of the unlimited wealth, actual or potential, possessed by every Englishman. The new-comer's next experience, therefore, was a very uncomfortable quarter of an hour until he had adjudicated between one set of incogniti and another, and had engaged a dubash. If the visitor was to be a permanent resident of Madras, he would send his dubash to secure a house complete with servants, palanquins, carriages and horses, while he looked out his letters of introduction ; if he was merely calling on his way to Calcutta, he would proceed at once to deliver his letters. A letter of introduction was the wedding garment of early Anglo-Indian society, a *sine qua non* of entry into the polite world ; once presented the adventurer had a warm and generous welcome, but if he possessed none, or had lost them on the voyage out, as the Fays nearly did, or found the recipients departed up-country, as might easily happen, he had no entry into society, no invitations to public or private breakfasts or dinners for an indefinite period. Formerly he might have applied direct to the governor and been entertained by him, but the size of the settlements now forbade such promiscuous hospitality. The Anglo-Madrasis were lavish but exclusive. Nor could the wanderers stay at an hotel in the cosmopolitan style of to-day, for no hotels existed until after the turn of the century. If the new arrival had an official appointment he might be accommodated in the far from palatial writers' buildings or sent to the cadets' quarters, or if an officer he would join his regiment ; otherwise he would be reduced to one of the taverns which existed in the Black Town.[6] These were establishments kept by 'Portuguese' or half-caste Christians, and devoted to the selling of arrack, toddy and punch, the provision of bad dinners, the encouragement of gaming, the fleecing of new-comers and the general promotion of squalor. To adapt Hamilton's description of the Calcutta Hospital, 'many pagodas went in thereat, but few there were that came out again.'

> Here Boatswains, Gunners, Mates and Common Sailors,
> Comport with Stewards, Midshipmen and Taylors ;
> And self-dubb'd Captains, Bailiffs, Barbers join
> And drown reflection in adultrate wine.

The accommodation consisted of one large room in which eating, drinking, gaming, toadying and sleeping were indifferently carried on ;[7] hangers-on were always in attendance prepared to assist the staff in obliging the new gentleman at the rate of £1,000 a year. In addition the taverns acted as rendezvous for the Portuguese Christians, European soldiers and sailors whose fondness for arrack and toddy enlivened Madras nights and shortened their lives. In Calcutta these houses sprang up constantly near the barracks or the hospital, and were liberally patronized by the patients until the manager was deported as a 'vagabond European' and a nuisance.

The man whose social credentials were in order forthwith became one of the family of the first gentleman he had called on, until either he had secured a suitable establishment of his own, or his boat was due to sail for Calcutta. He would find himself borne away in a palanquin to his host's 'Garden House' on the Choultry plain or perhaps as far afield as St. Thomas's Mount.

The house he would find a large roomy mansion.[8] It would lie in the midst of its garden and was usually of one storey only, built on a ground floor of warehouses ; it would be fronted by an imposing classical portico and surrounded by 'piazzas' of classical pillars supporting the roof without any arches and with windows protected by Venetian blinds. Verandahs came in with bungalows and were first used in Bombay where the word was apparently derived from the Portuguese.[9] The roofs were flat, the general style classical and the whole exterior was finished with chunam, a plaster compounded of sea shells and lime, which gave a bright white polish. Madras chunam was the most famous, as it gave a marble-like finish, but the Calcutta chunam, though less brilliant, was also white and elegant. Indeed it was often more pleasing to the eye, since the Madras merchants were inclined to neglect their houses in the fort which were only used as offices and warehouses, and allowed the chunam to peel off in patches and produce a mottled and decayed effect. In Calcutta, on the other hand, the town houses were attached to the offices with the result that both were kept in proper repair. The effect of the chunam was magnificent, but it was also blinding, and at the end of the century a light brown plaster of sand and lime with white chunamed corner-pieces began to be substituted.[10] The change was made for reasons which are still upheld by modern medical opinion, and it is the more interesting in view of the policy of the builders of New Delhi to-day, with their forests of lamp-posts and seas of whitewash. Already, it is interesting to notice, the dazzling white has been replaced by a faintly blue-tinted colour.

Inside the houses had arras floors to keep out the white ants, open-raftered ceilings which were preferred for cleanliness and through fear of insects, glass windows with Venetian shutters, and double doors or curtains in the doorway.[11] There was little furniture apart from the rich Persian carpets as the householder displayed his wealth and taste on his table rather than round his walls or in his drawing-room. Here, attended by a large staff of servants and indulging in a continuous round of social entertainments, the visitor would pass his time happily enough.[12] He would rise at sunrise and ride before breakfast, which was at eight or nine o'clock, after which his host would depart in his palanquin or carriage, to the fort if he was a government official, or to his adjoining office if a merchant. The morning was spent by others in making calls of gallantry and escorting ladies to the 'Europe shops', miscellaneous stores which sold Europe goods brought by the last season's ships. At two or three o'clock was dinner, the principal meal of the day. In the early days it had been at one, but grew slowly later to five or six o'clock, thus swallowing up tea, until it established itself at half-past seven or eight.[13] Supper then disappeared, tea at five o'clock was revived, and the place of the mid-day meal was taken by tiffin, nominally 'two or three glasses of wine and light curries', but often substantial enough to destroy the appetite for dinner. After dinner the company retired to rest, rose again at 5 p.m. to take tea and then to drive or ride, to see and be seen on the St. Thomas's Road, and then paid formal calls and supped at ten o'clock. For entertainment there were, after 1785, private and public balls on great occasions like Christmas Day or the King's Birthday, lotteries and occasional theatrical performances; for sport, riding, driving and shooting. The visitor would never enter Black Town where lived the Indian population, and a number of Armenians, Portuguese and European merchants and sailors, and would only go to the fort on official business. He would frequent the esplanade in a palanquin, carriage or on horseback—but never on foot. On his way perhaps he would pass the old 'Nawab Walajah', Mahommad Ali, Nawab of Arcot, sitting aged and dignified, in white muslin robes in a European carriage on his way to his mansion, the Chepauk Palace. There he would probably meet a band of European creditors who would be turned away empty with the customary courteous assurances that something would undoubtedly very soon turn up.[14] Mahommad Ali's debt, the origin of which dated from the old Carnatic wars, and the growth of which was not unconnected with rumoured douceurs by successive governors until Macartney broke the tradition, had long been a public question in Madras. It was eventually funded and finally taken over by the Government.[15] The Nawab himself was tall and dignified, of a light colour and a pleasing countenance; he was courteous and hospitable to Europeans, and was popular and respected in Madras.[16] There can have been few princes so noble in appearance and so disappointing in action, so rich in promises and so poor in performance. His whole policy was comprehended in the formal ending of Persian diplomatic letters—'What can I say more?'; government by deputy was his cardinal political principle, and complaisance his paramount virtue. He maintained an agent in London to plead his cause and another in Madras to correspond with the Governor, and his palace and service long remained a refuge for dismissed officials, a promised land for adventurers and a cave of Adullam for the discontented.[17] He had been deeply implicated in the Pigot plot of 1776, and in most of the shady financial transactions before and after that time, and his life was a continual round of petitions, protestations and remonstrances to the Council, and of private arrangements with its individual members; yet in spite of, or perhaps because of, this, he remained popular with the English till the end, and at his death received appreciative notices from the youthful Madras press.[18] To some he appealed by his dignity and as an interesting historical survival, to others he was a useful person in the political game as the pathetic victim of English rapacity and ambition,[19] to others again he was a source of profit, but what really endeared him to the English was something else—his dignity, his grand manners and his generosity, even though at his creditors' expense, which all invested him with the one thing needful in their eyes—the character of a gentleman.

With the rest of Madras, the Armenians, the Eurasians, and the Portuguese, the visitor would have little to do. Polite society hardly knew of their existence. Of Indians, except as servants, he saw nothing. In this way time would pass pleasantly enough until his ship was ready to sail for Calcutta.

The approach to Calcutta was very different from that to Madras. When still hardly within sight of land the ship cast anchor at Diamond Harbour and waited for a pilot, glad not to have struck one of the sandbanks which surround the mouth of the Hughli. With pilot on board the ship proceeded to Fulta, where passengers were transferred to budgerows, long, heavy oar-driven boats which took them up to Calcutta. Unless some friend had dispatched his private budgerow down river, the journey was apt to be uncomfortable as well as monotonous, for the public boats paid little attention to comfort and were often crowded. They passed between low banks lined with trees with no variation but a few villages to enliven the scene, tigers roared and jackals screamed at night, while mosquitoes buzzed their high-pitched rasping drone on the steamy air of the boat. The result to minds filled with vague ideas of the City of Palaces and the wealth and magnificence of Bengal was first keen disappointment and then indignation. But on nearing Calcutta the scene changed and its effect had all the force of contrast and the unexpected. As the boat entered the Garden Reach the former desolation gave way to prosperity ; large houses lined the banks, Colonel Watson's derelict docks were passed, until Calcutta, a mass of white buildings lining the right-hand bank of the river, came into view. The first impression was commonly even more favourable than that of Madras ; Calcutta was already frequently called one of the finest cities not only in Asia but in Europe and the world.[20]

On landing the same proceeding was largely followed as in Madras. Dubashes and servants thronged the river steps at which the traveller landed ;[21] each man felt for his letters of introduction and proceeded at once to visit the nearest friend in order to secure a shelter for the night. The unfortunate without them proceeded as before to a Portuguese tavern or punch house. The old hand returned from leave probably escaped all this by being met by a friend's budgerow at Fulta, and would very likely find his old banian (the Bengal dubash or steward) waiting to greet him.

Once settled he would live much the same life as at Madras, but with certain marked local differences. To begin with the arrangement of the town varied. The White and Black towns were not kept apart geographically, though they remained socially distinct as in Madras, but the one grew round the other. In old Calcutta the fort had been the core round which the principal merchants, some Indian and Armenian as well as European, lived, and beyond which again grew out the native city. After the capture of Calcutta in 1757 the English merchants began more and more to

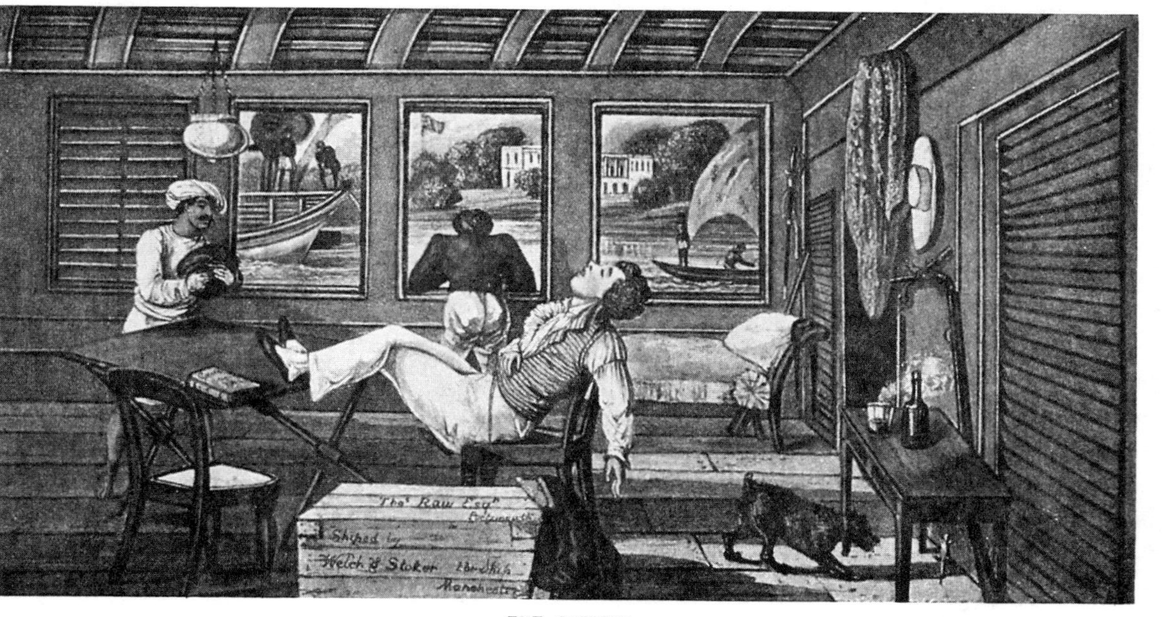

THE GRIFFIN

[*face p.* 48

live outside the city altogether, and the garden house craze began; the river downwards along Garden Reach and upwards towards Barrackpore was lined with English country houses; Danish Serampore and even French Chandernagore became residential suburbs. Indeed officials were so apt to seek repose and inspiration there that an order was passed forbidding government servants from leaving the city without permission.[22] When the fort was rebuilt, after the recapture, no houses were allowed within, unlike Madras, where houses existed but were only used as offices and not inhabited by the English. Within were only 'godowns' for stores, and the government buildings. The imposing Government House of Wellesley, Writers' Buildings, the new church built in 1786 and the general offices, grew up near the fort as the central official and business core of the city. In 'Black Town' as in Madras, also resided besides Indians, Armenians, Portuguese, Eurasians, and the poorer class of Europeans. The Calcutta houses were in the same grand style and of the same large dimensions as those of Madras, the town houses lining the esplanade along the Chowringhee Road being commonly of two storeys, the lower used as store rooms and the upper approached by a stone staircase.[23] It was only at the end of the century that the coolness of ground floor rooms was discovered.[24] In the country the houses had usually a ground floor only, and were arranged on the usual modern plan—a lofty central hall surrounded by lower rooms descending in tiers to the verandahs. But they were not yet called bungalows, a name which was then specially applied to temporary one-storeyed thatched buildings made of 'kacha' or sun-dried bricks.[25] These first became popular in the provinces with the growth of civil stations and military cantonments, where by their combined comfort and cheapness they suited the purse and the taste of the migrant soldier. In 1810 the word was still one to be italicized in a book of travel, although it was then beginning to usurp the old name of 'Garden House'.[26] Around the houses were verandahs, as in Madras, still usually called piazzas, and in front were classical colonnades. The English Calcutta houses of the later eighteenth century presented an interesting mixture of English and Indian features, of obstinate adherence to customs and attempts at adaptation to the climate. The classical style, of course, admitted easily of transplantation, being in England itself an exotic, and one has to admit that despite much mixture a sense of dignity and some fine general effects like those of the Governor-General's house and other Calcutta public buildings were attained. It was at any rate better than that of the Public Works Department and the missionary Gothic of the early, or the insincere Orientalism of the later, nineteenth century.

But the lofty classical piazzas with their pillars rising to the whole height of the house, airy and shady as they were at mid-day, let in the sun's rays too easily in the early afternoon. 'More air and less light' is a maxim of tropical architecture, and as a result there occurred a very interesting series of changes and experiments in the last years of the century. To remedy the glare caused by the height of the pillars, Venetian blinds were introduced and placed over the windows.[27] In the new bungalows the verandahs were lowered and the shade obtained in this way. Folding doors came in as being more effective against the dust. Glass had been in common use by the English since the mid-century. The great feature of the period was, however, the discovery of new appliances for reducing the heat. Tatties, made of fine strips of bamboos threaded together, were hung in the great inter-columnal spaces; kus-kus, a thick matting material emitting a peculiar smell when wetted with water, was applied to doors of both houses and palanquins, and the art of 'central cooling' a whole house by means of it and a breeze through one open door began to be practised. Another discovery was the swinging punkah, said to have been invented by an Eurasian clerk who, exasperated by the heat in his office in Fort William, tied his desk to the roof, attached a string to it and thrust it into his astonished servant's hands with the command to pull.[28] The earliest mention of its use is by Hickey in 1785,[29] and it spread later to Madras and Bombay. The Church, true to its cautious tradition, adopted them for the Calcutta church only in 1801 on the recommendation of Lord Wellesley.[30]

With all these adaptations, however, the English clung obstinately to English habits, and tended to do so more as the size of the settlements increased. Though they used comparatively little furniture in their houses, they never dispensed, even in their earliest days, with tables and chairs. They never adopted the system of inner courtyards and only slowly realized that the ground floor was cooler than the first storey. As soon as cooling apparatus like tatties and punkahs improved, they began to lower the ceilings and reduce the windows, which by 1800 distinguished the old houses from the new and made the former much sought after.

Each house lay in its own gardens, which were the pride and delight of all Anglo-Indians. Here again nationalism asserted itself; the English idea of a garden was not a fresco of ornamental water and playing fountains and shady pavilions like the Moghul, a Dutch garden in marble, but one of well-kept lawns and laden fruit trees, as in 'England's green and pleasant land'.[31] So they spent much toil and time in trying to keep lawns green during the hot weather, and in trying to grow grapes in the sandy soil of Madras.

The gardeners, or ' mollies ', were usually Hindus, whose skill in irrigation compelled admiration, but whose knowledge of horticulture was limited. The Chinese gardeners, whose patience and knowledge filled up the gaps in the mollies' attainments, were esteemed the best. In the gardening art the English were little influenced by the Moghuls whose gardens they hardly saw until they were in decay, but from the Dutch in their East Indian stations and at Chinsura they both borrowed new ideas and brought many seeds.[32]

The *Madras Dialogues* in 1750 gave the following vegetables as grown in Madras—' Cucumbers, Country Beans, Peases, Colewort, Cabbage, Corriander, Lettice, Mint, Radish, Garlick, Melon, Leeks and Chitterlings '.[33] Williamson mentions—' Cabbages, Cauli-Flowers, Lettices, Celery, Carrots, Turnips, Pees, Cucumbers, French Beans, Radishes and Potatoes as being acclimatized, and Love Apples, Egg Plants, Gourds, Calavans, Yams and Sweet Potatoes ' as being used. He also mentions the following fruits—' Guavas, Peaches, Nectarines, Grapes, Apples [but not Pears], Pine Apples, Mangoes, Oranges, Citron Limes, Pomegranates, Byres, Commingahs and Curruidahs '.[34]

Near and behind the house would be the servants' quarters and the stables ; poultry and possibly turkeys (very difficult to rear in the damp Bengal climate) were kept, and the really select mansions would be completed by a piggery, where pigs were both carefully bred and fattened.

The new-comer, having secured a house through his banian, would now leave his host to commence his establishment. On his arrival he would find a complete, and, as it would seem to him, very extensive staff of servants already installed by his steward. His expostulations would only lead to endless explanations as to why the sweeper could not be allowed to make the bed, the bearer would refuse to clean the boots or the clerk to dust his papers, why one man was required exclusively to fill his hookah, another to cool the wine, and a third to wait at table. Physical force might cut short the explanations, but it never cut down the number of servants ; in the last resort the servants had a strange power of taking joint action, and had their own ideas of the strike and the boycott.

Faced with this involved and subtle hierarchy, made doubly obscure by the ingenuity and as it seemed to nearly all Englishmen, the deceit of the banian, the new arrival soon gave up the effort to understand and to control in bewilderment and despair. Henceforth the banian was supreme, and provided he managed with reasonable prudence, was in a fair way to making the fortune that his master dreamed about. The banian, a Bengali Hindu of the commercial class and often a Brahmin, was the chief of the establishment. His importance lay in his control of the whole financial side of the establishment, which gave him great power over the servants by means of his control of the monthly wages, and over his master by means of the loans which most new arrivals raised on the security of their future prospects. Often the banians took no regular salary, being content with the control of the total turnover and the commission of a half anna to the rupee on all payments. Yet the English detested them as they did no other class of Indian. That characteristic of a mercantile nation, a dislike of being over-reached was very evident in later Calcutta. With his steward speaking fluently his own Bengali English, full of the most plausible and elaborate explanations of the most obscure business, whose sweet reasonableness increased in proportion to the doubtfulness of the transaction, with the expenses rising steadily in excess of his income, in spite of the most earnest efforts of the steward, with loans and their interest steadily mounting and due to the same most obliging and sympathetic steward, the average Englishman soon acquired a settled conviction of the superhuman cunning and skill of the banians.[35] This belief became part of the creed of all Anglo-Indians and the banians were looked on with a reverential awe, which was as far in excess of the real facts as the average continental opinion of the skill and subtlety of English diplomacy.

After the banian came the darogah or gomastah.[36] He was the general superintendent of works; like the banian he took no wages but received a commission on all his transactions. The new arrival would certainly make the acquaintance of the munshi, or interpreter, who was employed both for teaching and translating purposes. Of the more purely domestic staff the most magnificent were the outdoor palanquin bearers. These were headed by the jemmadar; he was often an old and trusted servant, who walked beside the palanquin, and was sometimes admitted into the confidence of his master. The palanquin bearers were from four to six in number and were preceded by 'soontah-burdars' bearing silver batons about thirty inches long, with the upper end carved to represent bludgeons.[37] If, however, it could be afforded a 'chobdar' was substituted who carried a silver pole four and a half feet long.[38] At night the retinue was increased by 'mossaulchees' or link boys.[39] Inside the house the head servant was the khansamah. The cook was the 'babachy'[40] and was usually a Mohammedan. At table there was the 'kitmatgar', who stood behind his master's chair at dinner; and did it sometimes so successfully that dinner parties were almost suffocated for want of air! Another essential servant was the 'hookah burdar', who kept and brought in his master's hookah after dinner, and accompanied his master to all his entertainments. In his office worked his clerk or 'kranny',[41] usually a Eurasian, and there the master daily interviewed his cash keeper and business manager, the 'sarkar' who corresponded to the Madras dubash. His small wage was liberally augmented by the 'dustoorie' of half an anna to the rupee which he charged on everything. For the menial office work there was the 'duftaree',[42] for messages, then as now a large part of Anglo-Indian business, there were 'hirkarrahs' and 'piadas' or 'peons'. The garden was in the charge of the molly and the various offices of groom (syce), grass cutter (gauskot), horse breaker (chaubuckasswar), dog-keeper (dooreah), camel-driver (surwan), water-carrier (bheesty), door-keeper (durwan) and watchman (chokydar) were all performed by different men. Besides these, there were a number of occasional servants attached to houses for particular duties. They were the darzi (tailor), the dhobi (washerman), the hajaam (barber).[43] The sweeper as now was the 'mater'. If the settler possessed a boat, as was usual, he would also employ a 'manjy' or steersman, a 'goleeah' or bowman, and a number of 'dandys' or rowers. Women servants were the 'ayahs' or ladies' maids, who were usually Eurasian, and 'dhyes'. Finally there were frequently slave boys[44] and women who acted as pages and ladies' maids. They often spoke English and were often given their freedom but that they were frequently ill-treated is evidenced by the number of advertisements describing and advertising for missing slave boys. The Company traded in slaves until 1764 and did not prohibit their export by proclamation until 1789.[45] European servants were not numerous or successful in Bengal. They were employed chiefly as postillions, coachmen, butlers and stewards, but were very expensive since they needed a house and servants of their own and they often saved money and then set up in some business without warning. An English butler had the additional disadvantage of understanding the conversation at the dinner table, which gave him in Bengal society endless opportunities for mischief-making.[46] European women were not much better; it was complained of them that they always deserted to get married, some even at Madras on their first arrival ashore. Ladies were advised to take from England an ayah wishing to return to India.[47]

A day of the Bengal Anglo-Indian is thus described in Macintosh's *Travels*.

> About the hour of seven in the morning, his durwan (doorkeeper) opens the gate and the viranda (gallery) is free to his circars, peons (footmen), hurcarrahs (messengers or

spies), chubdars (a kind of constable), houccaburdars and consumahs (stewards and butlers), writers and solicitors. The head bearer and jemmadar enter the hall and his bed-room at eight o'clock. A lady quits his side and is conducted by a private staircase, either to her own apartment, or out of the yard. The moment the master throws his legs out of bed, the whole force is waiting to rush into his room, each making three salaams, by bending the body and head very low, and touching the forehead with the inside of the fingers and the floor with the back part. He condescends, perhaps, to nod or cast an eye towards the solicitors of his favour and protection. In about half an hour after undoing and taking off his long drawers, a clean shirt, breeches, stockings, and slippers are put upon his body, thighs, legs and feet, without any greater exertion on his own part than if he was a statue. The barber enters, shaves him, cuts his nails, and cleans his ears. The chillumjee and ewer are brought by a servant whose duty it is, who pours water upon his hands and face, and presents a towel. The superior then walks in state to his breakfasting parlour in his waistcoat; is seated; the consumah makes and pours out his tea, and presents him with a plate of bread or toast. The hair-dresser comes behind, and begins his operation, while the houccaburdar softly slips the upper end of the snake or tube of the hucca into his hand;[48] while the hair-dresser is doing his duty, the gentleman is eating, sipping and smoking by turns. By and by his banian presents himself with humble salaams and advances somewhat more forward than the other attendants. If any of the solicitors are of eminence, they are honoured with chairs. These ceremonies are continued perhaps till 10 o'clock; when attended by his cavalcade, he is conducted to his palanquin, and preceded by eight to twelve chubdars, harcarrahs and peons, with the insignia of their professions and their livery distinguished by the colour of their turbans and cumurbands (a long muslin belt wrapt round the waist) they move off at a quick amble; the set of bearers, consisting of eight generally, relieve each other with alertness and without incommoding their master. If he has visits to make, his peons lead and direct the bearers; and if business renders his *presence only* necessary, he shows himself, and pursues his other engagements until two o'clock when he and his company sit down perfectly *at ease* in point of dress and address, to a good dinner, each attended by his own servant. And the moment the glasses are introduced regardless of the company of ladies, the houccaburdars enter, each with a houcca, and presents the tube to his master, watching behind and blowing the fire the whole time. As it is expected that they shall return to supper, at 4 o'clock they begin to withdraw without ceremony, and step into their palanquins; so that in a few minutes, the man is left to go into his bedroom, when he is instantly undressed to his shirt, and his long drawers put on; and he lies down in his bed, where he sleeps till about 7 or 8 o'clock, then the former ceremony is repeated and clean linen of every kind as in the morning is administered; his houccaburdar presents the tube to his hand, he is placed at the tea table, and his hair-dresser performs his duty as before. After tea he puts on a handsome coat, and pays visits of ceremony to the ladies; returns a little before 10 o'clock; supper being served at 10. The company keep together till between 12 and 1 in the morning, preserving great sobriety and decency; and when they depart our hero is conducted to his bedroom, where he finds a female companion to amuse him until the hour of 7 or 8 the next morning. With no greater exertions than these do the Company's servants amass the most splendid fortunes.[49]

The life of the young Company's servant is illustrated by the diary of Charles Metcalfe on his arrival in Calcutta in 1801.[50]

1801

Tues. 6 *Jan.* Went with Plowden to see Miss Baillie at Barlow's. Received an answer from Crommelin. Dined at home.

7 *Jan.* Went with Plowden to Brooke's. Saw Golding. Dined at Thornhill's. Got a Dhobee.

9 *Jan.* With Plowden in the morning. Was introduced to Sir Alured Clarke and General Baynard. Dined with the Governor-General who talked much about Eton. Went to Lady Anstruther's ball.

10 *Jan.* Shopping in the morning. Got a cocked hat (20 rupees). Dined and passed the evening at Dr. Dick's.

Sunday, 11 *Jan.* Called on Mr. Bazett. Dined with them.

12 *Jan.* Strolling about in the morning. Went to the levee. Dined at home and passed the evening at Colvin's.

13 *Jan.* Dined at College. Went to the Governor's ball.

14 *Jan.* Dined at Sir Alured Clarke's. At Dick's in the evening.

15 *Jan.* Dined at Mr. Graham's. Went to Brooke's ball. Sat up till sunrise at a second supper.

16 *Jan.* Dined at Tucker's. Went to bed very much fatigued, not having slept the previous night.

17 *Jan.* Dined at College. Sat at Higginson's. Had a Moonshee.

Sunday, 18 *Jan.* Dined at home. Had a Moonshee.

19 *Jan.* Dismissed my Moonshee, finding him of no use. Determined to teach myself. Went on board the 'Skelton Castle', the 'Malartique', and the 'London', taken from the French; and the 'Countess of Sutherland', a very large ship, in

company with Plowden, Impey, Hamilton and Chester. Dined at home. Went to Lady Anstruther's.
20 *Jan.* Dined at Dick's.
21 *Jan.* Breakfasted at Bristow's. Wrote Journal. Dined at Bristow's.
22 *Jan.* Tiffed at Hamilton's. Dined at Plowden's.
23 *Jan.* Answered my uncle Monson's letter. Ditto Richardson. Dined at home. Went to the Governor's ball.
Monday, 26 *Jan.* Dined at Barlow's. Great A's rout.
27 *Jan.* Dined at Bazett's.
28 *Jan.* Dined at College. Spent the evening at Hamilton's.
29 *Jan.* Dined at Brooke's.
30 *Jan.* Dined at Butler's. Ball at Brooke's.
31 *Jan.* Tiffed at Law's.

Mrs. Fay gives an equally interesting account from the lady's point of view.

> The dinner hour as I mentioned before is two and it is customary to sit a long while at table ; particularly during the cold season ; for people here are mighty fond of grills and stews, which they season themselves and generally make very hot. The Burdwan stew takes a deal of time ; it is composed of everything at table, fish, flesh and fowl ; somewhat like the Spanish Olla Podrida. Many suppose that unless prepared in a silver saucepan it cannot be good ; on this point I must not presume to an opinion, being satisfied with plain food ; and never eating any of those incentives to luxurious indulgence.
>
> During dinner a good deal of wine is drunk, but a very little after the cloth is removed ; except in Bachelors' parties,[51] as they are called ; for the custom of reposing, if not of sleeping after dinner is so general that the streets of Calcutta are from four to five in the afternoon almost as empty of Europeans as if it were midnight. Next come the evening airings to the Course, everyone goes though sure of being half suffocated with dust. On returning from thence, tea is served, and universally drunk here, even during the extreme heats. After tea, either cards or music fill up the space, till ten, when supper is announced. Five card loo is the usual game and they play a rupee a fish limited to ten. This will strike you as being enormously high but it is thought nothing of here.
>
> Tredille and Whist are most in fashion but ladies seldom join the latter ; for though the stakes are moderate, bets frequently run high among the gentlemen which renders those anxious who sit down for amusement, lest others should lose by their blunders.

> Formal visits are paid in the evening; they are generally very short, as perhaps each lady has a dozen to make and a party waiting for her at home besides. Gentlemen also call to offer their respects and if asked to put down their hat, it is considered as an invitation to supper. Many a hat have I seen vainly dangling in its owner's hand for half an hour, who at last has been compelled to withdraw without any one's offering to relieve him from the burden.[52]

This was the fashionable life of the settlement but it was not the whole life. For small though the settlement was it was yet divided into a number of classes which tended to grow sharper in definition as time went on. The eccentricities of Colonel Fierie-Phlaime, the tall stories of Major Corker, the customs of Flassipore, the gaucheries of the half-caste ambitious of social recognition, and the vulgarities of the boxwallah, so dear to the nineteenth century Anglo-Indian satirist, were only just emerging into their developed form. But though the nature of the distinctions have changed, the fact of distinction was as obvious then as ever it is now; the change was more one of division by hierarchy and position than division by occupation. Thus the sharp distinctions between trade and government service which still leads to such subtle social distinctions as that between retailer and wholesaler, did not then exist, because until the time of Cornwallis every official was a trader. In fact the commercial was the more popular service as being the most lucrative. Clive made much money on a commission for provisioning his company;[53] Rennell weighed the possibility of a fortune through trade as one of the prospects for his padre brother. Indeed, officials like Palmer could go into trade for good and remain acceptable in society,[54] and the successful merchant was equally tolerated. Even the Eurasians could find highly placed friends if they were sufficiently affluent.[55] Nevertheless, the society was already sundered by gulfs deep enough to make it a very fair imitation of the Hindu caste system which all its members affected to despise. The first broad distinction was between the official and military classes; the first regarded the second as foolhardy wine-bibbers, the soldier the officials as industrious quill-drivers, office recluses who had only pride to cover up their lack of all touch with reality. The army was the stronghold of a vigorous Philistinism; in the civil service existed whatever could be found of culture. Within the army itself was a division between Company's and Royal officers, which was a source of much grievance to the Company's officers until they were merged into the Indian army after the mutiny.[56] A further division was attempted between officers in Indian and European regiments, but this was rigorously suppressed from motives of prudence.[57] Speaking generally there was a broad division between the soldier who thought the civilian was losing what his sword had won and the civilian who felt sure that the blundering hand of the soldier would shatter all the intricate and laborious webs of his diplomacy. Both were socially approximately equal, and so the jealousy was acute. In the Presidency towns the officers lived in much the same style as the civilians but in the mofussil cantonments they developed a social life of their own which centred round the regiment and developed all the characteristics of the public school spirit long before Dr. Arnold.[58]

Next to the soldiers and civilians came the professionals—the lawyers, doctors, engineers and chaplains. They formed the middle class of the settlement, but it was a middle class too small to develop ideals and habits of its own. So their tastes and outlook and their style of life were simply reduced copies of the officials. Amongst them, however, was found much of the culture which existed. Only the lawyers can perhaps strictly be said to compose this middle class, since the doctors and engineers were mostly Company's officers with military rank, who rose regularly in the military hierarchy. The life of the more prosperous and profligate lawyer is illustrated by William Hickey, that of the less successful and less professional by Mr. Fay.

So far the colour of this society was aristocratic (in position though not of course in birth) and the great ambition of a man was to gain admittance into the round of breakfasts and dinner parties, concerts, balls and routs which made up the fashionable life. But instead of the thriving independent commercial life of London, owning the real wealth of the country, occasionally throwing up great merchants who bought lands and titles and so passed into the caste of gentlemen, but in the main noticing little and caring less for the life of the fashionable, there was in Bengal only a small class of European shopkeepers, who were reinforced at the end of the century by a few large commercial houses.

These possessed neither the bulk of the wealth nor the independent spirit of the settlement. So when the officials ceased to be traders a great gulf rapidly opened and became fixed between the official and the 'box-wallah' which is so prominent a feature of nineteenth century Anglo-Indian literature.[59] Instead of the commercialism of the merchant balancing the jingoism of the gentleman, to produce a policy practical as well as spirited, fruitful of wealth as well as of glory, the opposite process to that of Holland took place; the gentry were not exiled to their estates by the merchants, but the merchants were confined to their shops by the officials. The strength of a middle class is the union of commercial with professional interests but in India they were kept rigidly apart. The process was not complete till the turn of the century, but from the time of Wellesley, with his contempt for the 'cheesemongers of Leadenhall Street', it continued without a check. To Anglo-India since then pride and glory, power and prestige have always been more important than conciliation and understanding, co-operation and compromise. This is why imperialistic viceroys have tended to be popular amongst Europeans in India and liberal viceroys unpopular.

The ideals of the later settlements were becoming increasingly aristocratic, and even those who were excluded from polite society by a wall of class prejudice accepted the same standards and imitated the fashions as far as they could. But apart from the despised commercial class there was a much larger class of Europeans whom writers as a rule conveniently forget. They were classed at the time as 'Low Europeans', or the more desperate of them as 'European Vagabonds', they existed in considerable numbers, and they clearly caused the Government considerable embarrassment, both by prejudicing Indian opinion against Europeans by their lives, and by harassing the Government by their misdemeanours. They consisted of time-expired soldiers turned tavern-keepers, of small shopkeepers, of European servants who had set up on their own, of sailors and craftsmen brought to Calcutta by trade and the prospect of rapid fortunes, and even sometimes of convicts whom the Australian colonies tried to dispose of in India.[60] They were closely connected with another world, the Eurasians or Anglo-Indian community, and indeed they often inter-married with them and swelled their numbers. Inevitably many of them fell out of employment, when they entered the class of 'European Vagabond' and caused trouble by their brawls with and oppression of Indian coolies. They were responsible for much of the ill-repute in which Europeans as a whole were held by Indians, though in this respect some held the rich to be primarily responsible.[61] The Bengal villagers welcomed Carey at Debarta because he was unlike other Europeans 'who were worse than tigers'[62]; according to Dubois the decline of Christian missions in the eighteenth century 'must be imputed in a great degree to the immoral and irregular conduct of the Europeans in every part of the country';[63] an Indian could remark to a chaplain, 'Christian religion! Devil religion! Christian much drink, much do wrong, much beat, much abuse others';[64] a merchant could say to Swartz: 'You astonish me, for from what we daily observe and experience we cannot but think them [Europeans] with very few exceptions, to be self-interested, incontinent, proud, full of illiberal contempt and prejudice against us Hindus, and even against their own religion, especially the higher classes'.[65] Finally there is the retort of a girl pupil of a Hindu dancing master when told by Swartz that no wicked and unholy person could possibly enter the kingdom of Heaven—'Alas sir, in that case hardly any European will ever enter it'.[66]

The misdemeanours of the vagabond class occupy twenty-five volumes in the India Office records.[67] They consist chiefly of brawling, drunkenness and total contempt of law and authority, frequently commencing with initial debts, though some of them are of a far graver character. The authorities were alive to the scandal of their conduct, but were handicapped in dealing with them by their lack of power over the Company's own servants. For many years the worst punishment was deportation to England, and it was not till 1799 that a punch-house-keeper named William Smith who barricaded himself in on being ordered home and shot a sepoy, was executed for murder. In consequence of this leniency and the frequent conflict of jurisdictions a perusal of the records surprises most by the frequent pardons and not infrequent total evasion of justice.

As early as 1767 Clive noted the vagabonds which infested both Calcutta and Madras, and recommended them for deportation.[68] But the evil did not abate; in 1789, S. Price, the Marine Paymaster, wrote to the Secretary of the Governor-General that English seamen arrived at Calcutta in foreign ships soon became unemployable and died in the hospital of drink.[69] He suggested a guardship in the Hughli to take men off to other merchant ships. Cornwallis ordered strolling Europeans to be confined in the fort without rigorous imprisonment. But in 1792, Middleton, the magistrate at Dacca was again asking that 'some measure be adopted to prevent these low Europeans traversing the country in the manner they now do, by which means they get into disputes with the inhabitants of villages and the consequences which sometimes ensue generally originate from their own bad conduct'.[70] Two examples will show something of the conditions. In 1789 Michael Macnamara complained of being thrown overboard from a budgerow. On inquiry he was found to be 'a worthless character and drunken vagrant' who lived on his wits and maltreated boatmen. The boatmen were prosecuted but Macnamara was so insolent to the magistrate of Dacca that he was sent down to Calcutta with the already quoted recommendation.[71] The case of Tobias Henry Wagner well illustrates the scope for an adventurer at that time. First a trader at Dacca, he had then an indigo factory where he oppressed the ryots. Then he tried to obtain Rs. 12,000 from the minor Rajah of Cooch Behar on the plea of furthering his interests in Calcutta. He was ordered to be apprehended, but remained at large till 1801, when Colonel Obie, the Danish Governor of Serampore, reported his arrival as an emissary on his way to Calcutta to complain of injustice on behalf of the Rajah of Cooch Behar. His second attempt had evidently been more successful, for he had received Rs. 10,000 as a douceur for the Supreme Council. In 1802 he was taken at Chinsura, whereupon he produced papers to prove the sanction of a former Commissioner of Cooch Behar for exacting ferry, opium and liquor duties and holding lands in farm, all of which was against regulations. He was, however, still said to be negotiating with the Bengal Government through an attorney in Calcutta and in the circumstances was allowed to remain there.[72] In 1800 the Government was much exercised by the arrival of twenty-three ex-convicts from Australia, and one convict who swam out to the ship after it had sailed, and lived concealed for nine days, his only subsistence being water obtained by dipping his handkerchief in a water cask. The convict was placed in irons in Fort William, and the ex-convicts were sent home to England ; the Council protested very energetically both to the Company and to the Governor of New South Wales. Their protest provides an interesting foretaste of the White Australia policy from another point of view ; London objected because they 'feared colonization', but Calcutta because of the inconvenience and loss of prestige involved in letting loose such men on the country.[73]

One more community made up the hierarchy of European society. This was the miscellaneous Eurasian community of mixed descent, variously known as creoles, mustees, Portuguese, Anglo-Asiatics, East-Indians, Indo-Britons, but usually simply as half-castes. The Eurasian community[74] had its origin in the coming of the Portuguese, who intermarried freely with the people to form the Goanese race of modern times on the west coast, and the Portuguese communities of Madras and Bengal. Unions, regular and irregular, were all but universal. 'The inhabitants of Goa,' said Mandelslo in 1638, 'are either Castizes, that is Portuguese, born of father and mother Portuguese, or Mestizes, that is born of a Portuguese father and Indian mother. The Mestizes are distinguished from the others by their colour, which inclines towards the Olive, but those of the third generation are as black as the inhabitants of the country ; which happens also in the fourth generation of the Castizes, though there were no mixture among them.'[75]

In the eighteenth century the work of missionaries and increased contact with the growing English settlements recruited them from the ranks of 'pariah' Christians who wished to raise their status in life. 'Topasses,' said the Sieur Luillier in 1702, 'were Indian boys brought up and clothed in the French fashion, and instructed in the Catholic faith by missionaries ';[76] and the Danish missionaries did the same.[77] To wear a hat, boots and European dress, to be a Christian and to speak some European dialect, but usually the debased Portuguese of the settlements, passed a man off as a Eurasian, and conversely an Indian who became a Christian tended to be reckoned as a Eurasian forthwith. This was partly because it had not yet fully been grasped by the popular Hindu mind that an Indian could be a Christian, and partly because the prestige of the Europeans made the claim of relationship, however distant, a severe temptation to the intelligent and ambitious pariah, as it has continued to be almost to the present time. In 1790 the name Topass was still given to Portuguese and Indians who wore a hat and European dress.[78] 'Any man of colour, however dark, who wears a hat, passes for a descendant of the companions of the renowned Vasco da Gama,' wrote Major Blakiston.[79]

From the opening of the eighteenth century onwards, but specially during the second half, their numbers were further increased by the French and English. There was no colour prejudice among the French. Dupleix himself married a creole of Chandernagore, and in 1790 there were said to be only two French families in Pondicherry of pure blood, of whom the sons of one had married women of the country.[80] By the end of the period this new type of Eurasian had so grown in number that the Abbé Dubois in his classification of the class wrote that 'the Portuguese' consisted of the illegitimate offspring of Europeans, the descendants of low-caste Hindus, and a 'few' descendants of the Portuguese.[81]

After the early days of the settlement when mixed marriages often took place with 'Mustees' and sometimes with others, the original unions were nearly always irregular, except for a few exceptional cases like those of Skinner and Hearsay who married Mussulman or Rajput ladies of good family. These illicit unions can be divided, however, into those contracted by European soldiers during and after the French wars and those of the officers and officials. The former were with the lowest classes and were often only temporary in character, as the soldier moved from place to place. If a soldier married, it was usually with a Christian Eurasian girl. The children of these temporary attachments lived with their pariah or prostitute mothers until the age of fourteen, when many of them disappeared into the interior and others drifted into the bazaars.[82]

In Trichinopoly in 1780 there were sixty-four boys under fourteen, of whom only fourteen had entered Swartz's school, and only ten over fourteen were left.[83] In 1784 the *Report* of the Society for the Promotion of Christian Knowledge estimated that 700 Eurasians were annually born in Madras and the Coromandel coast.[84] With these conditions it is not surprising that they were said to combine the bad qualities of both races, and that, according to Carey, the Portuguese Roman Catholics should be 'universally despised by people of all ranks and descriptions'.[85] The situation was summed up by Dubois with his usual lucidity when he admitted the charge, but attributed it, not to any inherent rottenness of character but to a bad environment, bad examples, and neglected education.[86]

Very different from this were the surroundings and upbringing of the children of officers or wealthy Anglo-Indian officials. Their mothers, to begin with, were often permanent members of the household, presiding over a zenana, or perhaps, as in Hickey's case, having a separate establishment on the banks of the Hughli, where she joined her consort in entertaining his week-end guests. As the unions were permanent the children were often treated as members of the family and carefully educated. Many, especially if of a light colour, were sent for education to England, where it was said at one time that one boy in ten in the schools was coloured.[87]

Until 1800 there was no public opinion against these irregular unions. Palmer could write quite casually to Hastings of his 'natural children' and their progress. 'All,' he remarks, 'are good and sensible and have been well educated in England.'[88] The attitude to colour was illustrated in another letter about the natural children of Julius, whose case Palmer had undertaken. Two, 'almost as fair as English children', were to go to England; but the third was 'too dark to escape detection', and, although the strongest, was therefore to be educated in Bengal.[89]

Some remained in England and drifted on to the London streets 'in swarms',[90] but the majority returned. It was here that the tragedy began, for they had received the education of gentlemen and had to live the life of clerks. In many cases their fathers left India and so deprived them of all influence, and from 1792 they were officially debarred from employment in government service.[91] Deprived of parental support, and carefully unfitted by their education for the life they were compelled to lead, it is hardly surprising that many of them were unable to adjust their lives to their circumstances, and developed that mixture of arrogance and emptiness, of extravagance and poverty, that decayed nobleman outlook which has been traditionally associated with them.

For those who did not go to England, however, there were in both Calcutta and Madras orphan asylums of long standing. For the children of officers a special institution was founded in 1782 and supported by deductions from pay on a graduated scale.[92] But here again there was difficulty in finding work for the boys and even more for the girls on leaving. Officers' children were apprenticed to business firms, soldiers' sons were sent to the regiments as drummers and fifers.[93] Many girls married European soldiers[94] and thus reduced the earlier promiscuity ; some became ladies' maids, some the wives of officers, but many their mistresses owing to the growing English prejudice against mixed marriages.[95]

Thus the young Eurasian, while his father remained in India, often became a fashionable man about town. 'Many a young Bond St. dandy,' wrote the author of *Fifteen Years in India*, 'struts about with inconceivable self-satisfaction, and youthful British, Portuguese and French half-castes, with tawny face and neck stiffened almost to suffocation, jump from the sublime to the ridiculous in attempts at imitation.'[96] But when his father sailed for England, leaving his mother with a pension and no education, and himself with education and no pension, the bright day was done, the shades of the prison house began to close around him, and there was no other resource but to join the society of 'krannies' or subordinate clerks, or to live upon his wits. So all over India, side by side with the English settlements and stations, sprang up small societies of Eurasians (or Indo-Britons as they were known after 1827),[97] between whom and the gentlemen 'there was almost as great a distance as between Brahmin and Pariah'.[98] The 'gentlemen' consisted of the members of the covenanted service and two or three merchants, 'kranny society' of clerks, assistants to merchants, conductors (storekeepers), sergeants (who probably had Eurasian wives) and shopkeepers.[99] None had any prospects except the merchants' assistants.

In these circumstances the Eurasians could hardly be expected to be contented ; their discontent gave European society a rational ground for a disapproval to which their growing racialism already prompted them. In this disapproval is a note of fear very different from the attitude of the French at Pondicherry. While some disapproved of the sending of Eurasians to England for education, because it unfitted them for their Indian life ;[100] others feared that the unchecked increase of their numbers might eventually prove a danger to the government. Lord Valentia was in favour of 'obliging every father of half-caste children to send them to Europe, prohibiting their return in any capacity whatsoever'.[101] This would both remove the numerical danger and 'the expense that would then attend upon children would certainly operate as a check to the extension of zenanas which are now but too common among the Europeans'.[102]

During this latter period, the ceremonial life of Calcutta as well as the daily social routine underwent considerable social change. In the time of Warren Hastings, 'the good old days' of later Anglo-Indians when money was plentiful and time was cheap, large entertainments were common. There were grand official dinners on the King's Birthday,[103] on Christmas Day,[104] and on other special occasions, with a ball for the ladies; public breakfasts and dinners were given by the Governor-General and by the members of the Council ('Burra Sahibs')[105] in turn once a week, which strangers and anyone who had received a general invitation might attend, and in addition there were private dances and concerts in Hastings Street and Alipore.[106] Hastings himself moved simply amid all this display and wore nothing more ostentatious than a plain green coat,[107] but he knew how to assume state on occasion. Then though 'by nature uncommonly shy and reserved',

Hathi par howdah, ghore par zin,
Jaldi bahar jata Sahib Warren Hastin.

Lord Cornwallis brought a change. Along with such customs as private solicitation of offices[108] went public breakfasts as a preparation for levées. Open levées were substituted.[109] Cornwallis also frowned on public dancing, and discontinued after 1786 the customary Christmas dinner, ball and supper.[110] But ceremonial in the Government House was also much reduced, though Cornwallis reappointed Hastings' old staff.[111] The settlement had never expected 'so humble and affable a great man'.[112] But it is not surprising that 'his mode of life' prevented his becoming 'popular'[113] in the eyes of the majority. However, he did not entirely stop ceremonial as his account of the celebration of the King's recovery shows, when the illuminations were destroyed by rain, which did not prevent, however, 'some of the gentlemen who stayed late being nearly extinguished by the claret.'[114] Sir John Shore continued the Cornwallis régime with, if possible, even greater simplicity,[115] but with the coming of Lord Wellesley began a period of magnificence which has been continued with occasional breaks and reactions since. Under his inspiration arose the new Government House at Calcutta, where dazzling entertainments were held as soon as it was completed.[116] The 'stupidity and ill-bred familiarity' of Calcutta society, encouraged by Shore and Cornwallis, jarred on him, and caused him 'to expel all approaches to familiarity with a degree of vigour amounting to severity'.[117] Illuminations at one ball alone cost £3,248, and everything else was in proportion. The century which had come in with the sometimes riotous dining of obscure factors at a common table closed with an oriental adaptation of Vauxhall and the Brighton pavilion.

CHAPTER IV

BOMBAY

IN the eighteenth century Bombay was the Cinderella of the English settlements in India, the unhealthiest, the poorest, and the most despised. The first burst of prosperity under Gerald Aungier had been succeeded by Keigwin's revolt in 1683-4, the ambitious Moghul War of Sir John Child, the siege of Bombay by the Sidi, and the final purchase of peace from Aurangzeb by the dismissal of Child. The period of depression which ensued lasted until well into the eighteenth century, and the tradition of poverty and dullness survived its close. Unlike the other settlements there were few dramatic incidents to give a glamour to its history, and except for the defeat of the pirate Angria, they were usually disasters like the Sidi's invasion or the Convention of Wadgaun in 1779. Bombay had a reputation for parochialism, and its inhabitants fulfilled one test of smallness by being usually ashamed of their city and by wishing themselves in any other part of the Company's dominions. Throughout the century Bombay remained remote and unenvied by the rest of India, and it even allowed Calcutta to usurp its obvious position as the Gateway of the East.

The first reason for this is to be found in the political situation. Bombay was from the time of its acquisition surrounded by powerful neighbours who jealously watched its growth. The Moghul port of Surat remained an important rival far on into the eighteenth century, although in 1709 Bombay finally became the headquarters of the new United Company. It was not until 1736 that the Parsi shipbuilder Lowji Lassaramjee Wadia could be persuaded to take charge of the infant Bombay dockyard,[1] and not until 1759 that the English obtained control of the whole city of Surat. Even in 1773 Surat could be reckoned to contain anything from 400,000 inhabitants and upwards, and to be at any rate more populous than either Paris or London,[2] while Bombay had still not much more than 100,000.[3] Indeed, since the English virtually controlled both cities, it seems that it was only the gradual silting up of the Swally river on which Surat stood that finally turned the commercial scale in favour of Bombay.[4] On the south, the Portuguese regretted their cession of Bombay almost as soon as they had made it, and by their hold of Bassein and Salsette did much to diminish its value as a port and to throttle its infant trade. When the Portuguese were ejected from Bassein in 1739,[5] it was by the Marathas and not by the English, and the city remained as cramped and overshadowed as before. The Marathas themselves were too strong to be defied with impunity, and trade was further hampered by the hostility of the Mohammedan Sidi, and the depredations of the Angrias from their pirate stronghold of Gheria till their final destruction in 1756.[6] Time and fortune both favoured Bombay, but it was not until after the third Maratha war in 1782 that free communication was really established with the mainland,[7] and not until 1803 that the Maratha power was finally broken. The amazement which Colonel Goddard's march across India from Calcutta to Surat in 1779 created well illustrates the isolation of Bombay right up to the end of the century; an overland post to Madras via Hyderabad was only established in 1788,[8] and the first Maratha wars were largely precipitated by the delays occasioned in the sending of despatches from Bombay to Calcutta by sea. When these facts are remembered it is not surprising to find that though the first Parsi had arrived in Bombay by 1675,[9] the shipbuilder Lowji did not remove from Surat to Bombay until 1736, and that it was 1803 before a traveller could make the very modern observation that Bombay was almost entirely owned by the Parsis.[10]

The second cause of the early obscurity of Bombay was its climate, which gave rise to the proverb 'Two monsoons are the life of a man'.[11] This was partly due to the naturally damp and enervating air, and partly to the marshes on the landward side of the island which were, of course, malarial swamps. Their reclamation was not attempted before 1721, although swamps were vaguely considered responsible for 'pestilential vapours' which induced the prevalent fevers. Partly it was also due to the obstinate English adherence to their own food and drink, though they well knew both the dangers of their diet and the virtues of temperance in the tropics. Niebuhr thus described their attitude: 'It is true that many Englishmen die here very suddenly, but in my opinion the fault is chiefly their own: they eat much succulent food, particularly beef and pork, which the ancient legislators have forbidden for good reason, to the Indians; they drink very strong Portugal wines, at the hottest time of day: in addition they wear as in Europe tight-fitting clothes, which are useless in these countries, since they are much more sensitive to the heat than the Indians with their long and flowing garments.'[12]

But Calcutta was equally troubled with swamps, and all English merchants had equally unhealthy habits. What gave Bombay its notoriety was its toddy trees, which by their thickness shut out the sea breezes, and the peculiar method of manuring them with decaying 'buckshaw'[13] fish which 'impregnated the neighbouring wells' and caused a 'most unsavoury smell'. 'And in the Mornings,' adds Hamilton, 'there is generally seen a thick Fog among those Trees, that affects both the Brains and Lungs of Europeans, and breeds Consumptions, Fevers and Fluxes.'[14] All the early travellers agreed on the ill-effect of these methods, but the Council did not want to diminish the shade by cutting down the trees, while the Company derived a revenue of Rs. 25 per thousand coconuts.[15] Presented with the painful dilemma, of either losing their coconut revenue or of providing a constant succession of recruits, the Court corresponded for many years with the Bombay Council about it. In 1709 the Council tried the burying of the fish in earth,[16] but the next year they resorted to more drastic measures, and reported with pride the beneficial effects of the prohibition of buckshaw altogether, though there were more Europeans on the island 'than for sixteen years past'.[17] This policy, however, led to a decline of the coconut crop, which in 1722 only yielded an average of eighteen each from 20,000 trees. The Council therefore experimented with dried or 'coot' fish which were placed round the trees in small quantities and well covered with earth. After two months they asserted that there was 'no manner of smell',[18] and the next year they wrote that the experiment was still successful.[19] But how far the success of the experiment was medical as well as financial is open to doubt, for in 1750 Dr. Grose was still calling Bombay 'the burying ground of the English' and attributing its reputation to the manuring of the trees with *small fish*.[20] In fairness, however, we must add that this is the latest reference to the practice we have. Apart from the fevers and fluxes which these conditions naturally gave rise to, other common diseases were cholera, scurvy, 'barbiers' or 'berbers'—a kind of paralysis—and small-pox, while gout, the stone, and tetters or worms are also mentioned.[21] New-comers were specially liable to fevers, fluxes and prickly heat.[22] In the second half of the century Bombay was notable for liver complaints, 'which are more frequent and more fatal here than in any other part of India'.[23] English diet and particularly drink, were largely responsible for most of these; at the very beginning of the period Ovington reported that fevers were especially common after 'a strong debauch',[24] and at its close we hear of hundreds dying from intemperance, particularly soldiers on account of the cheapness of arrack and country spirits.[25]

A third reason for the unpopularity of Bombay was its demoralization at the beginning of the century. From the time of Gerald Aungier a series of disasters almost depopulated the island, and left the survivors without hope or public spirit for nearly a generation until the coming of the vigorous Charles Boone;[26] and the tradition thus created lingered on right through the century. That Aungier's régime came to be regarded as a golden age is itself the best proof of the subsequent decline and the evidence amply confirms the tradition. Keigwin's rebellion in 1683-4 was the first great shock, and Child's Moghul war was the second: at its close the island had lost its trade, its reputation, and most of its inhabitants, Indian and European. The population which had grown from about 10,000 in 1660 to an estimated 40,000 or 60,000 in 1678,[27] had shrunk to 16,000 in 1716;[28] and not until 1744 was it rather optimistically estimated at 70,000. Among the Europeans the depopulation was equally great;[29] of seven or eight hundred in Bombay before the Moghul war Hamilton says that not sixty survived,[30] and Governor Boone writes in 1718 that of 600 men which the island required there were then only 120 available.[31] But instead of endeavouring to repair their disasters, the survivors quarrelled and intrigued against each other and made as much for themselves as possible while yet there was time. Matters were complicated by the rivalry of the New and Old Companies, the old President at Surat, Sir John Gayer, refusing to recognize the authority of the new Governor of Bombay, Sir Nicholas Waite. Sir John Gayer was arrested and confined for many years at Surat, but in 1708 Sir Nicholas Waite was in his turn arrested by his own Council. From the papers and depositions dealing with his arrest he appears to have been a distinctly difficult man to work with. When asked the reason of a discrepancy in the accounts Sir Nicholas 'rose in a passion and protested that he would not concern himself, or transact any more business with them, than what was absolutely necessary'—namely the ordering of the payment of the monthly accounts—locked up the Consultation room and conducted all business himself from his lodgings.[32] John Symonds deposed that before leaving Bombay for a trading voyage, Sir Nicholas thus addressed him: 'Don't you know 'tis the custom of this place to be false, and to cut one another's throats; perhaps you may take me for your enemy, but egad I am not, and whoever tells you so is not your friend—I tell you there is Aislabie[33] (for that was his manner of speaking never to mention any person with respect) will cut your throat for a groat, and mine too if it was in his power, he's as false as the Devil, and the only instigation [*sic*] of my confining you, and there's your friend Goodshaw he sets up for a wit, and Hammer he calls me the old knight . . .'[34] On his return Sir Nicholas 'fell in such a passion, swearing and calling me a damn'd impudent rascal, and swore by God he knew nothing of my going to the southward'.[35] He declared that there was a conspiracy against him, and withdrew from all public business until his intransigeance provoked the very movement he feared. The councillors themselves were not very much better; Jeremiah Bonnell was suspended in 1701 by his fellow-members Morse and Callow, John Lock was suspended for striking Sir Nicholas and refusing to apologize,[36] and Morse later explained his absence from Council on the ground that 'his intellect was disordered by liquor'.

Besides a rather more than average turbulence, in early Bombay there was rather more than average corruption. The confidential letters of Governor Boone and the factors of Bombay to Woolley, the secretary of the Court of Directors, reveal a society which with its charges and counter-charges and its universal suspicion must have been in a continual effervescence of scandal and gossip. This is Mr. Boone's private opinion of Bombay.

> It has been the custom of this settlement, contrary to what I have known in others, That the Purser, Master Mariner, Steward and Master of Attendance buy up the necessary stores their employ requires and conscientiously spare them to the Company at 50 per cent advance, if I am not much deceived. The breaches are in a very bad condition, I will do my utmost to get them finished, but he that undertook them deserves hanging more justly than a common thief; If Mr. Strutt[37] had been the good servant he pretends to he should have opposed the presenting him with Rs. 2,000 to which he now acknowledges no pretension. . . . Here is a great want of regulation in the settlement, in Madras and Bengal such enormities would have been taken notice of, but were I to do all this at once they would load me with curses and backbitings. The Second is Bookkeeper but they allow his assistant £100 per annum. The Chief at Mahim had ¼% on all duties, this I have ventured to take off. The Paymaster has had certain perquisites which I shall reduce. Everyone in Council allowed a House, Pallaqueen fellows, and the keeping of a Horse, this swells our expenses prodigiously besides several other things which my time would not permit me to inquire thoroughly into.[38]

A few months later Boone discovered a credit of Rs. 435,149 which his predecessor Strutt had given to the broker Vanwallidas in order that he might take it away again and so gain the credit of economizing.[39] One of the responsible parties disclaimed all responsibility and the other pleaded ignorance. Governor Boone, however, was a man of real energy and determination who rendered good service, but even he did not hesitate to rate his own work at quite its full value. On the discovery of the next lot of frauds, he confesses to Woolley that he 'expects encouragement' and asks for a 20 per cent reward. He adds the postscript 'you know the country custom is one fourth part'.[40] The rest of the letters are nearly all concerned with applications for more lucrative posts, better pay or modified conditions and with reflections on the other correspondents; they are all written by most devoted servants of the Company who have long suffered the greatest hardships in uncomplaining silence, and they are not infrequently reinforced by a 'patch of Chints', 'beteelas' or 'two Moche stones' for Mrs. Woolley 'as a small acknowledgment of your favour'. From the frequency of these postscripts one surmises that she must have strongly approved of her husband's large Indian correspondence.

Besides all this there are hints of darker things. Ovington's horror at the pitch to which 'all vicious enormities' have grown may be suspected of professionalism but it found confirmation in both private letters and public records.[41] Strutt spoke significantly of 'arrack to keep the soldiers from the pariah houses' and more sinister vices were not unknown.[42]

These conditions could not have been very attractive in themselves, but when to them we add the fact that commercially Bombay did not pay, and that politically it was overshadowed by powerful neighbours, it is hardly surprising to meet with a chorus of depreciation from writers through the century. Boone summed up the general feeling of the early settlers when he wrote, 'I cannot find terms to express the misery of this island, here are great complaints'.[43] Twenty years later Bombay was still a 'narrow barren island';[44] at the end of the century it was still a 'losing concern',[45] and Governor Duncan 'would never have gone there had he known the state it was in'.[46] Bombay owed its existence to its harbour, and its continued maintenance to its dockyard, which alone induced the Company to suffer its annual loss on the settlement. The Parsi shipbuilder rather than the English merchant was the true maker of Bombay.

But the uniqueness of Bombay life did not lie merely in its wars with its neighbours or in the squalor of its early conditions. Even after its recovery from the gloom of its early years, its isolation from the other settlements, its comparative poverty and its closer connexion with the mercantile, as distinct from the princely class of Indians, gave it a distinctiveness and an individuality which it has never quite lost even to-day. The isolation and comparative poverty remained throughout the century; the chance fact of its cession by Portugal and the consequent independence of any Indian state, while it rendered its existence precarious and its growth difficult, saved Bombay from the sublime chicanery of a Nawab of the Carnatic or the gilded decadence of Lucknow. On the other hand, the tradition of the Surat factory, where the English long dealt as equals with Hindu, Mahommedan and Parsi merchants, gave them a more cosmopolitan outlook than in the other two Presidencies, and provided a solid basis for social intercourse and mutual co-operation. The difficulty with which the prosperity of Bombay was built up was very different from the early wealth of the other settlements and their sudden expansion into military centres. In Madras and Calcutta Indian merchants were glad to reside as a favour, and the Government would therefore make their own terms, but in Bombay they had first to be attracted from the larger city of Surat which was also nearer the great trade routes. Indian merchants could not be attracted by a trade which already existed, they had to be attracted in order to create trade. So Bombay developed a spirit different from the other two Presidencies, a cosmopolitan spirit of co-operation based on mutual respect and necessity instead of a spirit of imperialism founded on military glory and the pride of possession.

The first distinctive feature of English Bombay was its houses. Owing to its Royal origin Bombay was not divided like Madras and Calcutta, into a fort or factory with a Black Town attached and garden houses in the suburbs. The fort was Bombay Castle, which was built after and not before the English occupation and was a fortress rather than a market place. The English and Portuguese lived at first in the centre of the town, where the Indian city gradually grew up around them ;[47] later they built garden houses on Malabar Hill and elsewhere, but they retained town houses in Bombay.[48] There was never a sharp distinction between White Town and Black as in Madras, and there is in fact no mention of a Black Town until the end of the period ;[49] for Fort and Black Town were substituted the Castle and the city, for English merchant princes and Indian dependents, English governors and the cosmopolitan governed. The houses themselves were less pretentious than those elsewhere but by no means small or uncomfortable.[50] This is amusingly illustrated by travellers' reports ; those who knew only Bombay found them handsome and comfortable and those who knew the east coast as well thought them small and unpretentious.[51] The details of the houses also varied. They had sloping tiled roofs instead of flat,[52] wooden verandahs supported on wooden pillars instead of the heavy 'piazzas' of Calcutta and Madras, and they lacked the splendid classical porticoes of the other settlements.[53] But they used 'chunam' for their walls both inside and out,[54] and glass or small transparent shells for their windows[55] instead of the local iron or wood lattice work. Bombay had also distinctive servants. The upper servants were either Parsis or Mahommedans, the cooks usually Portuguese or Goanese, the ladies' maids Malabar girls instead of Portuguese or Eurasian, and the gentlemen's personal servants Malabar or 'caffre' (negro) slave boys.[56] The negroes who were perhaps the most distinctive feature of the Bombay servant world, were specially imported from Madagascar in English ships, and were also brought from the Red Sea as a speculation by Arab traders. The Government used them both as labourers and soldiers, and drew up the most careful regulations for their proper treatment. In 1789 there were 431 slaves in Bombay.[57] On arrival they usually became Roman Catholics, being much attracted, we are told, by the images of saints which they saw the Portuguese and the black Christians wearing on their breasts. English servants were rare, and when they appeared were considered a portent by the Indian servants and made their masters the envy of the settlement.[58] As in Madras, soldiers were sometimes borrowed from their regiments as coachmen, who were otherwise usually Parsis.[59]

Another Bombay peculiarity was a reputation for inhospitality. Colonel Rennell wrote in 1761 that the 'few inhospitable habitations serve to cover the heads of those whose chief end is gain and the destruction of their fellow creatures'. Le Couteur in 1790 far more deliberately complained that the people of Bombay 'are reserved in their manners and show no hospitality to strangers. It may be objected perhaps that it is rash, if not ungenerous, to pronounce in so decisive a manner against them, but the character they have borne at all times sufficiently warrants the censure'.[60] Against this there is the evidence of Forbes who as an old resident might be considered prejudiced, of Chaplain Cordiner who only resided in Bombay twelve days, and of Mrs. Graham who visited India at the very end of the period. The explanation of these conflicting views is perhaps that the Bombay settlers by the smallness of their numbers and the generosity of their hospitality towards each other, acquired at once an open-handedness which spent itself on each other and a clan spirit which looked with suspicion on strangers. To a resident like Forbes or to people well armed with introductions like Cordiner and Mrs. Graham, Bombay would therefore be hospitable enough, but the young officer without connexions like Rennell or the casual visitor like Le Couteur[61] might easily find themselves unknown and disregarded. In mid-century Bombay it was the custom for the principal inhabitants to dine with each other in turn, dinner also including supper as a corollary.[62] The more congenial a society the less it will feel the need for any reinforcement from outside, and this was probably the root of the trouble. The man with proper credentials was well entertained, but woe unto him who had no introductions.

The Bombay carriages were also distinctive. Owing to the scarcity of horses 'hackary' carts drawn by white oxen were used instead of the ordinary English chaises and gigs. The oxen 'trotted and galloped' up to seven or eight miles an hour, but had to be periodically stopped in order to remove the foam from their mouths to prevent their suffocation.[63] In 1754 Admiral Watson was granted a chaise and oxen while in Bombay harbour. By the end of the century the use of horses had spread to the rich Indian merchants who prided themselves on their speed and dash,[64] but hackary carts were still sometimes used even by the Europeans.[65] But what distinguished Bombay more than anything else from the other settlements was the Parsi community. Though early to appear, they were slow to settle in large numbers; when at last they really established themselves, they soon became one of the most influential elements of the town. More than any other factor they contributed to the wealth of Bombay, and they gave it the atmosphere of cosmopolitanism and racial tolerance which it still possesses. Their outlook on life was more sympathetic to the English than that of the Mohammedans with their love of glory and memories of departed empire, or of the Hindus with their pacifism, 'superstitions' and absorption in religion. They had no purdah system to close their houses to strangers, no prohibitions of pork, beef, or wine—those essentials of English regard—to embarrass social and convivial relationships, no caste distinctions to segregate themselves from the outside world and from each other. Even in their own customs they were less 'bigoted' than the other communities and were the first to adopt European clothes, food and manners.[66] Exiles of many centuries, they had been compelled to rely on their own exertions for their existence, and on the goodwill of alien governments for their protection. In consequence they were at once peaceful and independent, conciliatory and enterprising. They therefore had no scruples in coming to Bombay and no dreams of independence when they had established themselves. Unlike the Christian minorities of modern Turkey they had no independent motherland to look to for aid, they had all the political powerlessness of the Jews without the odium of their religion and occupations. Further, they had as a supreme claim to the regard of the English, the fact that they could do the things the English most valued better than the English themselves. Thus they monopolized both the shipbuilding and the trade of Surat, having many English ships and captains in their service;[67] at Bombay they controlled the Company's shipyard all through the century, where their work was pronounced at least as

SCENE IN BOMBAY

[*face p.* 75

good as any in Europe,[68] and they were frequently partners in English commercial houses.[69] Their munificent philanthropy, their clan spirit as shown in the care of their poor also appealed to the free living Englishmen of the time. It is hardly surprising, therefore, that good relations were established with them from the first. We hear of a silver rule and a shawl being presented by the Company to the shipmaster Lowji[70] and later to his son and successor,[71] and by 1810 the English and Parsis were frequently dining together and drinking 'great quantities of wine and particularly Madeira'.[72]

The life of early Bombay, as we have seen, was bound in shallows and in miseries. By about 1740, however, it had attained a subdued prosperity, and though still considered valuable for its relation to the rest of India rather than for itself,[73] could be considered in 1754, 'perhaps the most flourishing of any place in the universe'.[74] From that time it grew steadily without any of the sudden changes which transformed the other settlements from factories into seats of empire almost overnight. The difference which Forbes noticed between Lord Valentia's description of Bombay and his own recollections was one of degree and not of kind; Bombay experienced development and not revolution. There are several travellers' accounts of Bombay of which we will select two, written respectively in 1761 and 1774, to give an impression of the town's external appearance.

> This town is situated upon a peninsula the greatest part of which is occupied by the Fortifications, Powder Mills, etc. The town all lying low and swampy is generally esteemed unhealthy for European constitutions, and I think it sufficiently evinced by the memorials in the churchyard which I had the curiosity to examine; and find that few survived the age of 38. . . . The Fortifications fall very far below those of Pondicherry both in design and execution. There is a dock capable of taking a 70-gun ship and a small yard in which the work is performed by Indian artificers, who are observed to use but two kinds of edged tools, tho' their work is durable and neat. There is also a large Market Place where most sorts of Indian and European goods are sold by Black merchants who in general live in tolerable houses: the Governor's house is a large commodious building adapted to the Country, as are several others set apart for the use of the naval Commanders. The Houses are all built of stone and good cement made of a sort of lime called by the natives Chinam, which is said to be more durable than the common European cement. The Church is an incontestable proof of

our having long since discarded all outward show of religion, and the temper and disposition of the inhabitants testifies that they have resolved never to discover their inward thoughts if any, at least but to themselves. The common methods of travelling, both here and in every part of India is in a Palanquin which is a light frame of wood about the size of a small couch, and, is used like a Sedan chair with this difference only, that the traveller extends himself on bedding placed there for that purpose. Besides these there are some chaises belonging to the governor.

The Magistrates of Bombay are styled the Governor and Council, the latter of whom are generally chosen out of those of the inhabitants on whom nature has bestowed corpulent bodies ; to this sort of people the natives also pay a kind of adoration, so that a man of a moderate size must never expect preferment here.[75]

This is the account of Abraham Parsons in 1774 :—

The town of Bombay is near a mile in length from the Apollo gate to that of the bazaar, and about a quarter of a mile broad in the broadest part of the Bunda, across the green, to the Church gate, which is nearly in the centre, as you walk round the walls between the Apollo and the Bazar gate. There are likewise two marine gates, with a commodious wharf and cranes built out from each gate, besides a landing place for passengers only. Between the two marine gates is the castle, properly called the Bombay castle, a very large and a very strong fortification, which commands the bay : the works round the town are so many and the bastions so very strong and judiciously situated, and the whole defended with a deep and broad ditch, so as to make a strong fortress, which, while it has a sufficient garrison, may bid defiance to any force which may be brought against it. Here is a spacious green, capable of containing several regiments, exercising at the same time ; the streets are well laid out, and the buildings (viz. the gentlemen's houses) so numerous and handsome as to make it an elegant town. The soil is a sand, mixed with small gravel, which makes it always so clean, even in the rainy season, that a man may walk all over the town within half an hour after a heavy shower, without dirting his shoes. The esplanade is very extensive, and as smooth and even as a bowling green, which makes walking or riding round the town very pleasant.[76]

On the esplanade, there were numerous tanks and wells, so that besides the crowd of Europeans in carriages, on horseback or on foot, it was occupied by groups of washermen beating their linen on their peculiar washing stones, with strings of better class women coming from their houses to draw water.[77]

At that time the English merchants lived in the town, but from about 1770, the taste for garden houses developed.[78] They spread along Back Bay until they reached the various cemeteries of Bombay —English, Portuguese, Armenian and Mohammedan. Behind was a thick wood of coco-nut trees, and in front the shore was used for Hindu cremations, the remains of which were washed up by the tide and lay scattered on the strand.[79] The garden houses spread inland all over the island and in time to Malabar hill.

Old Woman's Island or Colaba was still separated from the mainland and was chiefly remarkable for its lighthouse.[80] Salsette belonged to the Marathas until 1782, and even then continued to be administered on the Maratha system, which made development difficult.[81] It was connected with Bombay by a causeway built by Governor Duncan from 1798 to 1805. Elephanta island belonged to the English but was little appreciated before the visit of Niebuhr in 1764, who complained of its neglect by earlier travellers. With the growth of the interest in Hindu archaeology, it became a regular resort for visitors.

Bombay was less favourably placed than elsewhere for a health resort. Apart from a sea voyage, the chief resource was Old Woman's Island, the sea breezes of which were considered very bracing.[82] But it enjoyed the distinction of springs within reach on the mainland at Dillinagoga[83] which were said to be as hot as the Bath waters. There were no arrangements for bathers ; bathers simply camped near the springs for as long as they wished—but their reputation was great enough to attract people from Bengal.

The English society of Bombay was arranged on a strictly hierarchical plan from the Governor, through the senior and junior merchants to the factors and writers, the common soldiers and sailors. Rules of procedure were as strictly observed at the end of the century as at the beginning, so that Mrs. Graham could complain that no general conversation was possible at a Bombay dinner, since the same people invariably met and sat next to each other at every dinner party. Bombay was, however, peculiar in the larger place it gave to military officers in its earlier days. The chief military officer was a Major instead of a Captain,[84] and he commanded more and better troops[85] than the Madras and Calcutta captains. As the army was relatively larger at first, it was relatively smaller later ; Bombay thus avoided the extremes both of early mercantilism or later militarism. Apart from these officials there were a few free merchants, the common soldiers, whose behaviour and health were a constant anxiety to the authorities, and a considerable floating population of seamen. The compartments of Anglo-Indian society were so hermetically sealed that it is easy to forget that this class formed the majority of the European population at all the settlements. Their chief resorts were the 'Roman Catholic' taverns[86] and the pariah houses, and their mortality bills equalled, through the neglect of the authorities, the mortality of the authorities themselves through intemperance.

The unofficial population apart from these was always small. In 1720 the list of 'free merchants, seafaring men, etc. at Bombay' including women, totalled fifty-nine; in 1750 it was fifty-two. In 1785 the non-officials excluding women and common sailors, totalled only seventy-two, made up of five free merchants, nine seafaring men (chiefly supercargoes) three attorneys, three tavern-keepers, a gaol-keeper, and the master of the charity school. The floating population of seamen varied much from year to year. In 1766, 239 seamen in the Company's service at Bombay are enumerated, in 1792 there were 150 officers manning forty-three ships on the Bombay coast.[87] There are no statistics for sailors at the end of the century, but they probably tended increasingly to be replaced by lascars.[88] About the soldiers we have more exact information. In 1737 there were 500 soldiers and 300 sailors employed by the Company besides 115 at Mocha;[89] in 1767, 1,961 infantry and artillerymen, which in 1775 was reduced to 1,512.[90]

The official population of Bombay was not much larger than the unofficial. In 1746 there were eighty-nine on the civil list[91] which the Company wished to reduce to sixty-nine,[92] under the impression they were supporting 111 men. 'The whole European population,' wrote Cordiner in 1798, 'would not exceed one thousand.'[93]

In 1766 the daily life of the Bombay factors, says Forbes, was a mean between early discomfort and later luxury. Early rising was the rule, with a ride before breakfast. In the morning all attended at their offices from nine to twelve. Dinner was at one o'clock after which the writers returned to work from two to five o'clock. Tea was then taken, after which a walk or ride on the esplanade prepared the way for supper and a social evening.[94] The principal men dined with each other in town, and always stayed to supper. Later the hour of dinner was moved to the evening as in Calcutta, and its place was taken by 'tiffin' at two o'clock, but the old habit of a hearty midday meal survived with the result that the dinner was often hardly touched.[95] The cadets only mounted guard once or twice a week,[96] and mostly spent the mornings in calling on each other with the aid of ' punch ' and arrack and water. Later on they were sent to Versorah or Salsette, where the unhealthy conditions often carried them off.

On occasions like Christmas Day the Governor gave a dinner to all the gentlemen on the island.[97] The island had not the reputation for wealth which Calcutta and Madras enjoyed ; young adventurers looked on Bombay as a sort of exile, and it was quite natural to find that the man who kept the best table in Bombay in 1771 had made his fortune in Bengal.[98]

In their society ladies played a slowly increasing but not very distinguished part. At first there was a good deal of intermarriage with Portuguese Christians[99] but this died out among the upper classes. They were often replaced by ' dulcineas ', sometimes European, but more often Indian or Portuguese. The number of European ladies slowly increased, but in 1809 they were still in a minority of one to three men. Mrs. Graham dismisses them curtly as being like those of an English country town, ' underbred and overdressed,' and with the exception of one or two very ignorant and 'grossiére '. ' The men are in general what a Hindoo would call of a higher caste than the women.'[100]

The amusements of Bombay were much the same as elsewhere : in Bombay itself riding, dining, dancing and card playing, in cantonments with the army hunting, shooting, cock-fighting and dog-fighting.[101] Of Indian amusements they enjoyed nautches and hookah smoking. But there was one amusement of the early factors which seems to have been unique.[102] Sallying forth into the banian's quarters of Surat they pretended to shoot sparrows and pigeons, whereupon the distressed banians came out of their houses and offered them money to go away. The same stratagem was practised by a Bombay soldier in 1764 who led an ill-looking dog through the streets with threats and curses, whereupon the banians offered him gifts in order to save the dog.[103] This delightful trait was appreciated by a man like Forbes, who prohibited the shooting of birds in the territory of Broach.

The century was for Bombay one of preparation. On the whole, in spite of its inauspicious start, the work had been well done, and though the English in Bombay might have the minds of the average English country town, Bombay was ready to become, in spirit as well as materially, the gateway of the West.

CHAPTER V

THE MOFUSSIL

DURING the first half of the century the interior was largely a closed land to Europeans. None penetrated except on business; these included only occasional embassies, the few Europeans who took service with the local princes as soldiers, and especially artillery-men like Manucci, missionaries like the Roman Fathers in Tanjore, Agra and Bengal, and finally the agents of the chartered companies. The European soldiers were absorbed into the general population and disappeared, ambassadors and professionals were rare and passing visitants, the missionaries lived lives of isolation and often, like the Jesuit missionaries at Madura or later Dubois, adopted the manners of the country so that only the merchants were left to form any permanent settlements.

These mercantile settlements were subordinate factories to the Presidency towns; their business was to act as buying and selling agencies and to despatch goods to the main stations. Their time in the north was much taken up by disputes with the local Moghul authorities, but in the south there were only local chiefs to deal with, and the monotony of life was relieved by the periodic arrival of ships to load their goods. Subordinate factories were usually in charge of a senior merchant or member of Council, and they lived on a smaller scale than the collegiate factory life of the larger settlements. In Bengal the chief subordinate factories were at Patna, Dacca, Kasimbazaar, Balasore and Hughli, on the west coast at Surat, Calicut, Anjengo and Telicherry, and on the east Fort St. David, close to the town of Cuddalore, and Masulipatam. In addition there were factories controlled from India like Gumboon in the Persian Gulf and Fort Marlborough in Sumatra.

The life of these factories was a miniature model of the larger settlements; those employed in them hoped to return to head-quarters, and their principal peculiarity was a greater tendency, from their isolation, to breed 'characters' from among those who stayed in them long. Such a one is described in a letter to the Secretary of the Directors in 1715.

> Indeed Adams is the best man for the place [Telicherry] barring his knavish character. He is almost a Native, very well beloved by them, very active and unweary'd; at Calicutt the Natives come to him for Justice between one another;

> or if anyone were sent under Him for a year or two to see the Business beforehand and then Adams removed (if that fitt) 'tis I think the most feasible way.[1]

Later Governor Boone wrote of Adams: ' Beside he is Master of the language and a man of great interest in the Country.'[2] Another mofussil eccentric of a rather later date—the famous John Whitehill, was described by Eliza Draper.

> He's an Extraordinary Character, Unequal, but there is a great Mixture of Good I might also say of sublime in it—for He's generous, Highly so, and literally despises Money, but as it serves to promote his Happiness—which wholly centres in his Friendships—once attached, he is steady in these as the sun is regular in its course—but then He's passionate and Jealous, even to Madness—if the Objects of his regard seem to give any other individual a temporary Preference this is the source of extreme Misery to himself, and to all who live with Him—for the heart—the Heart my Coz :—is a free Agent, and will assert its liberty of Choice in spite of the Chains imposed upon it by Gratitude, Interest or the love of ease. In short He is one of those Beings whom his Friends would sacrifice life or Fortune to serve or Oblige, rather than devote their whole time to Him (be secret as the Grave, as to this Communication) and unfortunately nothing but their time would either satisfy or even Amuse him. . . . He's capable of all the great Exertions to purchase Affection but alas! He can neither relinquish his foibles or suppress them, to secure Esteem.[3]

The best description of subordinate factory life is given by the same authority, when at Telicherry.

> I'm by turns the Wife of a Merchant, soldier, and Inn-keeper, for in such different capacities is the Chief of Telicherry destined to act. . . . The Country is pleasant and healthy (a second Montpelier), our house [a fort and property of the Company] a Magnificent one, furnished too, at our Master's expense and the allowance for supporting it Creditably, what you would term Genteely, tho' it does not defray the charge of our Liquors which alone amount to six hundred a year; and such a sum, vast as it seems, is not extravagant in our situation, for we are obliged to keep a Public Table, and six months in the year, have a full house of Shipping Gentry, that resort to us for traffic and Intelligence

> from all parts of India, China and Asia. Our Society at other times is very confined, as it only consists of a few Factors and two or three Families; and such we cannot expect great intercourse with, on account of the heavy rains and terrible thunder and lightning to which this coast is peculiarly subject six months in the year. 'Tis call'd that of Malabar, and was before the troubles with Hyder Ally, the source of immense wealth to its principal inhabitants; the French and Dutch as well as ourselves have each a settlement on it. Mahé is not more than seven Miles distant from us (Yet very few Civilities pass between us and the Monsieurs) and Cochin (a Sweet Spot) about two Days' sail.[4]

With the rise of the Company's political power in the middle of the century the mofussil settlements entirely changed their character. Special passes were still necessary for residence in the Company territories,[5] and settlement was not allowed, but the number of Europeans up-country steadily increased. They consisted firstly of diplomatists, soldiers, officials and adventurers. The diplomatists were the residents at courts like those of Murshidabad, Benares, Lucknow, Gwalior and later Delhi, the soldiers were Company's troops, European as well as Indian, who were stationed in cantonments in Oudh and Bengal; the officials were the Collectors who from 1772 administered Bengal, Bihar and Orissa and the Commercial Residents[6] who carried on the Company's business until 1833, and the adventurers were men of all nationalities who took service with the various princes of India, both north and south, and who tried to carve out fortunes for themselves in the growing political anarchy.[7]

The Residencies were much sought after for their financial advantages, and were accounted the most lucrative posts in the services until the time of Cornwallis. The Resident of Benares, according to Cornwallis, received Rs. 3,000 from the Company, but four lakhs in all, exclusive of the monopoly of all commerce and the power of granting ' perwannahs '. ' It is supposed,' he wrote, ' that they were not ungrateful to the friends of the Governor-General. There is no reason to suppose Mr. —— took more than his predecessors—God knows what he gave.'[8] According to Hickey his friend Potts was ' screwed up ' by Sir John D'Oyley to three lakhs with 90,000 rupees for furniture for the Murshidabad residency, which was then considered the most lucrative post in the Company's service because all the Nawab's transactions passed through his hands. It was at these courts that there was most contact between the upper classes of both races, and a very cosmopolitan spirit was developed.[9] In the cantonments on the other hand, the society was exclusively English and predominantly masculine ; there the habits of Madras and Calcutta, modified to suit camp life, prevailed, and fashions lingered on which were waning in the capital until the slowly percolating feminine influence finally saturated camp life also. Between the two was the united residency and cantonment where Orientalism and Imperialism, like two seas, met.

The leading example of this union was at Lucknow, which on account of its magnificence, its extravagance, its luxury and its cosmopolitanism, may be called the centre of mofussil life. Here was a Nawab with the whole revenue of a province to draw upon to satisfy his private whims, a Resident through whose hands a million pounds were said to pass annually, a British garrison from the times of the Rohilla war near by at Cawnpore,[10] and last, the French adventurer General Martin. He and the Nawab were the twin luminaries of this society, the Nawab with strong European tastes, the Colonel adopting a ' semi-native ' way of life.[11] Asaf-ad-daula developed a passion for mechanical toys and English objects of all kinds which were all placed together in a special room ; ' watches, pistols, guns, glassware, furniture, philosophical machines, all crowded together with the confusion of a lumber room '.[12] In addition he had a menagerie, which contained, besides a tiger and other animals, a large English dray horse, which being kept as a curiosity for his extraordinary bulk, was fed unsparingly and in consequence became enormously fat and unwieldy.[13] The next Nawab, Sa'adat Ali,[14] from long residence in England had adopted English habits and lived in the English style. According to Lord Valentia he was not always treated with the respect due to him by the Europeans, and had to resort to buying up all the houses on the river in order to control their tenants.[15]

Claud Martin, the twin luminary of Lucknow, was born in 1735 at Lyons, came to Pondicherry in 1752 and probably joined the English army after the fall of that town in 1761. After various vicissitudes he was allowed, when a captain, to remain in Oudh in charge of the Nawab's arsenals. From this time he remained in the Nawab's service, rising steadily meanwhile in the English army, until in 1795 he became a Major-General on a Captain's pay. He died in 1800 worth thirty-three lakhs,[16] most of which he devoted to founding the La Martinière schools in Lucknow, Calcutta and Lyons. The means by which he amassed his wealth are interesting.[17] He had first his salary from the Nawab, amounting to Rs. 1,860 a month. As superintendent of the arsenal he would follow the usual custom of taking a commission on all purchases. He further derived a large income from indigo cultivation, which he practised on hired or purchased land, either himself or by agents. These were his regular sources of income. In addition, however, he probably took considerable commissions on the purchase of curios from Europe. Lord Valentia, indeed, accuses him of profiteering, but while he is acquitted of this charge by S. C. Hill, it seems probable, in the light of the parallel case of Dr. Blane mentioned by Mirza Abu Taleb Khan, that he at least did not do it for nothing.[18] Indeed, at a time when commissions on all public purchases were customary, there is no reason why he should not have done. Next he probably received presents from suitors to the Nawab's court in order to obtain a hearing. He was connected with most of the loans which the universal habit of obtaining everything on credit made endemic,[19] and he acted as a sort of aristocratic insurance house, charging 12 per cent on valuables left with him for safety. This rate was not exorbitant, but in the circumstances it doubtless brought in a large sum. Gambling is also attributed to him, but it rests on the sole evidence of Zoffany's picture of Colonel Mordaunt's cock-fight at Lucknow.

Martin was a great builder. His fortress-like palace of Constantia at Lucknow (now La Martinière College) which has alternately impressed critics by its size and scandalized them by its mixture of styles,[20] became in 1800 his tomb, to circumvent, it is said, the Nawab's intention of appropriating it. In addition he had a country house on the Gumti, the Farhad Baksh, of which only ruins survive.[21] Twining wrote of the Farhad Baksh: 'it had the appearance of a fortified castle, and was indeed constituted with a view to defence, with drawbridge, loopholes and turrets and water when desired all round.'[22] Shore gave an excellent description of both the man and the house in a letter to his wife.[23]

> In the evening of yesterday I din'd with General Martin; who is a most extraordinary character, and everything about him. The house is built on the bank of the R. Goomty, and boats passed under the room in which he dined. He has under-ground apartments,[24] even with the edge of the water, the most comfortable in the world in the hot weather, and the most elegantly decorated. As the water rises, he ascends: the lower storey is always flooded in the rains, and the second generally; when the water subsides they are repaired and decorated. The two rooms containing the company, consisting of somewhat more than 40 ladies and gentlemen, were covered with glasses, pictures and prints: in short you could see no walls three feet from the floor.

> He had a pair of glasses ten feet in length and proportionately wide ; and estimated his glasses and lustres only, in the said rooms, at Rs. 40,000 or £4,500. It would require a week at least to examine the contents of his house. The old General is a Swiss, and talks English about a degree better than Tiritta, interlarding every sentence with 'What do you call it ?' 'Do you see ?' . . . He is, however, a man of much penetration and observation ; and his language would be elegant if it corresponded with his ideas. His singularities are amusing, not ridiculous. There was dancing in the evening ; and a very pretty exhibition of fire-works on the opposite side of the river, which pleased me, would have delighted and frightened Charlotte.

The General kept four Eurasian concubines and a regular staff of eunuchs and slaves. He also brought up a number of the children of Europeans who had left Lucknow and made provision for them in his will.[25] His charity was mostly posthumous, but in his life he was a generous entertainer ; his breakfasts and dinners were famous. His tastes were shown at the sale of his effects which included 4,000 Latin, French, Italian and English books, Persian and Sanskrit manuscripts, works of Zoffany and Daniels, and 150 paintings in oils.

Round these two men together with the Resident, a more ephemeral but almost equally important personage, revolved the society of Lucknow. The adventuring element disgusted Lord Valentia, but the greater part of this society was composed of the officers of the subsidiary force and their families. 'They lived,' wrote Twining in 1784, 'in a style far exceeding even the expense and luxuriousness of Calcutta ; they dined alternately with each other and kept a band to play who had learnt English and Scotch airs.'[26] On specially auspicious occasions, such as the purchase by the Nawab of 'Constantia', the whole settlement was entertained by the Nawab.

Apart from these few cases of cosmopolitanism, the army in general lived an entirely separate life, either in cantonments or in camp. A number of officers have left diaries and journals of their campaigns both in the Mysore and Maratha wars, so that we can obtain a very fair idea of their life.

The officer who went forth to war against Hyder Ali had a very clear idea of the importance of personal comfort. In 1780, during the most critical period of the Company's fortunes,[27] a captain was accompanied on campaign by a dubash (steward), a cook and a 'boy', a horsekeeper, a grasscutter, a barber, a washerman and 'other officers'. Fifteen to twenty coolies carried the baggage and a 'dulcinea'[28] sometimes completed the party. He often had a palanquin and the following items of luggage—'A good large bed', mattress and pillows, camp stools and chairs, a folding table, shades for candles, six or seven trunks with table things and a stock of linen. He also carried with him some dozens of wine, brandy and gin, tea and sugar, a hamper of live poultry, a milch goat and finally an extra tent for excess of luggage and servants. Some of the luggage was necessitated by the fact that there was no officers' mess at that time, each officer providing for himself,[29] but it helps to explain the difficulty of the army in keeping pace with the mobile forces of Hyder. During the Maratha wars a subaltern's kit included a tent twelve feet square with walls six feet high, and a bell tent for baggage and servants. Four bullocks or a stout camel were required for this, another camel or four bullocks to carry liquors, clothes and cooking apparatus, and another camel for mess trunks and camp furniture. The total outfit consisted of a horse, eight or nine servants and three camels or ten bullocks for the baggage.[30]

All officers had marquees, which, after the day's march of from ten to twelve miles, were pitched in lines as in England, with a bazaar in the rear. The soldiers naturally did not fare so well; six large tents were provided for each company of Europeans and three for each of sepoys.[31] Their baggage and knapsacks were carried for them by servants, who, it is said 'spoke English well and often became very attached to their masters'.[32] They had only to mount guard in their own quarters, but they had to live under canvas of only a single thickness during the hottest weather. Their tents were ten degrees hotter than the officers' double-lined tents,[33] and they suffered much from dysentery and sunstroke.[34]

The bugbears of camp life were 'cotton ground' and storms at night. The former, called by wags the Holy Land, was 'a jet black soil, which in dry weather was full of holes dangerous to ride over, but in rain a deep and almost bottomless puddle'.[35] Flooding was prevented by small earthen embankments made round the tents, but a second irruption, that of the officers' own servants, could not be prevented. Whenever a sudden storm occurred an officer's servants crowded into his tent for shelter. When their number is remembered, the congestion must have been considerable and was not at all appreciated by the occupant, but protest was useless, for if they were driven out the whole staff forthwith decamped, leaving their master next morning indignant but impotent.[36]

The day was usually spent in marching or drilling. In 1780 the army usually set out after breakfast, was harassed by the Mysore horse about noon and arrived at its next camping ground for tiffin.

After tiffin the officers rested and slept and awoke refreshed for dinner.[37] In the last war against Tipu much the same procedure was followed. The army marched at daybreak to the sound of drums and fifes, the officers riding beside their men instead of reclining in palanquins, as was formerly common. If the enemy horse were not near the officers often indulged in sport, and the monotony of the march was relieved by the curiosity of villagers who turned out to watch the army and often brought out dancing troops from the neighbouring pagodas.[38] In camp, drill and manœuvres commenced at 5 a.m. to which officers sometimes turned out direct from the mess table.[39] These continued for several hours until the time for breakfast. After breakfast the officers engaged in private hobbies like sword exercise and then slept for two hours until dinner at 3 p.m. At 5 p.m. the regiment was turned out again for further drill until sunset.[40]

The two things which must impress the reader of these journals, apart from descriptions of the actual fighting, both from the frequency and relish of the references, are dinners and sport. The bottle and the gun were the twin emblems of camp life. In the eighteenth century there were no regimental messes; each officer catered for himself. It was the custom in consequence for the officers to dine with each other in rotation, and he was accounted the best officer who was most generous with his tiffins and dinners.[41] An invitation to dinner usually carried with it an invitation to the next morning's breakfast and tiffin as well, and for these joint meals, the possessions of all the officers concerned would be pooled. With the new century the custom of messing together began; the messing was done by contract with a banian at a fixed charge per head, but once or twice a week there were grand dinners when guests were admitted.[42] On these occasions our authors become lyrical in their descriptions of the courses, their statistics of toasts and of bottles, and in their records of endurance feats. Drinking, which was on the decrease in the settlements by the end of the century, flourished unchecked in the army; Wellington's famous estimate that each man must have his bottle of wine per day was a minimum rather than a maximum. The dinner hour grew gradually later in camp as in the settlements, and after 1800 it became fixed at 8 p.m. instead of the earlier three o'clock. One such dinner is graphically described by Major Blakiston.[43] The guests arrived at 7 p.m. and were welcomed by the playing of ' The Roast Beef of Old England ' by the band. Officers and guests mingled on the verandah, enjoying the last puffs of the breeze and a first taste of Madeira until eight o'clock, when dinner was served. Fish and soup was followed by a ' huge ' turkey which was considered essential to an Indian dinner at that time, or an equally huge ham with curries and rice. This was followed by plum pudding, after which the cloths were removed and hookahs were brought on. Each man had his own servant who stood behind his chair. Then the sergeants entered to present their orderly books, and the drinking began. The colonel or senior officer, who presided, drank with the different guests while each man drank with his neighbour. Then came the ceremony of the toasts. Every mess taxed its ingenuity to increase their number and each was honoured by appropriate tunes from the band. The first was to the Ladies, to the tune of ' Kiss my lady ', the next of the King, with the National Anthem, then the Duke of York and the Army, then the Duke of Clarence and the Navy with ' Rule Britannia ', then the Company with the tune of ' Money in both pockets ', then Lord Wellesley, Lord Clive, Lord Lake, ' General Baird and the heroes of Seringapatam ', and any other name which a well-heated imagination might conjure up. The company was now warming to its work ; everyone in turn was called on for a song, which was applauded by banging fists on the table and honoured by a toast and a tune at the end. At 10 p.m. the Colonel retired, after which ' a few choice spirits closed on the President ', and continued the proceedings with the aid of dishes of olives, anchovied devilled biscuits and devilled turkey. The Major escaped during a dispute about the next guard to a volley of ' Shabby fellow ', ' Milk sop ', ' Cock Tail ', etc., and left the remaining choice spirits to continue till the small hours of the morning.[44] The drinking bouts which seem regularly to have taken place resembled the ' daily superabundant potations of champagne and madeira ' in which Hickey's set indulged,[45] and which in the settlements had now gone out of fashion. The diarist records the drinking at Sarssney of three and a half dozen of claret and ' a proportionable quantity of Madeira ' by fourteen people in a bout which ended with breaking the candle shades and glasses, ' pranks which too frequently finish drinking parties in this quarter of the globe.'[46] This was doubtless an exceptional exploit, but other references make it clear that a bottle of claret a day was the normal share of each man.[47] Arthur Wellesley was considered ' very abstemious with wine ; he drank four or five glasses with people at dinner, and about a pint of claret after '.[48]

In the cantonments the troops lived in barracks and the officers in bungalows. At Cawnpore, the largest cantonment in Northern India, the compounds were called ' estates '.[49] As the political conditions became more stable cantonments acquired a settled and permanent character. The first officers had gone without meat, poultry and even vegetables, had dined at mid-day and drunk all night, but by 1800, there was a marked improvement both in comfort and manners,[50] attributed largely to the influence of Cornwallis.[51] Ladies also appeared at these stations, and their influence produced still further results in the same direction. In 1800, however, when their numbers were still small, gaming and heavy drinking were still customary, manners were still very masculine, and their presence was not always appreciated. At dinner they acted as a restraint on the conversation, and on their retirement the men not infrequently forgot to follow them. 'Many of the party saw no more of the ladies this evening; in truth they too much resembled the generality of Indian dames to afford much attraction. The bottle was not unusually preferred, and generally confessed to be best so.'[52] The same writer mentions a social war between the bachelors and married officers of Bareilly on account of the European mistress of one officer, and described the ladies there—'a more stiff set I never fell in with; plain, proud and ignorant, attempting the airs of gentlewomen though it was more than probable that previous to their arrival at our markets most of them could not boast a change of dickies twice a month'.[53] Ladies who ventured to these stations had also to be prepared to meet the traditional eccentrics. One such is described in 1805 at Ghazipore.[54] 'After the ladies had withdrawn, the bottle was pushed pretty rapidly, and our host spoke so *plainly* and loudly that we were necessitated to shut the drawing room door, and about ten the old fellow reeled away to pay his respects to the ladies, very far gone and unable to walk without assistance. . . . We left him about 12 fast asleep in his chair.'

The second amusement of the military was sport. In the cantonments racing and gaming were the two chief amusements. By the end of the century most of the cantonments had at least their annual race meetings. But it was in camp and on the march that the soldier revelled in an unlimited supply of game of all sorts for shooting or hunting. In the unsettled state of the country and especially of Northern India, and in the sparsity of the population, immense stretches which are now cultivated lay waste and wild. At the end of the century, for instance, it was not safe for a traveller to proceed from Delhi to Agra or Lucknow without protection by day and shelter by night. Game abounded and was not limited by rights which had to be observed. Big game shooting at that time was for the few, and was only conducted on elephants or from machans (platforms).[55] It was, of course, a favourite diversion of the princes who organized elaborate shoots for their European guests. At the hunts of the Nawab of Arcot, who attended 'with a wonderfully large retinue', Sir Martin Hunter wrote, 'a net about a mile long was stretched outside of a jungle, supported by poles of 8 feet high every 5 or 6 yards. This net was made of very strong cord as thick as my finger'.[56] On the Nawab's arrival on an elephant a thousand poligars (woodmen) dived into the woods, ' making a most hideous noise, firing off matchlocks, sounding horns and beating drums. The terrified animals—deer, boar, jackals, hyenas, foxes, hares, and sometimes tigers, were driven on to the net where they were indiscriminately shot down. ' I was much surprised,' added Sir Martin, ' that they did not shoot one another ; a regiment could not have kept up a more constant fire for nearly an hour.'[57]

The ordinary officer obtained ample sport by hunting and shooting. In the south wild hog, jackals, hyaenas, foxes, and deer were hunted or coursed. The wild hog was hunted by two sets of dogs, greyhounds and Poligar dogs, who were ' fiercer than a bull-dog and full as fleet as a foxhound '.[58] The greyhounds came up to the boar and engaged it until the poligars arrived and held on and the huntsmen were able to finish it off with spears and pistols. Sometimes the hunter stuck the pig at full speed, but this was not the general practice before the end of the century.[59] Foxes were coursed because no scent would lie half an hour after sunrise, and deer were coursed either with dogs in the Deccan,[60] who separated fawns from the herds and chased them, or else by specially trained leopards with their teeth drawn. The chief difficulty in hunting was the hounds, who seldom lasted more than one season, but were nevertheless sold ' at astonishing prices '.[61] They very easily took disease, the most common being the bile, staggers, rabies and mange.[62] The place of English hounds was in part taken by a country breed of Poligar dogs crossed with the English greyhound.[63]

In shooting the sportsman displayed a most catholic taste. In 1803 one records shooting the following in the course of a few successive days' sport in Northern India[64]—tiger (near Bareilly), hogs, deer, florikin, otters, hyaenas, alligators, turtles, partridges, hares, quails, nielghy, peafowl, snipe, ortolans, teal, pigeons (' from a bridge about which they swarmed '),[65] king-crows, mango birds, parrots and parakeets, sparrows and ' a small green bird very common in India '. On 16 May 1803 he killed seven brace of hares, twenty brace of black partridge, several deer and hogs before breakfast, and afterwards proceeded to fish at the Kiary Lake near Bareilly. A net was stretched right across the lake, and when the large fish jumped right over it, large ' choppers ' (covers of thatch made of grass and bamboo and used for huts) were fetched from the village and men were put on them with clubs to knock the fish on the head as they jumped over. Some jumped into the boat and were despatched with a boat hook. ' The quantity of fish we killed exceeds all belief,' exclaims our author, and concludes his page by expressing horror at infanticide and suttee.[66] In Northern India, especially, game seems to have been prolific. Broadly speaking, a man shot on service and hunted in cantonments.

Another class of mofussil dweller was the indigo planter. The indigenous Indian industry, whose centre was in Gujarat, declined in the eighteenth century, partly owing to the adulteration of the Indian dye as the result of high prices, and partly because of the discovery of a source of the dye in America. With the loss of America, however, the American supply passed into the hands of the hostile United States; while at the same time the cultivation of sugar and coffee was found to be more profitable in the West Indies. The West Indian industry was finally killed by the negro revolts and the wars of the Revolution period.[67] In these circumstances from about 1780 onwards the Company took up the cultivation of indigo. Planters were brought from the West Indies to selected Bengal districts, the Company's officers were allowed to trade in indigo, and subsidies and advances were given for a time. By 1790 the European indigo industry was well established, and spread rapidly northwards from Bengal as far as Delhi; the old Gujerat industry slowly languished and died.[68] From 1780 private planters were establishing themselves with government licences in Bengal, Bihar and Oudh (where they were more difficult to control), and providing for the officials a pretty problem in racial relations. The nature of these difficulties is shown by a Bengal government circular dated 13 July 1810.

> The offences to which the following remarks refer, and which have been established, beyond all doubt or dispute, against individual indigo planters, may be reduced to the following heads:
>
> *First.* Acts of violence, which, although they amount not in the legal sense to murder, have occasioned the death of natives.
>
> *Second.* The illegal detention of the natives in confinement, especially in stocks, with a view to the recovery of balances alleged to be due from them, or for other causes.
>
> *Third.* Assembling in a tumultuary manner the people attached to their respective factories, and others, and engaging in violent affrays with other indigo planters.
>
> *Fourth.* Illicit infliction of punishment, by means of rattan and otherwise, on the cultivators or other natives.[69]

Thomas Munro, in his evidence before the Committee of 1813, corroborated this.[70]

The cultivation was carried on by means of advances from the planters to the cultivators, who undertook to cultivate a fixed quantity of indigo at a fixed price. Oppression of the peasants might arise through compulsion or extortion in various forms. The ryot's only remedy was an appeal to the courts, where the planter's influence and his own poverty gave him very little chance of redress.[71]

At this time indigo planting was a lucrative and favourite occupation of the non-official European. Carey worked indigo for a time at Debarta, where his character gave the villagers much perplexity from its contrast to that of the average planter. Martin of Lucknow farmed indigo at Nadjaf Garh as his friend de Boigne did at Koil. The planters lived as a rule isolated and lonely lives, which goes far to explain their irregularities, and their object was to make a fortune and return as quickly as possible.

The last class of European in the mofussil was the military adventurer. The wars of the English and French in the middle of the century, and the gradual onset of the 'Great Anarchy' in Northern India in its latter half, favoured their appearance. They were of all classes and all nationalities, serving under established states like Hyderabad or Oudh, under rising military adventurers like Sindia, the Begam Samru or Ranjit Singh, or setting up for themselves like Thomas of Hansi. They reached their zenith under Ranjit Singh, who had French, Italian, English and Anglo-Indian officers; Kaye in his *Life of Metcalfe* gives a list of seventy such, and recent research in the Punjab Record Office has revealed many more.[72]

The most famous names were Raymond of Hyderabad, who saved that state from the Marathas, de Boigne and Perron in the service of Sindia, Martin at Lucknow, the notorious Walter Reinhardt, Skinner, Thomas, and in the Punjab Generals Allard, Ventura and Avitabile. Few but the highest returned again to Europe, and most adopted a semi-Indian mode of life. Some married into the best Mussulman families, like Major Hyder Hearsay, who married Zuhur-ul Nissa Begam, daughter of the deposed prince of Cambay and adopted as a daughter by the Emperor Akbar Shah II,[73] or Colonel Gardner, whose descendants live as zamindars in the United Provinces,[74] and lay claim to the dormant family barony. Col. Hearsay's son married the Nawab Mulka Humani Begam, daughter of Mirza Suliman Sheko and niece of Akbar II.[75]

The life of General Martin has already been described, but his case is hardly typical, since he lived in a large capital. Comte de Boigne's establishment at Koil (Aligarh), which Twining visited in 1794, illustrates better the typical adventurer's mode of life, or rather the mode he aspired to once he had gained sufficient wealth and success.[76]

> Dinner was served at four. It was much in the Indian style: pillaws and curries, variously prepared, in abundance; fish, poultry and kid. The dishes were spread over the large table fixed in the middle of the hall, and were, in fact, a banquet for a dozen persons, although there was no one to partake of it but the General and myself. [An elephant ride followed dinner. The next morning after breakfast the general called for his 'chillum' (hookah) which aroused the traveller's enthusiasm.] What a mean and vulgar thing does the tobacco pipe seem, when compared with this, even in the mouth of its great patron, Dr. Parr.

After this the general held a Durbar when vakils and men of rank paid their respects. His little four year old son, dressed as the child of an Indian prince, and 'of a Kashmirian tint', was brought in; de Boigne was unmarried, 'but he had it appeared his seraglio'.[77]

The Company's servants who spent many years in the mofussil, also sometimes adopted this mode of life. Such a one was Ochterlony, who possessed mansions at Delhi, Karnal[78] and elsewhere, and who is said to have startled Bishop Heber by his oriental habits, Fraser, whose friendliness to the Delhi families was not appreciated by his brother officers of the thirties,[79] and many others. Colonel Collins, resident at Sindia's court, was thus described by Major Blakiston.[80]

> Such was the state maintained by this representative of John Co. (known in Bengal by the nickname of King Collins) that he had a brigade of field pieces, worked by native artillerymen, attached to his escort. In front of a noble suite of tents, which might have served for the Great Moghul, we were received by an insignificant little, old-looking man, dressed in an old-fashioned military coat, white breeches, sky-blue silk stockings, and large glaring buckles to his shoes, having his highly powdered wig, from which depended a pig-tail of no ordinary dimensions, surmounted by a small round black silk hat, ornamented with a single black ostrich feather, looking altogether not unlike a monkey dressed for Bartholomew fair.

The military adventurers, from the brilliance and eccentricity of their lives, are perhaps the most fascinating of all the Europeans in India. But the magnificence of the few, and the halo of romance which time and military glamour have shed upon them, must not blind us to the majority, obscure officers and renegade soldiers, who led lives of hardship and often of degradation, and found in the end unhonoured and obscure graves, forgotten equally by the country of their birth and of their adoption.[81] As in the settlements, the wealth and luxury of the few were offset by the squalor and hardships of the more numerous but forgotten 'Low Europeans'. Amongst adventurers as amongst the settlement dwellers there was no middle class; a man was either a rajah or a serf.

Chapter VI

SIDELIGHTS OF ANGLO-INDIAN LIFE

Personal Rules of Life

Scattered in the records of the eighteenth century may be found a number of personal rules of life. Though some of them were more in the nature of counsels of perfection than seriously observed rules, they serve to emphasize the fact that not all the English lived irregular and dissipated lives, and that then as now the really busy man could not afford to live wildly. There was much sober living and hard work in the eighteenth century as well as much excess and merrymaking. Those who neglected these rules found places in the great cemeteries of the eighteenth century settlements, and the number who thus found early graves indicates the extent to which these rules were disregarded. But a regular life, then as now, had its votaries, and they were probably far more numerous than the ordinary picture of eighteenth century society would suggest.

In 1768 Mrs. Kindersley thus described life in Calcutta. 'In Calcutta at that time the custom was to rise early, to dine at one to two o'clock, to take a siesta afterwards and then to dress and take the air at sunset in carriages. Finally the evening was given up to social intercourse.'[1]

Captain Williamson thus advised the new arrival for his first year in India. The newcomer or 'griffin' should rise at dawn and should ride for one or two hours. Breakfast followed, at which melted butter (ghi), salt meats, fish and sweetmeats were to be avoided. He should then take up language study for an hour and proceed to his office for an hour in order to learn business. After dinner at two to three o'clock [the hour had moved to 6 or 7 o'clock by 1800] he should rest. An hour before sunset he should bathe by throwing a pot of water over his head, and then take an airing. His dinner, whether at two or at seven should be of plain food, at which not more than four or five glasses of the best Madeira should be drunk. The day was concluded by two hours language study, after which some bread and one glass of Madeira preceded sleep.[2]

This is specially interesting as providing a standard of what the Anglo-Indians themselves regarded as plain and simple living. How many observed it may be judged from the study of the obituary records.

Warren Hastings in 1784 wrote that he rode eight miles before breakfast and took a cold bath.[3] At meals he took nothing stronger than tea or water ; he took no supper and went to bed at ten.

Sir John Shore, in a letter to Lady Shore, dated 21 January 1787, wrote : 'I rise early, ride seven to ten miles, and breakfast by eight o'clock : after that business occupies my time till the hour of dinner, which is three. Our meals here are short : and in the evening, when the weather permits, which at this season of the year is daily, I walk out. The remaining time between that and ten o'clock, which is my hour of rest, I spend with my friends ; as I make it a rule not to attend to business of an evening. Suppers are by no means agreeable to me. At present, we have balls every week ; but I am not fond of them ; and indeed have been at one private ball only, which was given by Lord Cornwallis ; nor yet have I attended one play.'[4] 'Most men who worked hard in offices,' he wrote in 1789, 'worked for six hours a day.'

Cornwallis rode out on horseback at dawn, and attended to business during the morning until the time of dinner, about two. At sunset he drove out in a phaeton and then wrote or read for two hours. At nine he ate fruit and biscuits with two or three officers and went to bed at ten.[5]

Lord Wellesley wrote in 1798 : 'I rise early and go out before breakfast, which is always between 8 and 9. From that hour until 4 (in the hot weather) I remain at work, unless I go to Council or to Church of Sundays ; at 5 I dine and drive out in the evening. At present I drive out at 5 and dine a little after 6. No constitution here can bear the sun in the middle of the day at any season of the year, nor the labour of business in the evening. After dinner, therefore, nobody attempts to write or read, and, in general, it is thought necessary to avoid even meetings on subjects of business at that time. . . .'[6]

The Punkah

The punkah, or swinging fan, suspended from the ceiling and worked by a cord on a pulley, was introduced into Anglo-India towards the end of the eighteenth century. Colonel Yule in *Hobson-Jobson* gives quotations to show that this device was known to the Arabs ; it was invented by Caliph Mansur (A.D. 753-74) and was known as the Mirwaha-t al Khaish (linen fan). He also quotes from Bernier, who speaks of 'good cellars with great flaps to stir the air' in Delhi.[7] But Bernier suggests no mechanical contrivance and may have meant only the large fans which were held over a noble by a slave. There is no other reference to swinging punkahs in Moghul India, and no sign of their use in any of the

A FAMILY AT TABLE UNDER A PUNKAH

[*face p.* 96

extant Moghul palaces. Even if they were used in the underground apartments at Delhi, their use certainly never became general in the palace proper, and the orthodox Moghul fan consisted of a large flap which slaves held over a grandee as he sat at ease amidst his cushions. If the swinging fan ever existed in Moghul India, its use never spread to the Europeans.

At first the Europeans used the ordinary Moghul fans. Captain Fryer says that at Masulipatam the air was fanned with peacock tails by servants who also held umbrellas over them.[8] At Surat, according to Ovington, the factors were fanned with 'murchals' or fans of peacock feathers four to five feet long.[9] These large fans, together with small fly switches, were those in use until the eighties of the eighteenth century.

The exact date of the introduction of swinging punkahs is uncertain, but we can confine it within fairly narrow limits. They first appeared in Calcutta, where the first reference to them is made in 1785, but they could not have been used before 1780, as they do not appear in any of the inventories preserved in the India Office which extend from 1755 to that date. They were not in use at Nand Kumar's trial. On the other hand, they must have been fairly well known in Calcutta by 1785; William Hickey then records the opinion of Lord Macartney when on a visit from Madras, that the use of 'punkahs or hanging fans, suspended by ropes from the ceiling, to cool them while eating their meals' was very luxurious.[10] This reference incidentally shows that the punkah had not yet reached Madras. It penetrated to Bombay still later, where it is first mentioned as being in general use by Mrs. Graham in 1809.[11]

De Grandpré thus described the Calcutta punkah in 1790. In many houses there was 'a large fan hanging from the ceiling over the eating table, of a square form and balanced on an axle fitted to the upper part of it. A servant, standing at one end of it, puts it in motion by means of a cord which is fastened to it, in the same manner as he would ring a bell'.[12] The early punkahs consisted of a large frame of wood, covered with cloth or painted paper;[13] it was not till later that it was discovered that the decorative fringe of cloth attached to the frame produced on account of its pliability a better draught than the rigid frame. During the nineteenth century the frame grew smaller while the fringe grew larger until the final form of a large cloth hanging from a horizontal wooden bar was reached. This evolution is described by Mr. D. Dewar in his *Bygone India*.

In addition to the swinging punkahs, hand fans, made of palm with part of the stalk for a handle, continued to be used, and

Williamson also mentions fly-whisks or 'chowrys' made of wild oxtail hair, peacock feathers or grass roots (kus-kus).[14]

Smoking

At the beginning of the eighteenth century the smoking of hookahs seems not to have been so general as it later became among the Europeans. In the *Factory Miscellaneous Records* '1 Chamolet Hoake with a green baise' is mentioned in an inventory of 1675,[15] but the remaining references to smoking in the book (pp. 44, 51, 73 et seq., and 100), which extends to 1728, all refer to pipes. We read of 'a Box of Pipes', of '38 Tobacco stopers Brass and Iron', of 'one China Tobacco Pipe' and a 'Box of Pipps' belonging to Mr. E. Hanslopp, and 'a Parcell of Tobacco and Pipes' sold for Rs. 6. There are also one or two additional references to tobacco, but none to hookahs. It seems probable, therefore, that the early factors for the most part used their accustomed churchwarden clay pipes.

From 1728 to 1755 no inventories survive, but as soon as the series reopens in Calcutta in that year there are numerous references, both in the inventories and in books of travel. We may surmise, therefore, that the custom of hookah smoking came in during that time, probably as the result of the increasing contact with Indian life which the French wars brought about.

In Bombay hookahs were known in the middle of the century as 'Cream Cans', being named, it was said, after Karim Khan Zend, King of South Persia in the middle of the century, who invented it. Another variety was the Ailloon, which Niebuhr says also came from Persia.[16] The Hubble-Bubble was, according to the same authority, the poor man's hookah. Thus Eliza Sterne wrote in 1760 of her brother-in-law 'who will suck a Hubble-Bubble, draw an Ailloon, smoak a hooka or cream-can with you if you please'.[17] Williamson also mentions the 'Kalyan' as a western hookah smaller than the average, and with a larger bottom.[18] In Surat hookahs, according to Parsons in 1774, were called 'Nargils',[19] and in Calcutta a small hookah for a palanquin was called a 'Googoory'.[20]

By the sixties the fashion of hookah smoking had become firmly established. Stavorinus in 1769 says that at a dinner given to a Dutch Director in Bengal hookahs were placed before each of the company.[21] From then to the end of the century the hookah reigned supreme in Anglo-Indian society, the ladies smoking as well as the men.[22] Grandpré thus describes the etiquette of the hookah: 'The rage of smoking extends even to the ladies; and the highest compliment they can pay a man is to give him preference by smoking his hookah. In this case it is a point of politeness to take off a mouthpiece he is using and substitute a fresh one, which he presents to the lady with his hookah, who soon returns it.'[23]

The first sign of the decline of the custom was the action of William Hickey, who, when told on his arrival in Calcutta in 1778 that hookah-smoking was essential but that a few did not practise it, promptly refused to touch one.[24] From that time the custom commenced a decline which became perceptible after 1800. In 1802 Major Blakiston wrote that hookahs were too expensive to be afforded by many officers, requiring as they did, a special servant (the hookahburdar) in addition to the cost of the hookah and the tobacco.[25] D'Oyley, in *The European in India*, a few years later, says that not one in three were then smokers, although the custom had been almost universal. But the custom died hard. In the twenties of the nineteenth century retired Anglo-Indians still often brought their hookahs with them to England, and one lady is remembered by Burnell to have used it in Scotland for several years. In 1840 it was still common in Calcutta, and it lingered still later in the mofussil. In 1860 there were, according to Col. Yule, still six hookah smokers in the Madras Presidency; they had disappeared by 1878, though a few were still said to keep up the practice in Hyderabad State.[26]

The hookah was replaced by the cheroot or cigar. At first, according to Williamson, they were only used by the lowest Europeans, who presumably could not afford hookahs. The cheroot was like the Spanish 'segar', only rather more expensive. But the cigar slowly made progress; in 1798 Captain Elers mentions smoking a cigar,[27] and a little later writes of the hookah, that it is much better 'than the horrid, vulgar smell of common tobacco, which I abominate. I am not very fond of cigars, even when they are good, which at present is by no means common. They are more than half spurious'.[28] With these tastes, the cigar was bound to make its way as the hookah declined, or rather as the means to maintain them decreased.

Macintosh's description of a hookah has already been given; we will add one more, that of D'Oyley in *The European in India*. The ordinary hookah, he wrote, had a glass or composition bottom containing two quarts, which was two-thirds filled with clear, cold water. The snake or tube was ten feet long, and was composed of a bark like sycamore bound round a skeleton of pewter wire, and covered with a black or purple calico. The mouthpiece was of agate mounted on a wooden socket. At the other end the snake connected with a bamboo tube which pierced the top of the water chamber above the water level. Into the water another tube, a foot in length, was immersed to a depth of three inches. Above this tube an earthenware receiver or ' chillum ' was placed, which contained the tobacco. This was covered by a tile, upon which were placed four pieces of charcoal prepared from burnt rice. Finally a silver cover, which fitted the rim of the ' chillum ' covered the whole.

The Palanquin

Throughout the century the palanquin played a large part in Anglo-Indian life. It was the regular mode of conveyance from house to office, and on all small journeys of business or pleasure, and on long expeditions across country. With the growth of roads carriages of various sorts were used for afternoon airings, but the palanquin remained the essential means of transport within the settlements. Everyone down to the writer just arrived from England possessed a palanquin if he could.

The original palanquin was the ' dooly ', which was an ordinary string bedstead, five feet by two, covered with a light bamboo frame and draped with red curtains. From this the ornate palanquin of Calcutta and Madras was developed. First the shape was changed to that of a hexagon. Then the sides were raised, more ornament was added and the canopy was arched. Cushions were added inside, and curtains which could completely close the palanquin if desired. The occupant reclined at full length, and was often supplied with a specially designed hookah, at which he could puff as he was borne along to business. The ' naulkeen ' or ' naulkee ' was a further elaboration. The frame was five feet by four, the sides richly carved woodwork, while inside was a chair and pillows. This was carried by eight men.

Mrs. Graham in 1809 mentions a further development in Bombay. These palanquins had a wooden frame, and were fitted with windows and sliding doors within which one could either lie or sit. They were ' little carriages without wheels '. The decorations of course varied with the wealth of the owner ; gold and silver bells, embroidered curtains and tassels adorned the more wealthy.[29]

In Calcutta Oriyas were usually employed as bearers, but their monopoly was later broken by men from Patna and Dacca. The usual number in a set was seven, one cooking for the rest, one being the sirdar or head bearer. The actual carrying was therefore done by five men. The palanquin bearers were very independent and on occasion went on strike.

Medicine

So many general references have been made to disease in the eighteenth century that it is perhaps worth while to inquire a little further into the practice of medicine during that period.

Captain Fryer in Bombay in 1674 mentions 'Fluxes, dropsy, scurvy, barbiers, or the loss of the use of the hands and feet, gout, stone, malignant and putrid fevers' as the principal complaints.[30] Ovington at Surat speaks of fevers, specially 'after a strong Debauch', Barbeers, for which the cure was to haunt the 'hum-hums' (baths), 'which are here in great plenty,' and 'mordechine' or cholera, which he attributed to excess in eating fish and meat together, and which was cured by applying a red hot iron to the heel.[31] Captain Symson in 1702 mentions the same disease and the same cure; the red hot iron, he says, must be applied 'so close that it touches to the quick'.[32] He also mentions an interesting talisman against snake bite. Europeans, he says, often wore a snake stone in a gold heart hung by a gold chain from their necks. The stone was a dark, almost flat, artificial stone, 'composed of Ashes of certain burnt Roots, mix'd with a Sort of Earth found at Diu'. This was all re-burnt and made into a paste which hardened into a stone.[33] The rhinoceros horn was also regarded as an antidote to poisonous draughts. The Sieur Luillier also mentions scurvyl; 'it is a Distemper occasion'd by continual breathing the Air of the Sea, eating Salt Meals and drinking strong Liquors'.[34]

Here we may note the emphasis all through the century on the connexion of intemperance with disease. The connexion was apparently generally admitted and as generally ignored by all but a few throughout the period. After Ovington and Symson we find Niebuhr writing in the same strain of Bombay in 1764.[35] In Calcutta in 1765 Topham wrote that 'intemperance is the disease that destroys more people in those Parts than either Fevers or Agues'.[36] In 1780 Innes Munro wrote of Madras that the bile was much increased by the 'gross manner in which the English live here and their excessive use of mixed liquors'.[37] Similar instances could be multiplied including those of men like Hastings and Cornwallis, who preserved their health by means of a carefully regulated diet.

The same diseases, with the addition of liver complaints, continued to be common throughout the century. Thus Dr. Ives, a surgeon on Admiral Watson's fleet, writes of bilious and putrid fluxes, and of liver complaints. Fluxes he treated by vomiting and the administration of rhubarb and ipecacuanha. For the liver, fever was first abated by bleeding, the patient was then given a purge and treated with calomel.[38] Ives gives some interesting figures of illness in the Admiral's fleet. From 13 Sept. 1754 to 7 Nov. 1757, 6,062 were admitted into hospital, of whom 203 died.

The following table includes all the diseases which claimed more than fifty victims.[39]

Disease	*Number*	*Deaths*
Fluxes	1,819	97
Scurvies	1,103	11
Fevers (miscellaneous) ..	900	42
Intermittent fevers ..	547	17
Bilious obstructions ..	536	10
Rheumatism	103	2
Bowel inflammation ..	83	5
Bilious Colics	62	0
Venereal Diseases ..	58	2

Dr. Lind, in his *Essay on Diseases, etc.*, published in 1768, speaks of Bengal as the most unhealthy of the three Indian Presidencies. Intermittent fever was the chief disease, of which he says 800 Europeans died in 1762. He notes that those that stopped the use of the 'bark' relapsed, and suggests that the moon and tides may have some influence on fevers since patients in Bombay often died at low water.[40] Unlike Dr. Ives, he did not recommend bleeding. He considers that an unhealthy country has the following characteristics—sudden and great alteration of the air, thick and noisome fogs, swarms of flies, corruption of butcher's meat and a sandy soil.[41] He advises against exposure in the open air on a foggy night,[42] and recommends for protection from the sun a 'bladder dipped in vinegar'.[43] In unhealthy places a man should chew rhubarb, stop his nose with linen dipped in camphor and vinegar, and put up 'some bark, garlic and rhubarb in brandy'. He should vomit at the first sign of a chill. In the interior he advises the avoidance of marshes during the rain. Their connexion with fever had already been noted, but their relation to mosquitoes had of course not yet been thought of. This opinion was expressed by the Sieur Luillier, but later we find Surgeon Johnson disagreeing with Dr. Lind's theory and quoting Dr. Currie's 'New Theory' that marsh airs in themselves were neither noxious nor infectious.[44]

A few facts of medical history may here be of interest. The treatment of fever with quinine was first used in Europe to cure the Countess of Chinchon in 1638 of tertian malaria.[45] She was treated with a bark brought from Loxa, where its use had been known to the Spaniards since 1640, and where it was called 'quina-quina' by the South American Indians. The disease was first called 'pulvis comitessae' in honour of the Countess. In 1670 the Jesuits introduced quinine into Rome; thence it was distributed throughout Europe by the Cardinal de Lugo, and was in consequence known as ' Jesuit's or Cardinal's Bark '. The term ' Cinchona ' is derived from Linnaeus who thus mis-spelt the Countess's name in his Latin name of ' Cinchona officinalis '. A controversy as to its effectiveness for malaria was settled by Morton and Sydenham and by the cure of the Dauphin. In the early eighteenth century it was introduced into the East, but it was not until 1820 that the first alkaloid quinine was prepared from bark by Pelletier and Caventou. The term ' mal aria ' was first used by Francisco Torti in his treatise *Therapeutica specialis ad febres quasdam perniciosas*, published at Modena in 1712. He also recommended the use of Cinchona bark in its treatment, and with Baglivi described an Italian outbreak in 1715.[46] The connexion of mosquitoes with malaria was foreshadowed by Lancisci in 1717, but the clue was never followed up.[47]

Typhoid fever was first differentiated from typhus by Dr. John Huxham in 1755 in his *Essay on Fevers*. Typhoid was a ' slow nervous fever ', and typhus a ' putrid malignant fever '.[48] Dr. Huxham also recommended a diet of vegetables for scurvy cases. Drs. Lind and Ives both recommended lemon juice as a cure, and in 1795 it was supplied to the Fleet by an Admiralty order.[49] Inoculation was known from very ancient times. It is mentioned in the Atharva Veda and was known in the School of Salerno.[50] In the eighteenth century it was used spasmodically in England, and in 1769 it is mentioned by Stavorinus who says it was much practised in Bengal.[51] The contagious matter was made up into powders and either taken internally or else sometimes administered through incisions. The patient was cured in three weeks. Dr. Jenner's discovery, that girls with cowpox were immune from the small-pox was made in 1778, and his system of vaccination was introduced into India, according to Williamson, in 1802, where it slowly became popular.[52]

Major J. Taylor, a surgeon, in his *Travels in India* (1789) described the treatment for the usual diseases, in which he makes much use of ' Dr. James' Powder ' for colds, fevers and agues. He recommends a medicine chest for a traveller, with a description of which we will conclude this chapter.[53]

(1)	Extract of bark with rezin ..	1 to 2 lb.
	Extract of logwood	2 oz.
(2)	Opiate confection	½ lb. (not to be kept)
(3)	White vitriol	1 oz.
(4)	Acid elixir of vita	6-8 oz.
(5)	Camphor	2 oz.
(6)	Powder of snake root	
(7)	Prepared Chalk	2 lb.

(8)	Powdered Nitre	2 lb.
	Catharic Extract	2 oz.
	Glaubos or Epsom salts in a bladder.	
(9)	Calomel Preparation	2 oz.
(10)	Dr. James' Powder	2 oz.
(11)	Liquid Laudanum	½ pint.
(12)	Tincture of Senna	1 pint.
(13)	Borax	2 oz.
(14)	Magnesia	½ lb.
(15)	Tartar Emetic	1 oz.
(16)	Powdered Spanish flies ..	2 oz.
(17)	Adhesive Plaster for blisters	
(18)	Jalap (powdered)	2 oz.
(19)	Cream of Tartar, ½ lb.; salts of hartshorn; Goulard's extracts for cooling washes, 2 ounces of each	
(20)	Cathartic extract for costiveness	

Chapter VII

CHAPLAINS AND MISSIONARIES

Chaplains

It is said that the arrival of Bishop Heber in Calcutta caused some excitement among the Brahmins and sannyasis. At last, it was said, the Christians had sent one of their holy men, and their interest was not unmixed with anxiety for the prestige of their own faith. So one of the Brahmins was appointed to visit the Bishop and report to the rest. He reached the Bishop's house, but when he saw the size of the mansion, the number of carriages waiting at the door, and the throng of servants, he laughed, and returned to tell his companions that whatever dangers might threaten Hinduism, the Bishop was not one of them. Whatever the truth of this incident, it largely represents the Indian impression of Christianity in the eighteenth century. At the outset, Protestant missions did not exist, while the Roman Catholic missions were bound up with the political fortunes of the Portuguese. Always inclined to lean upon the secular arm, the Roman missions had followed in the wake of Albuquerque's soldiers, and the eloquence of St. Francis Xavier was soon followed by the inquisition at Goa. On the one hand the Roman weakness for ' compelling them to come in ' found full scope in the Synod of Diamper and its efforts to obtain the submission of the Syrian Church, on the other hand the Jesuit genius for experiment and adaptation resulted in the interesting Madura Mission. Its leader was Roberto de Nobili, known as ' the white Brahmin ', who endeavoured to win the Hindu intellectuals by learning Sanskrit, discoursing philosophy and observing all the high caste rules. But other bodies, the Capuchins, the Austin friars, the Theatines, the Franciscans, the Dominicans and the Carmelites, soon followed the Jesuits, and to the missionary entanglements in politics was added the traditional rivalry of the orders. They mostly had their headquarters at Goa, whose monasteries, schools and stately churches formed the largest part of the city.[1] In 1700 was just beginning that long decline, which lasted throughout the eighteenth century and reached its nadir in 1815 with the publication of the Abbé Dubois' famous jeremiad, asserting not only that the missions had lost two-thirds of their adherents in the course of eighty years, but that the remainder were Christians only in name.[2]

The only other European representatives of Christianity in India were the English and Dutch chaplains. At the opening of the century the Company was still largely under Puritan influence; the Directors showed much concern for the spiritual welfare of their servants, inquiring after their morals, and both supplying books applied for and recommending others themselves.[3] The early chaplains like Ovington were serious and devout men, punctilious in their daily prayers, preachings and their catechizings, and the new charter of 1698 in the same spirit provided that every ship of 500 tons burthen should carry a chaplain.[4] But with the new century the changing moral and religious atmosphere in England soon made itself felt in India. The tone of the Directors became more haughty, and they began to treat their chaplains in the Lutheran manner as the servants of all, instead of in the English way as the indispensable adjuncts of any gathering of gentlemen. Their tone and their methods became so peremptory that at last a protest was made to Archbishop Wake, which led to a change of attitude.[5] From that time the Directors maintained a typically mercantile attitude; what obligations they could evade they did, and what they could not they accepted with a good grace as part of the order of things. So for sixty years they carefully sent out ships of 499 tons in order to escape providing the statutory chaplain;[6] they frequently failed to observe the rule that 'every garison and superior factory' should have a chaplain; and they appointed Danish missionaries as chaplains instead of finding men of their own, but for the rest they accepted the position and treated the chaplains honourably and well.[7]

In the settlements themselves the chaplains were always of some importance. This was due primarily, not so much to the nature of their profession, as to the fact that they were professional at all. In the days when the doctors were often quack ex-soldiers like Voulton or adventurers like Manucci, the chaplains carried the whole weight of learning and the whole dignity of the professions in the settlements. They were the only people not avowedly connected with trade, and they represented the culture and learning as well as the solemnity and piety of England in India. In the early days their salary of £100 a year ranked them equal to the Second in Council and inferior only to the Governor;[8] in addition they had a diet allowance and the privilege of the use of a palanquin, though governmental respect stopped short at the provision of a 'roundell' boy for their umbrellas when they walked abroad.[9] The duties of a chaplain were to read prayers twice a day, to preach twice on Sunday, to catechize the children, to administer the Sacraments once a month and on the three major festivals, and to carry on the usual clerical round of funerals and marriages.[10] But they also very early showed an interest in education. Special masters were originally employed for the education of the European children (beginning with the ex-soldier R. Ord in 1678),[11] but the care of the Charity Schools and Orphan Asylums of Madras and Calcutta soon became part of the chaplain's duties and usually devolved on the junior chaplain.[12] Apart from this they had the conduct of all marriages, baptisms and burials. These duties in the early factories were not very onerous, and this fact, together with the hope and later the necessity of augmenting their salaries, tempted them into various extraneous activities. The most obvious of these was trade. Under the Charter of 1698 the chaplains were on the same footing as the other covenanted servants with regard to trade. They were prohibited from most of the important branches of the Europe trade, but might trade as they liked elsewhere as long as they did not neglect their duties. Private trading on the part of a clergyman was forbidden by law, but was winked at by the Company within limits. Evidence of its existence is scattered all through the century; Clive and Rennell both mention private trade as one of the advantages of the Chaplaincies. They recommended them to their relations, and John Owen of Calcutta shows in his letters that the practice was still regarded as permissible and customary. The practice seems finally to have been killed by the stricter notions of the Evangelical chaplains at the close of the century.[13] The extreme example of secularism was perhaps that of the Rev. R. Palk, who returned to Madras as the Governor himself. In distinction from the Directors, the local governments were usually friendly to the chaplains, and often collaborated with them in raising their salaries against the will of the Directors.[14] Another outlet for their energies was the provision of buildings. The Madras church already existed at the beginning of the century, being described by Lockyer as the equal of any in London except for the lack of more than one bell.[15] But at that time the church in Bombay lay roofless and but half-built owing to the difficulties of the Child wars, and the church at Calcutta had still to be built.[16] Later in the century the chaplains found the provision of education for the increasing number of European children an important question, and spent much time in raising the money and in managing the various male and female asylums which grew up. Later still, they turned to philanthropic work like the raising of money for famine relief, and finally as the century closed the new Evangelical chaplains bethought themselves of missionary work.

It is not easy to distinguish the life of a chaplain from the life of the settlement at large. The difference was one of function and not of status and mode of life, and to the average Hindu he would certainly be no holy man, but only a European more curious than the rest. The English lack of religious observance was frequently commented upon by the Hindus ; we find the Brahmins of Broach asking why the English, in distinction from all the other Europeans, never observed their religion,[17] and the English lack of religious observance was one of the difficulties encountered by Swartz, Martyn, and the Abbé Dubois.[18] The chaplain's way of living was much the same as the rest of the settlement. In Madras the chaplain had rooms provided for him at the back of the church, which in 1756 he complained were too small for a married man.[19] Inventories of their property show that there was little difference between them and the ordinary factor, except perhaps in the greater supply of and taste for books.[20] As the factories developed into settlements the chaplains became more numerous and more active, though perhaps relatively less important. They no longer ranked with the Second in Council, but instead became the chartered philanthropists of the settlements, from whom the organization of education and charity was naturally expected. Thus we find them connected, as before mentioned, with the orphan asylums of Madras and Calcutta, and organizing famine relief in Madras in 1782. The century ends as it began, on a note of deepened earnestness. As at the beginning the slowly breaking clouds of Puritanism still hung over the factories, at the end the breeze of the new Evangelicalism had begun to stir the stagnant waters of religious life. Enthusiasm had raised its head in England in defiance of all propriety and good taste, and Simeon's emissaries—the Evangelical five[21]—spread the infection to India. Under their influence the services became less formal and perfunctory ; elegant exposures of the 'deistical writers' were replaced by fiery castigations and warnings of the wrath to come, to the initial scandal and ultimate increase of the congregations. With this new zeal came a new interest in missions ; the chaplains were no longer content with the vicarious discharge of their missionary obligations by Danish and German workers, and began actively to sympathize with missionary ideals, and with the Baptist pioneers, Carey, Marshman and Ward, until Henry Martyn appeared in 1806, a missionary in the guise of a chaplain. With the revival of zeal came a revival of controversy, and the century which opened in Calcutta with disputes between High and Low Churchmen, 'where all religions were tolerated except the Presbyterian',[22] ended with the philippics of good Latitudinarians against Baptist conventiclists, and protests against the hell-fire preaching of Martyn.

The chaplains in the eighteenth century have been alternately represented as uniformly corrupt, the three-bottle orthodox going to seed in Bengal counting-houses, or as the scrupulous followers of 'duty's stern decree', an impeccable if somewhat uninspiring band.[23] The first view represents a mentality which likes to apply to the past standards it would never think of exacting from the present, while the second betrays that modern fashionable taste for unearthing all the peccadilloes of saints and discovering all the virtuous might-have-beens of rogues. The truth, of course, lies between the two. The chaplains could not logically be better as a body than the class in England from which they sprang, and they were not likely to be worse than the settlers themselves. The reply of 'corruptio optimi pessima' will not serve in this case, for the Church of England in the eighteenth century had no pretensions to great holiness. 'True piety without enthusiasm' was its ideal, as an eighteenth century epitaph put it; it represented the quintessence of normality, and was as much shocked by the enthusiasts who tried to rise a little higher as by the deists whom it considered to fall a little lower. 'The Church of England,' said an eighteenth century bishop, 'is a happy mean between the meretricious gaudiness of the Church of Rome and the squalid sluttery of fanatic conventicles.' Average virtue could only produce by reaction average vice, and since there was very little enthusiasm for good to begin with there could hardly be much enthusiasm for evil by reaction.

The official income of the chaplains and the efforts they made to increase it are proof enough against their apostolic simplicity,[24] but their various public and philanthropic activities are also a disproof of their complete lack of zeal. They were much less than fiery apostles of the faith, but also more than merely commercial parsons, and they certainly fulfilled the test of a virile priesthood in being as a whole slightly better than the rest of the population. The black sheep among them were occasional and not typical—the Rev. St. J. Browne, whose servant fell twenty feet off a terrace in trying to escape his blows, and who remarked to suggestions of rescuing him, 'Let him go to hell';[25] John Mitchell who masqueraded as a clergyman and married the daughter of Captain Williams on the strength of it,[26] and Chaplain Fordyce, whose career of calumny (punctuated by such remarks as that J. Fowke 'was a dark designing villain', whose 'nose he would slit the first time he met him', that 'he had knocked him under the table at the Governor's' and that 'he would put off his canonicals any time to do himself justice') was finally cut short on the complaint of Clive whom he had called 'a scoundrel and a coward'.[27] In general they were the sporting parsons of the eighteenth century England, transplanted to become the merchant parsons of India—honest, genteel, and dull. Apart from the Puritanism of an Ovington or the zeal of a Lewis at the beginning, and the Evangelicalism of a Brown and a Martyn at the end of the century, I have come across only one case of any intense religious devotion. It is the proposal of a 'Europe shopkeeper of Benares' about 1790 to erect with 'a few high Church friends' a chapel for their private devotions.[28] Was this some private whim, or was it perhaps one of the last faint echoes of the non-juring movement, 'lingering and wandering on as if loth to die', the gentle devotion of Ken and his friends, travelling from the dreamy towers and gardens of Wells to find a strange last resting-place in the citadel of hydra-headed Hinduism?

The church life of the settlement naturally varied in proportion to the changing spirit of the century. At the opening it was the focus of factory life, with the Governor's house as the social and ceremonial centre of the settlement. Attendance at daily prayers was compulsory, and on Sunday the services became a sort of state function. Attendance continued to be compulsory until far into the century; as late as 1744 'every Protestant absent from prayers without lawful excuse was to pay twelve pence for the poor, and to be confined one whole week within the house for every such default'.[29] The tradition was so strong that in the absence of a chaplain, factors were appointed as 'Readers of Divine Service' to read the daily and Sunday services. They had charge of the church registers and funds, they read the daily services and conducted baptisms and burials unless one of the Danish missionaries was available,[30] and what was probably most important from the factors' point of view, the two readers divided the chaplain's salary between them.[31] Marriages were the only ecclesiastical duty from which they were relieved, these being performed by the Chief Justice.[32] On occasion they even preached; in 1718 it was ordered 'that Mr. John Turton read prayers in the Church twice every Sunday and that Mr. Thomas Dunster read a sermon out of Archbishop Tillotson's works every Sunday morning'.[33] The familiar features of village church life reappeared in India; there is the weekly church parade, the gossip and the quarrels over precedence. Later there were complaints of perfunctory attendance, and the Directors issued stringent orders against laxity. With the expansion of Madras and Calcutta into fashionable settlements the church attendance became more and more a matter of form, and either a rendezvous of fashion or a resort of no one in particular. It became a convenient place for viewing new arrivals, but it dropped out as a centre of the social life of the settlements, to be replaced partly by the race-course, and partly by the Governor-General's levées and balls. The writer of *Hartley House*, though inaccurate in details,

CHURCH ENTRANCE TO DHARAMTOLLAH

[*face p.* 111

is probably correct enough in her general description of a church parade about 1787.

> The church is where *all* ladies are approached, by the sanction of ancient custom, by all gentlemen indiscriminately, known or unknown, with offers of their hand to conduct them to their seats; accordingly, those gentlemen who wish to change their condition (which, between ourselves, are chiefly old fellows, for the very young ones either choose country-born ladies for wealth, or, having left their hearts behind them, enrich themselves, in order to be united to their favourite dulcineas in their native land) on hearing of a ship's arrival make a point of repairing to this holy dome, and eagerly tender their services to the fair stranger, who, if this stolen view happens to captivate, often, not undergoing the ceremony of a formal introduction, receive matrimonial overtures.[34]

A little later, after the building of the new church in Calcutta, the ladies were moved from a pew in line with the Governor's to one in line with the Judges, the transaction giving rise to the following verse.

> The Ladies on the Lord relied
> To dignify their forms divine,
> But now, forsaken by their pride
> To court the praying maidens join.[35]

That all this had no connexion with religion is shown by the *Calcutta Gazette*, which in reporting the baptism of two infants in the church in 1787, thus solemnly writes: 'It is hoped that so laudable an example will become the general practice as the convenience of the new church now removes every possible objection which might have existed before; the solemnity of the place, must also naturally point it out as best adapted for those sacred obligations which the parties concerned enter into on such occasions.'[36] The extent to which the church had dropped out of the corporate life, and the gulf which separated it from any real devotion, was illustrated by the common saying, 'Is it Sunday? Yes; for I see the flag is hoisted'. One lady, Simeon reports, claimed great merit 'for every Sunday morning I read over the church service to myself while my woman combs my hair',[37] and another, twelve years in Calcutta and twice married, had never been to church because she had had no offer of escort from a beau.[38] Some of this was perhaps pious exaggeration, with a view to appreciating the more the work done by David Brown, but it points quite definitely to the supersession of the Church as a centre of social life. Nor was this altered by the new school of chaplains of whom Brown was the herald. They re-filled the church and confirmed the faithful; religion returned, but fashion still preferred the race-course and Lord Wellesley's levées.

Another side of church life was developed in Madras, where the Church functioned as a parish with its own Vestry and Wardens throughout the century. Their first care was the European poor, for whom they administered the charitable fund called the Church Stock and developed the organization of charity schools and 'asylums'. They did good work, until at the close the zealous Kerr so overdosed his parishioners with vestry meetings[39] that their legality was finally questioned and the whole parish as a legal entity abolished in 1805.[40]

As every nation its government, so on the whole every congregation gets the ministers it deserves. The East India Company's chaplains were neither saints nor prophets, and they were perhaps not even religious in the true sense at all; they probably thought more of their precedence as next after the Second in Council, of possible secretaryships for the augmentation of their salaries, or of the arrival of the ship from China or the Philippines containing the hoped-for profits on their respondentia bond, than of their ecclesiastical routine work or their Sunday sermons.[41] But they were not as a class either unprincipled adventurers or scandalous livers; like their confrères in England they were in general competent members of the most genteel of the professions. They had an honourable record of church building, of charitable and educational work; they supplied what the settlements wanted, a sense of respectability and of being on calling terms with the Deity; and for the rest they behaved reasonably in an Age of Reason, and kept Religion and Atheism impartially at arm's length.

Missionaries

At the opening of the eighteenth century, as has been said, the only Christian missionaries were the members of the various Roman Catholic orders.[42] Even their duties were only partly evangelistic, for they had in addition to their Indian congregations the spiritual charge of the Portuguese or 'Topasses', descendants of mixed marriages from the time of Albuquerque onwards. The Roman Church was organized into the two Archbishoprics of Goa and Cranganore, the two bishoprics of San Thomé and Cochin, all appointed by the Portuguese, and three Bishops *in partibus* appointed by the Pope, who were stationed at Bombay, Pondicherry and Virapoly. Their chief strength was naturally at Goa where two-thirds of the whole population of the Portuguese territory were Catholic; they were found all round the coast to Madras, and small stations were maintained by the Italian Capuchins and others at Agra, Lucknow, Patna, Bengal (where they came into contact with the Calcutta factors), Nepal and even in Tibet.[43] But their chief work was undoubtedly the Madura mission, which in 1700 still maintained its se rate existence and characteristics. Roberto de Nobili, the founder of the mission in the seventeenth century, was an extreme example of the attempt to be all things to all men; his aim was to win the Brahmins by becoming a Brahmin himself. He and the members of their mission until their final Papal condemnation in 1744, completely abandoned the European mode of life, donned the saffron robe of the sannyasi and lived the life of learned Brahmins, with Brahmin servants and vegetarian diet.[44] But to maintain the 'pious fraud' of the 'white Brahmins' it was necessary to disclaim all connexion with the Jesuit missions on the coast;[45] Pondicherry could only be visited in secret, and it was the indiscretions of these coast Jesuits together with the discovery of their connexion with the white Brahmins which largely destroyed their influence. The Tanjore persecution broke out and shattered the mission at the opening of the eighteenth century. In 1704 the Jesuit methods were condemned by a Papal bull, and though the Jesuits resisted its application with their customary tenacity and suppleness, they could only delay its final confirmation until 1744. While the mission lasted, the missionaries showed great ingenuity in Christianizing Hindu customs and great complacency in tolerating others. The caste system was maintained to the extent of refusing the Mass to Pariahs in Brahmin churches, and establishing separate congregations of Brahmins and Pariahs in the same towns; baptism was administered after a thirty or forty days' course in the style of a guru and his disciples, and symbols like the sacred thread were retained as a triple cord of gold representing the Trinity, with two silver strands to represent the human and divine natures of Christ. The other missionaries on the coast did not go so far as this,[46] but the Jesuits were accused by the Capuchins of Madras[47] of compelling Pariahs to receive the Sacrament at the doors of the churches, retaining caste marks, allowing men to wear jewels and the women 'talis' which they blessed, with a cross on one side and an idol on the other, and encouraging the Indian taste for noisy processions at marriages and funerals and on saints-days.[48] The Abbé Dubois, who disapproved of these concessions, thus described a Christian procession.

> Their processions in the streets, always performed in the night time, have indeed been to me at all times a subject of shame. Accompanied with hundreds of tom-toms, trumpets, and all the discordant music of the country ; with numberless torches and fireworks ; the statue of the saint placed on a car which is charged with garlands of flowers, and other gaudy ornaments, according to the taste of the country—the car slowly dragged along by a multitude shouting all along the march—the congregation surrounding the car all in confusion, several among them dancing, or playing with small stocks, or with naked swords ; some wrestling, some playing the fool ; all shouting, or conversing with each other, without any one exhibiting the least sign of respect or devotion. Such is the mode in which the Hindu Christians in the inland country celebrate their festivals. They are celebrated, however, with a little more decency on the coast. They are all exceedingly pleased with such a mode of worship, and anything short of such pageantry, such confusion and disorder, would not be liked by them.[49]

Apart from these experiments and an occasional missionary in the interior like the Abbé Dubois himself, the main body of the priests on the coasts lived in the European manner. They seem to have lived in the main devoted and sober lives ; we hear of few scandals among the Catholic priests working in the settlements, though the old quarrels of Jesuit and Capuchin, bishop and monk, French and Portuguese continued interminably and they all retained their genius for political entanglements. If to make a mistake is worse than a crime the Roman Catholics in India were some of the guiltiest people in the world. Among them all only two were Englishmen, the Jesuit, Padre Stephens in the sixteenth century at Goa, and the Theatine, Padre Milton, who seems to have been generally disliked by the settlers.[50]

The priests were chiefly brought into contact with the English as pastors of the Portuguese congregations near the English settlements. In both Calcutta and Madras there was a considerable Portuguese population, Madras in particular receiving many of the inhabitants of San Thomé, who abandoned the town after its capture in 1662. Captain Fryer reported a Portuguese population of 3,000 in 1680,[51] which in 1787 had become 17,000, in Madras out of a total of 100,000 Roman Catholics on the Coromandel coast.[52] Besides the Portuguese proper, there were the native Tamil congregations, but the dividing line tended always to become more blurred, and any Pariah who had learnt a European dialect and bought a 'Christian' hat, as Dubois says, could and often did, pass off as a Portuguese.[53] These were the two classes from which the English, specially in the early days, drew largely for their wives, girls whose charms as Prof. Dodwell says, promised an early old age, 'shrill, sluttish and obese'.[54] The merchants often married into the older and often wealthy Portuguese families, the soldiers wedded the poorer Portuguese and Topasses.

This is perhaps a convenient opportunity for summarizing the English attitude towards Roman Catholics in eighteenth century India The Directors were more hostile to them than the Councils, and there developed something of a conflict between the doctrinaire bigotry of the Directors and the considerations of expediency urged by the Councils. In 1675 the Directors wrote that the English were being married, buried, and having their children baptized by Romish priests, 'which we look on as a thing so scandalous to the professors of the Reformed Religion, that we cannot but disallow all such practices'.[55] Offenders against this rule, and all married to Catholics who did not bring up their children as Protestants, were to be sent home on the first ships. This regulation was not repealed until 1721, when it had become manifestly impossible to enforce, but the prejudices of the Directors only slowly subsided. In 1751 they wrote to the Madras Council that the Roman Catholic church 'in the very heart of the settlement has been very injurious to us . . . it is to be demolished . . . and not retained on any pretence',[56] and in 1758 in similar circumstances at Calcutta they prohibited all Roman Catholics and priests from entering the fort so long as the French war lasted, and took it as a virtue that they did not exclude them altogether.[57]

The attitude of the settlers themselves was quite different from this. The principles of the Reformed Religion wore very thin in the East Indian factories, even in the seventeenth century. The prevalence of marriages with Portuguese and other Catholics can be gauged both by early lists of inhabitants,[58] and by the Councils' efforts to reconcile the Directors' orders with their own judgement. In 1680 they recognized marriages with Roman Catholics by Company's servants as valid, but required both parties to promise to bring up their children as Protestants.[59] But as time went on they found an increasing difficulty in keeping the Roman Catholics out of anything ; all trace of religious animosity disappeared, to be replaced by a mixture of opportunism, snobbery and nationalism. Thus in 1705 they considered the rule against Catholic officers 'obsolete', and cited the case of several India captains and supercargoes in order to justify the promotion of Sergeant Dixon to Ensign, only salving their consciences by suggesting, ''tis not unlikely his preferment may make him return again to the Protestant religion '.[60] In 1719, when the chief officer of the 'Falconbridge' became a Roman Catholic because his bride, the daughter of a Frenchman at Madras, refused to be married there on account of the 1680 regulations, Council thought of it as a social rather than a religious scandal, 'which practice we apprehend to be of very dangerous consequence; many of the young gentlemen in the Company's service being of good families in England, who would be very much scandalized at such marriages',[61] and in 1721 the Regulations were repealed, though the President's consent was still required.[62] As the century advanced, however, a new complication was introduced by the increasing rivalry of the French and English companies. Nationalism entered into the relations of Catholics and Protestants, and Catholics came again under the suspicion of disloyalty. So the Capuchins, who had hitherto been favoured by the Government against the Portuguese Jesuits,[63] lost ground as being French in the Anglo-French struggle for supremacy. In 1751 the Madras Council considered the Portuguese Church 'a very remarkable nuisance' which 'ought by no means to be returned (to its owners)',[64] and the Calcutta Government experienced the same feelings of disgust and suspicion after the fall of Calcutta.[65] In 1751 the Company sent out, as they thought, Protestant mercenaries from Switzerland and Germany, only to find on arrival that many of them were Catholics.[66] The connexion of Catholicism with French influence continued through the French wars, and is well shown in the Madras Artillery Regulations of 1747: 'No Indian, black or person of mixt breed, nor any Roman Catholic of any nation Soever' was to be admitted into the artillery laboratory, and the same regulations barred all Roman Catholics from the artillery and forbade either marriage with a Catholic or the conversion of a wife to Catholicism.[67]

From this time, however, interest in Roman Catholics as such declined. On the one hand the political danger subsided with the French defeat, on the other the increasing number of English women in India reduced the number of mixed marriages among the upper classes. Romanism was no longer dangerous, it was only superstitious. It was considered only less ridiculous than Hinduism, and the conversion of Catholics was nearly as meritorious as of Hindus and indeed much more reasonable. The 'abominations of Heathenism' and the 'mummery' of Rome are usually bracketed, though no one else reached the sublime impartiality of Henry Martyn when he wrote, 'So much for this Mussulman Lord; now for Antichrist in another shape, the Popish Padre, Julius Caesar'.[68] Swartz frequently baptized Roman Catholics as well as Tamils, and Kiernander in Calcutta worked almost entirely among the Portuguese Catholics of Bengal.

For the Romanists the century closed amid deepening gloom. The dry wind of nationalism had dried up the springs of devotion, and the tempests of the revolution left no surplus energy for foreign adventures. Sees became vacant, gaps were not filled, Indians had not been trained to the priesthood,[69] and the surviving missionaries, without resources and without hope, helplessly watched enthusiasm languish and congregations dwindle. The traveller Twining saw one such, the Padre Juvenal of Agra, in 1790 and has left a pathetic description of him.[70] He was the only priest of the mission; he had never more than twenty and now only twelve converts. Like his Jesuit predecessors, his chief work was baptizing infants about to die, who he believed were thus snatched from the hell to which the millions around him were infallibly doomed. Indeed he preferred this work to the baptizing of the healthy children who were only too likely to apostatize later and so suffer greater damnation. His chief interest was botany, for which he had made two journeys to Tibet. He so despaired of any success that he had applied for permission to return, but had been answered by the Holy Father 'recommending patience'. So, forbidden to tread again the streets of Rome, 'his own dear land', he lived on in his own hired house in that city of departed glory, hopelessly preaching to an uninterested and almost equally hopeless people.

The Royal Danish Mission was established as a private religious whim by King Frederick IV of Denmark, and the first missionaries, Ziegenbalg and Plutschau, arrived in 1706. They met with every opposition from the Danish Company's Governor which lasted till 1714, but in spite of it they persisted, and at Ziegenbalg's death in 1719 he had collected a congregation of 428, half Portuguese, and half Tamils both Sudras and Pariahs.[71] The Danish Mission was in many ways remarkable. It was founded and directed in Copenhagen, drew its missionaries from the Lutheran Pietists of Halle, and its income largely from the English Society for Promoting Christian Knowledge. Incidentally it shows how much nearer the eighteenth century could come to reunion with its 'indifference' and 'rationalism' than the present day with its Lambeth 'eirenicons' and stimulated mass emotions. Later the Society for the Promotion of Christian Knowledge itself took some of the German missionaries into its service and continued their support until they were taken over by the Society for the Propagation of the Gospel in the nineteenth century.[72] It did not, however, send out any Englishman, partly because they were not to be had, and partly because they did not wish to risk friction between

Anglicans and Lutherans.[73] One may smile at this vicarious missionary zeal, but such a natural spirit of tolerance and brotherliness can well stand a comparison with the average modern missionary society, with all their devotion and desire for fellowship. The S.P.C.K. had its reward, for one of its missionaries was Christian Frederick Swartz.

The Lutherans worked impartially among caste and pariah Hindus and Eurasian Roman Catholics, and they often acted in addition as chaplains to the British troops. They soon became respected members of the settlements, a part of the accepted order of things. They lived a simple life in the European settlements on an infinitesimal salary diversified only by preaching tours in the country round. Their chaplain's fees they usually handed over to the mission funds, but they had one peculiarity in being allowed to trade, or as we should express it, to speculate in commercial ventures. This often benefited the mission, but occasionally led to disaster, as in the case of the venerable Fabricius, who spent the last two years of his life, after fifty years' service in Madras, imprisoned for debt,[74] and of Kiernander, whose mission church in Calcutta was attached for debt, and was only saved by Charles Grant.[75] Otherwise they seem to have differed from the other Europeans only in their greater simplicity, their more regular lives, and their more intimate contact with Indians. Benjamin Schultze (who worked in Madras from 1728-43 and wrote the rare and curious *Madras Dialogues*) thus described his house : ' The house (Capt. Hanson's sold for 600 pagodas) has all the necessary conveniences which I could wish for ; there is a great hall which serves for a place to meet in ; beside my lodging my colleague has an apartment in the lesser house ; and in the forepart of the same house is the charity school'.[76] In general, missionaries lived in any houses they could get ; thus Swartz at Trichinopoly occupied a room in an old Hindu building ' just large enough to hold his bed and himself and in which few men could stand upright',[77] and Henry Martyn occupied an old pagoda on the banks of the Hughli when he first arrived at Calcutta.[78]

The life of these men was a constant round of preaching, visiting, exhorting, and except for those in Madras and Calcutta, of travelling. The most energetic of them all, Swartz, thus described his daily programme at Trichinopoly in 1768. Every morning he sent out his four catechists whom he called helpers, two Pariahs and two Sudras, on their different missions. Two went preaching, one attended the Tamil school and one visited the Christians. In the afternoon he and all the helpers preached the Gospel. On Tuesdays ' we stir ourselves up by meditation and prayer, and to this end we are engaged on the first epistle of Paul to Timothy'.[79] In 1771 he had forty children in an English school taught by 'two pious soldiers' as well as thirty children in the Malabar school. On Sundays and Fridays he preached to the Tamil congregations; on Sunday evening he had prayer with English soldiers in which a chapter of the Bible was explained verse by verse, and finally he conducted the public service for the garrison and held after it a special prayer meeting for his twenty English converts.[80] In addition to this he constantly itinerated, for 'a missionary should be constantly going to and fro among them'. In his later life at Tanjore his work was thus described by his nephew Kohloff. 'He rose at 5, breakfasted at 6 or 7 on a basin of tea made in an open jug, with hot water poured on it, and some bread cut into it. One half was for himself, the other for Kohloff. The meal lasted not five minutes. He dined on broth and curry very much as the natives. He never touched wine, except one glass on a Sunday.[81] What was sometimes sent to him he reserved for the sick. His temperance was extraordinary, habitual and enjoined on his catechists and brethren. He supped at eight and after reading a chapter in the Hebrew Bible in private, and his own devotions, retired to rest about 10.'[82]

With the English soldiers, who were the despair of Martyn and Brown, his relations seem also to have been very happy. At Trichinopoly, Chambers reported that he at first read the lessons to the garrison and sermons from English divines in whom he discovered an Evangelical spirit.[83] When he knew the language better he preached extempore, first in an old Hindu building, and then in a church subscribed by the garrison itself. When one remembers Henry Martyn's difficulties with the troops one can agree with Chambers that 'it is indeed astonishing, when we consider the manners of our troops in India, how he has been able to persuade whole garrisons'.[84]

The only one who worked in Calcutta was Kiernander, who removed thence from Cuddalore after its capture by the French in 1758, and was supported by the S.P.C.K.[85] He worked chiefly among the Portuguese Roman Catholics, and was joined by two ex-Roman priests. He is remembered by the old mission church which he built with the fortune of his second wife. Like Fabricius he went bankrupt late in life owing to the injudicious investments of his sons, but his church was saved by the efforts of Charles Grant.

The Danish missionaries were generally respected and seem to have been a singularly devoted and able band of men. Though only Swartz and perhaps Ziegenbalg rose to greatness, none of them sank like many of the chaplains below a high standard of devotion and ability, and the breath of scandal has touched none of them.

The only other missionaries in the eighteenth century were the Moravians, who after forty years of effort at Tranquebar in face of Danish opposition, eventually withdrew,[86] and the Baptists of Bengal. The first of the latter was John Thomas[87] whose eccentricities earned a frigid welcome for Carey from the Evangelical chaplain Brown,[88] and the second was the Baptist pioneer William Carey who arrived in 1793. Carey believed in supporting himself, and paid the price of his enthusiasm by much hardship before establishing himself with his family of seven as an indigo planter at Madnabati. He stayed there[89] until he moved to Serampore in 1800 to join the mission party which the Danish Governor, Colonel Obie, an admirer of Swartz, had invited to settle there. Marshman thus described his meeting at Madnabati. 'The sight of a house increased my perturbations. At length I saw Carey! He is very little changed from what I recollected, rather stouter than when in England, and, blessed be God, a young man still. He lives in a small village, in a large brick house, two storied, with Venetian windows, and mat doors. Fountain (his lay assistant) lives in a (bamboo and mat) bungalow a quarter of a mile away. Mrs. Carey is wholly deranged. Their four boys talk Bengali fluently. Felix is 14 or 15. We arrived in time for the Bengali morning-worship. Carey preached at 11.0 in the Hall (ground floor of his house). I was much moved by the singing. There is a Mission school of about thirty.'[90]

The relations of the European community in general with the missionaries went through the various gradations of suspicion, contempt and wonder. The first Danish missionaries were thwarted by the Tranquebar authorities in every way for their first six years, and the Moravian brethren who arrived at Tranquebar in 1760, and worked for a time also at Serampore, were so harassed by public and denominational hostility, that they retired in despair in 1803.[91] Nor were the English at first much more friendly. The Council of Fort St. George in 1711 wrote that 'The Danish Mission is an imposition on the credulous; the collections for them, not being properly applied'; and hoped they would be stopped in England.[92] The sort of missions they approved was that represented by the Rev. G. Lewis's proposal to educate Indians as Protestants, which the Directors thought 'so noble a design' that they ordered Madras to submit a 'plan to them' and even 'would not grudge some charge to effect it'.[93] But when the English grew used to the idea of Protestant missionaries, and still more when they were supported by 'the Right Rev. the Lord Archbishop of Canterbury and all the Episcopal clergy[94] and later by British money[95] as well, suspicion slowly gave place to respect and friendliness. Later the Madras missionaries Fabricius and Breithaupt, and Kiernander at Cuddalore did occasional duty for the chaplains and later still Swartz was a Company's chaplain. So the Madras Council wrote that 'the Danish missionaries have not wanted our assistance on all occasions, though we must still continue of opinion that they spend a great deal of the Society's money to little or no purpose',[96] and the S.P.C.K. thanked the Company for sending missionaries and various stores passage free.[97] Apart from the Government the general attitude was one of superstitious respect with a background of benevolent scepticism. Most men agreed on the sublimity of the missionaries' purpose, but everyone thought any hope of success chimerical, and was inclined to criticize missionary methods accordingly. Manucci set the tone: 'There can be no doubt that the missionaries who come from Europe bring with them much zeal. They expect on their arrival in these Indian lands that their labours will be very fruitful. But they know nothing and have no experience of these people, nor the fitting way to deal with them'.[98] He made the very modern remark that 'with the profession of Doctor it is possible to do some service for God', but it was for a less modern reason that he had himself in this way baptized 15,000 infants, who were all bound to die.[99] The sceptical view persisted all through till we find Lord Cornwallis at the end giving a testimonial to Swartz but complaining that missions were of no use,[100] and Lord Valentia commented on both their good conduct and lack of success.[101] Even some of the missionaries like Dubois and Kiernander held the same opinion.[102]

At the end of the century missions came under attack as dangerous to the political peace of the Company's dominions. The Bengal Government, oblivious of the work of the still subsidized Swartz, prohibited preaching in its territory, drove the Baptists to Serampore, and the Company tried to forbid all missionary activity in the Charter of 1793.[103] But the fault was not altogether on one side, for the Company was first alarmed by an attempt to compel them not only to permit but to promote missionary work, and the Bengal missionaries were very different in outlook from the quietist Lutherans. The man who could sing hymns before the Rajah of Tanjore, preach under Hyder's eye at Seringapatam, and persuade English soldiers to build their own church without offence, was very different in outlook from a Brown, 'who never would endure that they (Indians) should unchecked obtrude their abominations on the notice of the Europeans', and the tone of whose lectures 'Anti-kalee', 'Anti-Durga', etc. can well be imagined,[104] and a Martyn who used the parable of the servant beaten with many stripes to refute what a munshi had said about Mohammedans not remaining in hell for ever.[105] 'This is Mohammedanism', said he, 'to murder as infidels the children of God, and to live without prayer. . . .

Now that I am more cool, I still think that human nature in its worst appearances is a Mohammedan.'[106] And on hearing the sound of the cymbals of a Hindu temple, he said, 'Never did such sounds go through my heart with such horror in my life. . . . I shivered at being in the neighbourhood of hell; my heart was ready to burst at the dreadful state to which the Devil had brought my poor fellow-creatures'.[107] One can hardly fail to sympathize with the Government, sitting, as it thought, on a far from extinct volcano, when it had to deal with such zealous but intolerant champions of the Christian faith. It was not through the prophets of wrath, but through the preachers of a more excellent way, Swartz in the south and Carey in the north, that Christian missions were to take root in India.

The greatest of the eighteenth century missionaries was undoubtedly Christian Frederick Swartz, and it is perhaps worth while to examine his life a little more closely. So little indeed was found to say against him in the eighteenth century that it is surprising that the twentieth has not thought it worth while to repair the omission. Swartz was born in the Sonnunburg, Neumark, in 1726, and entered the University of Halle in 1746. There he met Schultze, recently returned from Madras, and came under the influence of the masterful Dr. Gotthilf Francke. Missionary recruiting by mass suggestion was not then in vogue, and it was at Dr. Francke's request that Swartz became a missionary. He began to learn Tamil, was ordained in 1749 and in the following year left London for Tranquebar. Four months after his arrival he preached his first Tamil sermon, and henceforward for forty-eight years his life was one long round of preaching, teaching, disputing, journeying, and shepherding his flock. There were no frequent furloughs with enthusiastic summer conferences to attend or crowded cathedrals to preach in in those days; Swartz never left South India again. In 1767 he left Tranquebar for Trichinopoly as a missionary of the 'Honourable Society for the Promotion of Christian Knowledge', and in 1779 he removed to Tanjore, where he stayed till his death. This is the whole chronicle of his outward life.[108]

Swartz's work was of the most varied kind, and demanded the most varied attainments. A German, he had first to learn Tamil; Tranquebar required a knowledge of Danish, Trichinopoly of English; Portuguese was necessary for the work among the 'black' Christians; and in Tanjore his increasing contact with princes caused him to add Persian and Urdu. In addition to this he spent the first five years of his Indian life in reading the Hindu sacred books in order to understand the Hindu system. His work included the care of Indian congregations composed half of Portuguese, and half of caste and Pariah Hindus; at Trichinopoly and Tanjore he was also chaplain to the English garrison and conducted special services for ' converted soldiers '. Besides this he spent much time in itinerating, preaching and training catechists, and in his later days he ran schools for both Malabar and English children. Caste problems in church, disputations with Catholic priests, controversies with Brahmins, church building, and embassies to courts were all part of his day's work, and through it all he remained the same indefatigable, hopeful and humble man. Homage to holiness is easily given in India and spiritual pride is never far behind it, but Swartz avoided the one as easily as he gained the other. What was his personal character? He had a German thoroughness which ordered his life by rule, an urbanity of temper which nothing seemed to ruffle, and a readiness of wit which often stood him in good stead and turned the laugh against his opponents. When preaching before the Rajah of Tanjore he noticed that he did not understand Persian well; at once he asked leave to speak in Tamil, and so gained the royal ear.[109] To the Brahmin's conundrum :—

' Mr. Swartz, do you not think it a very bad thing to touch a Pariah ? ' he replied :

' O yes, a very bad thing.'

' But Mr. Swartz, what do you mean by a Pariah ? '

' I mean a thief, a liar, a slanderer, a drunkard, an adulterer, a proud man.'

' O then we are all Pariahs ', remarks the Brahmin.[110]

At Tanjore he sat with his back to an idol under a tree. His listeners said, ' I ought not to sit so near the tree because their Schrami was there.' I said civilly, ' Why do you speak for him ? Let him tell me himself to go away '.[111] They laughed and came round me.

Indeed, sometimes this readiness of repartee and this urbanity of temper united to produce a flow of trite moralizings which must have been very trying to his friends. He was always, we are told by an admiring writer, ready to point the moral of the most trivial circumstance, and one can imagine the mixed feelings which the prospect of a meeting with him might arouse, or the occasional falls from the grace of good temper which a constant companion might suffer.[112]

With these traits he showed an independence of mind which marked him as no mere dreaming Pietist, talking languidly beneath trees or exchanging platitudes with Brahmins. He went freely from place to place and never held his peace because of authority. When at Seringapatam in 1779 on a mission from the Madras Government, he preached every Sunday to the Europeans there. ' I did not ask whether I might; but did it as one who in conscience was bound to do it. We sang, preached, and prayed and no one hindered us.'[113] Later he refused another diplomatic mission from Lord Macartney because he thought he had been used as a tool by Sir H. Rumbold. The consequence of this mingled frankness and charm, sincerity and consideration, was that he won the confidence of Indians to a degree which the most prudent Europeans had not attained. Ten years before the campaign against missions as dangerous to the State, twenty years before preaching was forbidden in Calcutta, the Rajah of Tanjore was giving Swartz a blank sheet of paper to make terms with Hyder Ali, and confessing, 'We all, you and I, have lost our credit. Let us try whether the inhabitants will trust Mr. Swartz.'[114]

In many ways Swartz was very modern-minded. He did not believe, any more than he practised, the denunciatory method of evangelism. 'Were we to address the Heathen in an angry or cutting manner, it would be just as if we were to throw sand in a man's eyes, and then exhort him to see with distinctness and accuracy. But when addressing them in love and meekness or when overhearing some evil speech we graft on it a representation of Christianity in its loveliness, they usually listen with attention and reflection.'[115] The furthest he got on the path of 'righteous indignation' as a missionary method was to write of Mohammad Ali's second son: 'He is a genuine disciple of Mahomet (that is, is inclined to cruelty)',[116] and to report 'our Iquasi-Muttu read for some time . . . out of a little book which explained the abomination of heathenism, and after some exhortation we left them'.[117] He saw the danger of the complete suppression of caste in the Christian church as well as the disaster of its tolerance, and followed a policy of suasion and moral pressure which was far more effective than Schultze's earlier, or Bishop Wilson's later, peremptory suppression. He could appreciate the good in non-Christians and non-Europeans and wrote with admiration of Hyder Ali's care of orphan children.[118] He appreciated the importance of education in missionary work, a point which Dr. Grose noticed as early as 1760 as distinguishing Protestant from Roman Missions,[119] and he believed in the desirability of single missionaries, at any rate till they had learned the language.[120]

But it was the whole spirit of the man which made him unique in the eighteenth century. His was a positive spirit, far more concerned with the Gospel he had to preach than with the wickedness of the heathen. He divided people into Christians and non-Christians rather than Christians and the lost; he explained their errors and preached salvation instead of denouncing their horrors and preaching the judgement. His journals are a record of continual journeys and conferences, punctuated at intervals by exclamations such as, 'Never O Lord Jesus, may it escape my mind how much it cost thee to redeem me.'[121] His antipathy to Islam and Hinduism was intellectual only, and he was always able to distinguish the heretic from the heresy ; he never talked of ' ferocious and profligate Mussulmans ' and ' wicked Brahmins ' and of never meeting ' with such contempt and disrespect from a native ' who argued about the lawfulness of putting people to death for blasphemy.[122] Who else but he could have thus ended a controversy with a Roman priest before a hesitating Roman Catholic lady ? ' He departed, wishing that I might become a saint, and I wished him sincerity of heart.'[123]

As one reads his memoirs and journals and notes his modernity of mind and charity of spirit, the twentieth century begins to melt into the first, and reveals something stranger and stronger than tolerance and humanism. There is the same exhortation without wrath, truth without dogmatism, zeal without bitterness, the same love of all men without dissimulation. There is the same calmness of possession, the same radiance of an inner peace, softly shining like the moon on an August sea. If Carey is the Origen, and Martyn the Elijah of Protestant Missions, Swartz is the Nathaniel, ' an Israelite indeed, in whom there is no guile '.

CHAPTER VIII

RACIAL RELATIONS

THE contact of two races so dissimilar in character, in culture and in institutions as the English and the Indian raises the problem of the contact of cultures in its most acute form. Mutual influence is easiest when two cultures are basically the same ; radical difference tends either to mutual repulsion, or to absorption of one by the other. In the case of India easy contact was made more difficult by the institutions as well as by the character of the two peoples. There was first the difficulty of institutions, and secondly the difficulty of character. The Hindus were so used to foreign invasions and the sight of alien communities settled in their midst, that they had become perhaps the most tolerant people upon earth ; a man was accepted as a part of India so long as he did not attempt to interfere with others, and was indeed expected to conform to his own rather than any other communities' customs. But the defensive and microscopic division of society into castes, whose life was their religion, and religion their life, at the same time made Hinduism as socially exclusive as it was communally tolerant. Foreign communities could be amongst, but not of the Hindus. Added to this there was the insularity of the English character, as marked in the eighteenth century as to-day, which made the English persist in their customs and habits of life even in most unfavourable circumstances. Count Keyserling's verdict on the modern Englishman finds a clear echo in Maria Graham's description of the English at the Cape: 'They live like the English everywhere, as much in the manner they would do at home as circumstances permit.'[1]

Politically the English love of liberty, sharpened on the whetstone of the struggle with the Stuarts, encountered a universal despotism ; morally the still lingering puritanism met an immense and complicated polytheism ; and socially their convivial habits and meat-eating tastes, the very characteristics which in Europe would have formed bridges of fellowship with other nations, aroused only the disgust of the Brahmin and the bania. With the Mussulman, these inhibitions indeed did not apply, but relations with them were soured beforehand by the tradition of hostility and bigotry which had descended from the days of the Crusades. Finally the contact of peoples so dissimilar was further complicated by political factors, such as the earlier pomp and later insignificance of the Moghul Court. Men's opinions of each other are influenced more than they know by irrelevant factors like power, prosperity and prestige, as modern Japan well illustrates. Over such chasms had the bridge of understanding to be thrown.

At the beginning of the eighteenth century the English merchants still lived in factories under the discipline of the President, and dined at a common table. They received goods from up-country and despatched them to Europe, but they went little abroad from their own settlements except from one factory to another and as occasional ambassadors to the Moghul Court. They had in consequence little social intercourse with Indians as equals; the men they saw were either agents like the dubashes of Madras or the banians and shroffs of Calcutta, servants and slaves, or superiors like an occasional Moghul governor who might visit the factory.[2] Then the guard was turned out, a great feast was prepared, and the Governor trod very delicately until the great man could be persuaded to remove to a safe distance. The Company's servants were frequently ignorant of the country languages, and the debased Portuguese which was the *lingua franca* of the coast was all that most of them acquired; complaints were made from time to time of loss and inconvenience caused by the factors' ignorance, and a chaplain was on one occasion proposed as an envoy to the Moghul Court because 'he was well versed in the Persian tongue'.[3] What social intercourse there was took place, therefore, between the Company's servants, the dubashes and the banians. The relations of Ananda Ranga Pillai, the dubash of Dupleix, with the French officials show at once how far and how small a distance they went.[4] He could talk familiarly with Dupleix, de Leyrit and the Councillors and his advice was obviously valued, he could invite Dupleix to a grand dinner with salutes of twenty-one guns between each course and the Councillors to wedding feasts; but it was a privilege for him to be permitted to talk with a Councillor's wife,[5] and of the ordinary give-and-take of social intercourse there was little or none. One Councillor was regarded as exceptional because he always treated Indians as equals.[6]

On the west coast of India, however, conditions were different. In Bombay the initial poverty of the island, the necessity of attracting Indian merchants, and the competition of Surat made the Company much more dependent on Indian goodwill, and in the Parsis the English found a race much closer to them in temperament than either Hindus or Mohammedans. At Surat the English merchants were in the midst of a populous city under a foreign government, and only one among several European competitors. Here the

English were the weaker party, trading by the grace of the Moghuls; Indians and English were on an equality, and it is not surprising to find that there was more in the way of real intercourse here than anywhere else. The English lived in a factory as elsewhere, it is true, but this did not prevent them from dining out and from entertaining strangers. The Moghul magnates were the most welcome guests with their common hunting and drinking tastes; one Governor after his first visit particularly asked to be given some of the excellent roast kid then provided, upon which the English President sent out for the fattest pigs which could be found, to the great satisfaction of the Governor on his next visit.[7]

Even the banians of Surat, a very important community, dined on occasion with the Europeans. The impressions of one such is thus described by Ovington: 'He was strangely amaz'd and surpriz'd at the opening of a Bottle of Bottled Drink, when he saw it froth and fly about. The President asked him what it was struck him with such Amazement, which was not, he told him, the sight of the Drink flying out of the Bottle, but how such Liquor could ever be put in '.[8]

The banians were held in considerable respect by the Europeans as astute and honest traders,[9] and friendly intercourse went to the length of practical jokes by young factors, who pretended to shoot birds near the banians' gardens in order to see them come out and pray them not to take life.[10] Finally the Company's chapel was bare of all images, in order not to offend Mussulman puritanism.[11] There is no other instance of such regard for Indian susceptibilities by any but missionaries for many a year afterwards. Apart from Surat, therefore, the English were quite separate in ideas as well as in social intercourse. As far as they thought at all, they thought of Mohammedans as profligate and of Hindus as superstitious, and of both as quite incomprehensible. The Indians on their side considered all Europeans in general and the English in particular to be winebibbers. Their reputation dated from Akbar's time, when an English adventurer in the Moghul army made his service dependent on adequate supplies of liquor, and his demand was admitted on the ground that Europeans must have been created at the same time as spirits,[12] and the idea was confirmed by the feats of Captain Hawkins at Jehangir's nightly drinking bouts. The one thing in which the English were unique was their lack of religious observance. The Portuguese, the French and the Dutch all made much of their priests and ministers; the English alone neglected them.[13]

It was in the matter of clothes and daily life that there was approximation between the two races. The early settlers wore 'banyan' coats and 'Moormen's' trousers as a matter of course in their houses, and some occasionally wore them in public.[14] In 1686 the writers of Masulipatam were expressly forbidden to lounge on the parade on Sundays in loose coats,[15] but as late as 1738 a Council meeting was held in Calcutta in loose coats with hookahs and drinks in attendance.[16] The last reference to this practice is a government order in the early nineteenth century prohibiting native dress in the United Provinces.[17] As a full dress it never became general, but for indoor wear it remained common throughout the century.

In thought and opinion there was separation and disapproval without contempt. The difference between European and Hindu outlook was too great, the prejudices of Mussulmans were too deep, for either race to have any great attraction for the other, but there was in it no trace of racial feeling or talk of inferiority. Francisco Pelsaert disapproved of the extravagant waste of the Moghuls,[18] Bernier and Manucci exposed the weakness of their armies, but none of them objected to living amongst, or even serving under, the Moghuls. Many of Shah Jehan's artillerymen were Europeans, whose discipline Aurangzeb peremptorily restored,[19] and the early embassies of the eighteenth century still show the greatest respect.[20] Even down to 1760 a European servant like Macdonald, with more than the ordinary servant's self-respect and all his pride of race, could work and mix familiarly with Portuguese, Parsi and Mussulman servants. There was no 'European Third' in the eighteenth century. The mutual opinions of Indians and English in the early years were largely compounded of ignorance and prejudice, but they contained in them little trace of racial bias. Europeans and Indians disapproved of each other's social systems, but they had not yet the tolerant pity which comes of a sense of inborn superiority. Pride had not yet been sanctified by science; patriotism still meant belief in one's own country as the best, but not the conviction that all other countries were inevitably inferior.

When the position of the East India Company changed towards the middle of the century, the character of racial relations changed also. On the one hand the old merchants occupied new positions, on the other the supply of Englishmen greatly increased, first as soldiers and then as administrators and traders. The result was to set in motion a double current, of increasing contact and knowledge of Indian life, and of increasing contempt of everything Indian as irrational, superstitious, barbaric and typical of an inferior civilization. The first was bred of contact with the Hindu and Mussulman aristocracy, the second with the servant class of the Presidency towns; the first was typical of the period between 1760 and the return of Hastings in 1785 and is represented by such men as Hastings himself, James Forbes, and Colonel Palmer with its prophet in Sir William Jones; the second perhaps reaches its zenith in Macaulay's famous description of Sanskrit and Persian literature. As the Anglo-Indian function developed from trade to empire, from embassies to administration, the criterion of judgement swung round from the naively patriotic belief that one's own customs are necessarily the best, to the equally naive idea that the strongest is necessarily the best. But before the political change was complete there was a period of political equality, when the East India Company was one of the chief powers in India without yet becoming the paramount power. The old traders had become diplomatists—and often financiers—and had not yet been ousted by the soldier turned empire-builder, the Dundas recruit from Scotland, or aristocratic governors from England. There was not only opportunity but necessity for intimate acquaintance with Indian manners and customs, and most government officials were thrown back by their work to a large extent on Indian society. The Indian Princes on their side had quite ceased to regard the Company as troublesome traders, and were displaying an increasing interest in European methods in order to discover the secret of European success. For the present, then, the tide of racialism was quite unperceived in the cross-current of mutual contact and interest, and there ensued a period of cosmopolitan intercourse. It was the Golden Age of the adventurer and the diplomatist.

This new social intercourse was more marked with Mussulmans and Parsis than with Hindus, owing to the caste difficulty of inter-dining. It had its centre at Madras, where the Nawab held his court in the Chepauk Palace, in Bombay, where the relations of Europeans with Parsis had long been closer than with any other communities, and at towns like Lucknow and Murshidabad where English residents were stationed at Indian courts.

In Madras Mohammad Ali, the Nawab of Arcot, was long the centre of intercourse, financial as well as social.[21] While his second son schemed to recover Tanjore, he borrowed from merchant speculators like Paul Benfield and from members of Council; he also kept an agent, and, it was said, several members of Parliament in his pay in London. He was so confidently asserted to have had a large share in the arrest and imprisonment of Lord Pigot in 1776 that a notice was issued in the hope of obtaining evidence against the Company's servants of 'the account of the Money said to have been given by the Nabob for the Revolution of 1776'.[22] This included four lakhs of rupees to Paul Benfield, three to Sir E. Hughes, two to Sir Robert Fletcher and similar sums to many members of Council.

Asiaticus thus describes his establishment: 'He keeps a very splendid court, where the English meet with every mark of attention and are often preferred to very lucrative posts about his person.'[23] At that time his guard was commanded by a European captain, two lieutenants and six cornets, with subedars and jemadars as subalterns 'who are men of high military reputation'. 'A dissatisfied group of creditors daily meet at the Nabob's. No sooner has the sun risen than every avenue to the palace is filled with palanquins and carriages and in the evening the same faces, the same surly looks are to be seen again. The Nabob receives everybody with politeness, apologizes for his want of punctuality (in paying), which he attributes to the loss of Tanjore, and repeats the hackneyed tale of the cruel treatment which he has received at the hands of Lord Pigot.'[24] In spite of his somewhat doubtful transactions, however, the Nawab was dignified, hospitable and of charming manners; and nearly every traveller who visited him was favourably impressed. Dr. Ives expressed the general feeling when in 1754 he described him as having 'no other mark of distinction, but a truly majestic countenance tempered with a great deal of pleasantness and good nature'.[25] Innes Munro wrote in 1780 that he 'looked on a newly arrived European with such a look of majesty, blended with sorrow, as one could not behold without compassion and regret'.[26] Grattan wrote to Hastings that he 'feels a sincere reverence and affection for him',[27] and Orme, though alive to his limitations, wrote, 'I pity no man on Earth so sincerely as I do this Nabob'.[28]

More scrupulous and more European was the cultured Serfagi, Rajah of Tanjore, who was educated by the missionary Swartz, in whose memory he wrote the first example of English verse by an Indian. He became a student of English science and literature as well as a patron of Indian art, and was English enough in his manners to give a banquet in the English style at his accession.

The Nawab of Arcot was only the first and most long-lived example of such social and convivial intercourse. 'Nabobs and Soubahs throughout India,' wrote the authors of *The European in India* in 1800, 'are in the habit of giving public breakfasts, and of occasionally inviting all the European gentry in their vicinity to grand dinners, nautches or dances, and other entertainments'.[29] On both sides there was much give-and-take; the English had long acquired a taste for nautches, and developed new ones for elephant fights and hookah smoking; the nawabs on their part experimented with English food and drink.[30] 'Many excellent Mussulmans,' say the same authors, 'are above prejudice, and often eat substantial slices of ham under the designation of Belatty Heron or English venison.'[31] Salabat Jung, chief of Ellichpur and a tributary of the

Nizam, entertained the officers of several regiments to dinner during the Maratha war and attended the dinner himself, an action which was favourably contrasted with the conduct of Hindu and Maratha chiefs.[32] Before the coming of Cornwallis many Indians were still in positions of authority in British India, and reciprocal entertainments were common.[33] After the dinner or the breakfast there were usually entertainments, the chief being cock and elephant fights, nautches and occasionally plays.

In the north the two chief centres of social intercourse were the Palace of Mubarak-ad-daula, the Nawab of Bengal at Murshidabad, and the court of the Nawab Wazir of Oudh. Significantly enough no memories of the Black Hole prevented European intercourse with the Mussulman princes; wherever they were assured of a luxurious and hospitable welcome they gathered like flies to the honey-pot. The same rule applied to the 'East Indians', at that time segregated from English society; 'anyone of this class,' says F. J. Shore, 'whose circumstances will allow him to give good entertainments, will not find the English (in Bengal at least) at all backward in partaking of them'.[34] At Murshidabad there was, from the time that the Company 'stood forth as dewan', a resident at the court of the fainéant nawab, and Europeans in his bodyguard; the office of Resident was considered so lucrative that great sums were expended in order to obtain it.[35] The friends of the Resident were entertained in the European manner by the Nawab, and amused themselves with purdah interviews with the Begams. This went on until Cornwallis laid the axe to the tree in 1787, and withdrew all the officers under the suspicion of deriving 'unjustifiable advantages'[36] A glimpse of the inner workings of the Residency is given by a report on the 'mhatute' tax prepared by a Select Committee in 1771. They compiled a list of illegal and recoverable disbursements totalling Rs. 636,705, and charged them to thirty-three names which included those of Clive, Carnac, Verelst, Barwell and the Resident Becher.[37] Benares was another centre of social intercourse, and until the time of Cornwallis rivalled Murshidabad in the brilliance of its financial prospects. But the chief Mussulman entertainer was the Nawab Wazir of Oudh, whose long contact with and semi-independence of the British power rendered him the most accessible and the best equipped for the task. From the time of Shuja-ad-daula there was a constant succession of residents, troops, adventurers and travellers coming from Calcutta to Lucknow, and the effect of a long-continued cosmopolitanism is shown, as nowhere else in India, by the flamboyant and exotic architecture of mixed Moghul and classical styles. The Resident was the permanent head of this society. The nawabs, on their part, from the time of

Asaf-ad-daula showed a lively interest in things European. They were fond of giving public breakfasts, sometimes with elephant fights to follow, and not infrequently entertained the whole European community to dinner.[38] Thomas Twining thus describes a grand breakfast party given by the Nawab in a tent in 1794. 'Besides coffee, fish, curries, etc., the table was covered with a profusion of sweetmeats and flowers. . . . Asiatic and European mixed together'.[39] After breakfast a 'greyish' white elephant was exhibited beside a very large black one. In the evening elephant rides across country, escorted by cavalry, were arranged, quite regardless of the crops and the villagers. Several days were thus spent 'in reciprocal visits and festivities'.[40] The third leader of Lucknow society was General Claud Martin; he was nearly as Indianized as the Nawab was Europeanized, and provided the European counterpart to the Nawab's cosmopolitanism.

In the upper provinces further amusement was provided by the recurrent appearance of fugitive Moghul princes like that of Shah Alam in Allahabad from 1767 to 1770, and of his son Mohammad Bakht in Oudh in 1784. Even the Emperor at Delhi habitually granted interviews to every casual traveller who penetrated thither. In Hindustan this social intercourse reached its fullest development with military adventurers like the Comte de Boigne, General Perron, George Thomas and Colonel Skinner, who spent their lives in the service of Indian courts or as independent adventurers among Indian princes. Social intercourse was constant and unrestrained, and the manner of life as much Indian as English.

The intercourse of Mussulmans with Europeans did not extend to European ladies as yet. The difficulty was Indian rather than English, for the English ladies did not share the scruples of later generations about mixing with men whose wives remained in purdah. Warren Hastings related to his wife his mistake in allowing the Nawab Wazir to see two English ladies, and his efforts to assure him that they were by no means representative of English beauty;[41] and Lord Valentia recorded the disgust of the Wazir's son at the appearance of two English ladies who insisted on attending a joint dinner at Lucknow.[42] In both instances the initiative came from the English side, the moral recoil from the Indian, and in both cases English public opinion sympathized with the Mussulman feelings. In this particular matter the freedom of the eighteenth century woman went too far, but on the other hand her lack of Victorian tastes and taboos removed one of the greatest obstacles to cordial racial relations. They had no objection to the hookah,[43] and occasionally smoked it themselves; they freely attended and enjoyed nautches; they adopted the fashion of the turban and carried it to London, and they used familiar Urdu terms like 'bibi'.[44] Society at that time was predominantly masculine and the women had perforce to accept the masculine point of view ; but the later change in their outlook was perhaps as much due to the increasing regard for propriety and sober deportment, the incipient spirit of Victorianism which the Evangelical Revival fostered among the fashionable in London and Calcutta, as to a mere increase in numbers and a higher standard of refinement. It is one of the misfortunes of the history of racial relations in India that as soon as Mussulman society began to rid itself of its traditional feelings about the unveiled woman, European society imported a fresh stock of prejudices about the veiled woman of the purdah, the joint product of the evangelical missionary and of new-born racial pride.

In Hindustan and Bengal the intercourse between Europeans and Mussulmans was almost entirely with princes and nobles. They had in a sense common trades as soldiers, as diplomatists, as members of a governing class, and common tastes in hunting, feasting, wine and nautches. The prestige of military success had given every European an entry into aristocratic Indian society, while the cancer of racial pride had not yet destroyed his enjoyment of it. But with the merchants and bankers of Bengal there was little intercourse at any time ;[45] the temperament of Bengali banians was too antipathetic to that of English adventurers for contact ever to advance beyond occasional formal dinners. In Bombay, however, it was otherwise ; into the relations between English and Parsi merchants crept something of the cordiality that existed between English and Muslim lords in Hindustan. At the beginning of the century, the Parsis still kept their own customs.[46] In 1770 the cheerful Macdonald was treating two Parsis in a 'Roman Catholic' tavern ;[47] by this time the Parsis had many Englishmen in their employ as ships' captains, and social intercourse was frequent.[48] They often borrowed carriages from the English for their weddings ('which were lent with great good humour'), and invited them to their feasts. At this time men and women were still segregated,[49] but by the end of the century they had become largely Europeanized in their manners as well as in their feasts.[50] Their dinners were now complete with tables and chairs, their rooms with mirrors and prints ; and what entitled them to even more respect, they owned 'nearly all Bombay'. Much wine, 'specially Madeira', flowed at these gatherings. They kept their own carriages and horses now and had two or three houses each ; their westernization was already largely complete except for their adherence to early marriage and their failure to educate their women.[51] The same social intercourse also extended to Mussulman merchants of Bombay ; one 'jovial, hearty fellow' named Chillabie,

LORD WELLESLEY AT THE NAWAB OF OUDH'S BREAKFAST PARTY AND ELEPHANT FIGHT

[face p. 134

'broke through the rites of his religion to have company with the English gentlemen and to drink wine' as early as 1772.[52] The difference between this and the aristocratic intercourse of the upper provinces was that, while the one continued to develop into the modern Bombay cosmopolitanism, the other after a brief period of brilliance faded away into the drab hues of racial and social exclusiveness.

With the Hindus there is not so much evidence of extensive social intercourse. Of the Hindu princes, the Rajputs were too distant to come into contact with the English, and the Marathas too independent and suspicious to encourage very cordial relations. Officers attending a durbar of the Peishwa had to remove their boots until the nineteenth century,[53] when their wounded feelings found vent in an arrangement by which uncovering the head was considered an equivalent; and they generally considered the Mussulman princes far more 'courteous and free' than the Marathas.

But the seal of social intercourse is personal friendship, and this, too, had its place in the life of the eighteenth century. At that time the best of the Company's officials were acquainted with Persian and many of them became genuinely interested in Persian literature. This is seen at its best in the encouragement given by Hastings to Oriental studies,[54] in the enthusiasm of Sir William Jones, Wilkins and Colebrooke, and in its popular and vulgarized form in the songs first learned from the nautch girls and translated into popular drinking songs.[55] Such knowledge and such tastes gave them common interests with the Vakils, Nawabs and Rajahs whom they met, and intimate friendships resulted. Beneram Pandit, the Vakil of Scindia, was intimate with Hastings, General Palmer and Chapman; Hastings in recording a meeting with him at Benares writes of him to his wife as 'one whom you know I reckon among my first friends'.[56] With the Nawab Asaf-ad-daula of Lucknow he had also a close friendship, though there was in it a note more of admiration of a younger for an elder than the equal relationship of scholars which existed between him and Beneram. Nor did these friendships cease with absence or with Hastings' departure to England. As late as 1802 the Nawab Wazir offered him through Palmer a pension to tide over financial difficulties,[57] and Palmer in his periodical letters to Hastings frequently mentions the 'anxious enquiries' of his old Indian friends. Beneram's brother Bissambu Pandit, Ganga Gobind Singh, Ali Ibrahim Khan, the incorruptible judge of Benares whom Cornwallis refused to supersede, and his son were others in the Hastings circle. Charles Turner, Chapman and Scrofton wrote about them in the same way. Faizulli Khan, wrote Turner in 1799, was learning Greek from the Armenian Padre Parthenio.[58] In 1789

Palmer forwarded a letter from 'that excellent man Tufferzul Hussain Khan'[59] who 'is respected and admired by all who know him'.[60] Chapman wrote of 'my friend and fellow traveller', Bissambu Pandit, than whom, wrote Thompson, 'none is more sincere in his devotion'.[61] In 1801 Palmer lamented the loss 'of that excellent man Taffazul Husain Khan and with him all that was wise and good among the Mussulmans'.[62] This is the language of friends and of intimates, untainted by any breath of patronage or racial pride. They appear in private letters between intimates where no possible motives for tact or circumlocution would operate. All the Indians concerned, it will also be noticed, with the exception of the Nawab Wazir, were officials or Mussulman gentry; men of culture, but not men of princely rank who might enjoy the freemasonry of aristocratic feeling. The Englishman did not yet wait for the Indian to learn English before he would talk to him, but learned himself Persian instead; he did not demand a complete 'western education' before a man could be considered completely civilized, but enjoyed and himself composed Persian poetry. Hastings, in public the Hastin Bahadur of pomp and occasional high-handedness, was in private the most unassuming and friendly of men. This is the reason that he was 'anxiously enquired for' twenty years after he had left India for ever, and that his name became a legend.

But as the century drew to its close, a change in the social atmosphere gradually came about. The frequency of grand dinners and 'reciprocal entertainments' decreased, the formation of intimate friendship with Indians ceased, except in obscure corners of the country where administrators like Sir Thomas Munro or diplomatists like Colonel Tod or land settlement officers were thrown back upon Indian society. The higher posts of the Government were filled with appointments from England, its designs became more imperial and its attitude more haughty and aloof. The gulf which Mussulman Nawabs and English *bon viveurs,* diplomatic pandits and English scholars had for a time bridged over began ominously to widen again. With it the attitude of the average Englishman changed also from one of disapproval of Hindu 'superstition' and Mussulman 'bigotry' or philosophic interest in Hindu mythology and the Golden Age and the histories of Moghul glory, into one of contempt for an inferior and conquered people. A 'superiority complex' was forming which regarded India not only as a country whose institutions were bad and people corrupted, but one which was by its nature incapable of ever becoming any better. An attitude of superiority requires not only that a people and its institutions should be bad but also that they should be incapable of improvement, and for this reason expressions of pity, of patronage or of 'long-suffering understanding' are often more expressive of that attitude of mind than the most full-blooded denunciations. Many hard sayings inspired by the heat of a temporary irritation can be forgiven, but it is the polite disdain which founds its tolerance on the basis of necessitarianism, that rankles in the mind like a festering sore. It is one of the ironies of Indo-European relations in India, that the purging of the administration coincided with the widening of the racial gulf. Cornwallis not only made a new aristocracy by the Permanent Settlement, he also made a new governing class by his exclusion of all Indians from the higher governmental posts. Corruption was stamped out at the cost of equality and co-operation. In his own mind, as in the commonly accepted view, there was a necessary connexion between the two measures; 'every native of Hindustan', he said, 'I verily believe, is corrupt'.[63] As with the land question, he found an intricate problem and honestly attempted to solve it, and as with the land question his solution had a fallacious simplicity which gave it an illusion of success. He thought English corruption could be solved by reasonable salaries, and did not stop to consider that the advantage of Indian goodwill made it at least worth trying as a remedy for Indian corruption also. He never thought of creating an Indian imperial bureaucracy on the model of Akbar's mansabdars, which by special training, proper salaries and the encouragement of equal treatment, promotion and honours, might have been bound to the Company as the Moghul officials were bound to the Emperor. His honesty enabled him to appreciate single-mindedness when he found it in individuals, as in the case of Ali Ibrahim Khan, but his knowledge of the country was not wide enough or his insight into character deep enough to enable him to perceive the great reservoir of loyalty and devoted service which might have been tapped to fertilize the parched garden of Bengal administration. So the garden was watered by thin sprays of efficiency from small watering-cans of duty instead of by the streams and fountains of co-operation and common ideals, until in our own days, instead of the rose trees and lotus flowers that had been looked for, came up stubborn cactuses of criticism and bitterness. Then as now first-class character was no substitute for third-class brains, nor did innocency of intention mitigate the effect of the blunders of ignorance.

This change in the social atmosphere was subtle in its effects and slow in its operation. The first step was the arrival of Cornwallis, who came as a reformer of abuses with plenary powers, and brought with him the view-point of the India House and Whitehall, no previous knowledge of the country, and a lack of that imaginative sympathy which would have made up for his ignorance. He lived simply and hated ostentation, but the atmosphere of the Governor-General's house became inevitably more English and more olympian; he had no close contact with Indians and did not notice their gradually increasing estrangement.[64] As his intentions became better known, distrust changed to respect, but the social estrangement continued unchecked. In his personal relations he was much influenced by Sir John Shore, whose strict views made him particularly critical of Indian customs and whose great knowledge was not allied with natural sympathy.[65] Measures like that of withdrawing all Europeans except the Resident from Murshidabad, while fully justified by the facts,[66] had the further effect of tending to separate the two races. Finally came the limitation of the higher government ranks to Europeans only. In 1790 the Nizamat courts with their criminal jurisdiction were abolished, and in the Zillah courts Europeans presided with Indian assessors. Indian magistrates were only employed up to a monthly salary of Rs. 50.[67] The old princely ceremonial was modified at the same time, no nazars were to be presented to princes in person except to the house of Timur; the Shahzada was informed that the customary honours paid to Moghul princes would not be provided if he visited Calcutta; Sa'adat Ali of Lucknow and the Nawab Mubarak-ad-daula on similar visits were refused the usual royal honours, and no one was appointed to welcome them.[68] The warmth of geniality and the punctilio of etiquette, so essential to friendly social relations, were now lacking; every Indian felt that he was no longer a *persona grata* at the Government House. The effect of the closing of the avenues of official and especially legal appointments was to drive the old governing classes into seclusion and to leave none but the clerk, the banian and the shroff to represent Indian character and culture to the average Englishman.

To Cornwallis succeeded Shore, whose rigid views nullified the advantage which his knowledge of the country gave him.[69] With Wellesley the process proceeded apace. He habitually adopted towards princes like the Nawab of Arcot and the Nawab Wazir of Oudh the tone of a hectoring schoolmaster, and could hardly be expected to notice at all the existence of those of lesser rank. By him Indians were excluded along with Anglo-Indians from the regular entertainments at Government House,[70] and even the vakils of the country powers felt the chill wind of official olympianism. With him the habit of speaking or writing of Indians as of some strange order of beings unaccountable in their constitutions and actions, to be dazzled by ostentation and to be impressed by invincible power, from being the custom of the Calcutta class of 'low European' became the fashionable and dominant attitude.[71]

The changed face of things was thus expressed by General Palmer in a letter to Hastings which is worth quoting in full :—

> But little or no attention is paid to the Vakils of the Native Courts by Lord Wellesley. They are not permitted to pay their respects to him oftener than two or three times a year, which I think is as impolitic as it is ungracious. The above mentioned gentlemen all retain the strongest attachment to you. And indeed that sentiment is general among the natives of my information. I observe with great concern the system of depressing them adopted by the present government and imitated in the manners of almost every European. They are excluded from all posts of great respectability or emolument, and are treated in society with mortifying hauteur and reserve. In fact they have hardly any social intercourse with us. The functions of magistrate and judge are performed by Europeans who know neither the laws nor the language of the country, and with an enormous expense to the Company. The Head Molavy in each court, on whose information and explanation the judges must decide, has a salary of Rs. 50 per month. And this I believe one of the most trustworthy and lucrative employments which a Native is allowed to hold in the Company's service. What must be the sensations of this people at our thus starving them in their native land.[72]

This change of feeling and attitude is confirmed from other sources, which provide many details to illustrate the general attitude. 'Europeans,' wrote Captain Williamson in 1810 with twenty years' experience of the country, 'have little connexion with natives of either religion', except for business.[73] No Hindus and few Mussulmans would eat with Europeans ;[74] they would not join the occasional nautches, wild-beast shows or feasts to which they still asked Europeans. Mrs. Graham, visiting Calcutta in 1810 after living in Bombay and staying in Madras, deplored that 'the distance kept up between the Europeans and the natives, both here and at Madras, is such that I have not been able to get acquainted with any native family as I did in Bombay. . . . This mixture of nations ought, I think, to weaken national prejudices, but among the English at least, the effect seems to be diametrically opposite. Every Briton appears to pride himself on being outrageously a John Bull'.[75] Amongst the Europeans the feeling was strong that Indians should always be subordinated to Europeans. The maintenance of 'prestige' had now become a dominant factor of policy, and as usual in such cases, was most piously believed in by those who had very little prestige to lose.[76] The necessity ' of upholding the British character ' was now so well understood that ' nothing, short of absolute compulsion would actuate a magistrate to commit a European woman on a charge for neglect of duty, inebriety, insolence or other such impropriety '.[77] In such an atmosphere there was no room for the breath of social intercourse. As the new century advanced, things grew worse rather than better, until the time of Bentinck, who achieved fame by permitting Indians to drive to the Governor-General's house in carriages.[78] By that time, in contrast with their attitude to the feasts of Warren Hastings' days, Mussulmans considered dining with Europeans degrading. On going to a station no Englishman thought of calling on the notables of the district, as was once done as a matter of course ; instead certificates of respectability were required of the notables before they could be guaranteed a chair when they visited the officer. In the courts no sitting accommodation whatever was provided for spectators or for any officials of the court except the judge.[79] In Calcutta many writers expected every Indian to salute them,[80] and many, it is said, were so ignorant of Hindustani that after several years they could not count beyond twenty.[81]

One of the causes of this social estrangement has already been given in the policy of Cornwallis towards Indian officials and the pose of Lord Wellesley as an empire-builder.[82] But these, after all, were more the symptoms of the change than the cause of it ; in themselves they could hardly have been decisive had there been no other predisposing forces at work.

One of them is to be found in the increasing number of women in the settlements. By another irony the same influence which improved the morals of the settlers increased the widening racial gulf. As women went out in large numbers, they brought with them their insular whims and prejudices, which no official contact with Indians or iron compulsion of loneliness ever tempted them to abandon. Too insular in most cases to interest themselves in alien culture and life for its own sake, they either found society and a house amongst their own people, or in the last resort returned single and disconsolate to Europe.[83] The average Anglo-Indian was equally insular, and his contact had usually first been established by the tyranny of solitude and in time sanctified by custom and tradition. So with the advent of women in large numbers a new standard was introduced, one set of customs and traditions died out,[84] and another equally rigid and not necessarily better took its place. A woman's reaction to strange conditions was instinctive rather than rational, but rationalization quickly followed. The attitude of airy disdain and flippant contempt had the background of fear which an unknown and incalculable environment inevitably excites in everyone, but above all in the ignorant and the emotional. For the men the establishment of English homes in place of the prevalent zenanas withdrew them still more from Indian ways of thought and living,[85] and the acquisition of homes and families gave them something to lose which they had never had before, and thus made them the victims of the same fear. It is this which accounts for the strange panics which from time to time agitate European communities in the east, and for their apparently unaccountable ferocity at times of crisis.[86] This change of attitude did not pass unnoticed at the time and is thus rather crudely described.

> Every youth, who is able to maintain a wife, marries. The conjugal pair become a bundle of English prejudices and hate the country, the natives and everything belonging to them. If the man has, by chance, a share of philosophy and reflection, the woman is sure to have none. The ' odious blacks ', the ' nasty heathen wretches ', the ' filthy creatures ' are the shrill echoes of the ' black brutes ', the ' black vermin ' of the husband. The children catch up this strain. I have heard one, five years old, call the man who was taking care of him a ' black brute '. Not that the English generally behave with cruelty, but they make no scruple of expressing their anger and contempt by the most opprobrious epithets, that the language affords. Those specially who, while young, are thrown much among natives, become haughty, overbearing and demi-Asiatic in their manners.[87]

This attitude fully developed is seen in the *Memoirs* of Mrs. Fenton, who was in Calcutta from 1826-30. On going to see a nautch at the house of ' Rupe Loll Mullick ' she remarks, that ' the natives consider it a great addition to their importance to have European guests. The poor animal who exists on rice and ghee all the year, contented with a mat for his bed, here may be seen playing the liberal entertainer '.[88]

Another contributory factor to this growing racial estrangement was the influence of the evangelical missionaries and chaplains. While their personal relations with Indians—at any rate in the case of the missionaries—were usually on terms of equality, their repugnance to Hinduism and Islam and all the ' abominations of heathenism ' was so great, and their denunciations of them so violent, that they propagated the idea of Indian society as irredeemably corrupt and degraded. Henry Martyn, the most violent of them all, lived the simplest of lives and frequently courted European censure by mixing with Maulvis and Pandits and by such little acts as walking about in the evening instead of riding and driving;[89] at the same time the violence of his denunciations confirmed the Europeans in their belief that few Indians were fit to associate with, that it was a waste of time to mix with them, and that the merit of missionaries consisted not in giving their lives to the service of India, but in condescending so far and giving up the privileges of a gentleman. The attitude of Brown who 'never permitted the heathen to obtrude their abominations on Europeans if he could prevent it', of the Lutheran Kiernander by his tacit abandonment of work amongst the Bengalis for the more congenial employment of converting the Roman Catholic Eurasians, both had the same effect. Swartz of Tanjore and Carey of Serampore rose above this attitude, but the one was too remote from European settlements, the other too suspect for his anabaptism to have much influence. And even Carey, as well as the eccentric Thomas, more than once was in trouble with the Government for his preaching and writing.

But the principal cause was the simple though often neglected fact of the rapid increase of the European community after 1760. The influx was largely military, but also partly official and commercial. The soldiers consisted largely of royal troops serving in India for a few years only with a maximum of national pride and a minimum of desire to understand the country; the rest formed a nucleus of an English settlement in Calcutta and Madras, which lived its own life, ran its own shops and newspapers, entertained itself at balls and routs and concerts, admired or criticized itself on the Chowringhee Road and congratulated itself at the Governor-General's receptions. Except for the Rajahs and Nawabs who entertained officers and who declined in social importance as they decreased in power and political prestige, none of these often met Indians except as servants or on terms of business. The social ideal changed from a desire to live like a Nawab to a desire to make each settlement and cantonment down to the smallest station a replica of an English model. As the ideal and ambitions of the majority swung from India to England (powerfully aided as already noticed by feminine influence) there was no influence left to overcome the natural insularity and exclusiveness of a highly self-conscious and self-confident community. India became an unknown country to the English inhabitants of Calcutta and Madras, and what is unknown a natural conservatism will always condemn. So in 1827 'it was the extremity of bad taste to appear in anything of Indian manufacture—neither muslin, silk, flowers nor even ornaments however beautiful'.[90] The sentiment became general, which is still sometimes expressed, 'How nice India would be if it wasn't for the Indians.' Calcutta fixed its gaze on the pomp of Vauxhall and

Brighton, and it had no time to perceive the treasures which lay at its feet.

Racial feeling assumes many forms. In its simplest form, there is pure colour prejudice, the repulsion felt by the sight of a man of strange colour.[91] This is a temporary feeling which disappears on further acquaintance. So in the early days Indians were always called ' blacks ' by Europeans,[92] but this did not affect their ordinary intercourse. But if the general condition of free intermixture is lacking, this colour sense may easily become a first barrier to intercourse, as in fact happened in the society of the later century. But since it depends on ignorance and novelty, it is comparatively of little importance.

The next variety is formed of a union of colour-feeling and the particularity which all nations have in varying degrees. Everything foreign or new is judged from the standpoint of familiar customs and condemned in proportion as it differs. This prejudice is strong enough amongst those of different nations in any circumstances, and it can therefore hardly be absent when those of different race make contact with each other. The man who calls the French frog-eaters and the Germans beer-swillers is likely to call the Italians dagoes, the Mussulmans ' profligates ' and Hindus ' superstitious '. This is specially characteristic of the uneducated, and in India it was particularly prevalent among the soldiers. But this general condemnation does not preclude individual intimacy, and so it was the same men of whose conduct Hindus most complained, the ' low Europeans ' of the records, who adopted the Indian mode of life most extensively and inter-married most freely.[93]

Beyond this instinctive level comes the stage where moral judgements begin to be made. This is the special sphere of the half-educated who judge one culture from the standpoint of another and condemn it before they have ever understood it. As this reaction is more subtle, it is proportionately more difficult to combat, since the defects it points out are real, while the virtues which exist are omitted or glossed over. Indeed, the more one's view is limited to the values and standards of one's own culture, the more convinced will one become of the defects of other cultures. This attitude was, of course, very rife in the eighteenth century, the Hindus being condemned for superstition, exclusiveness, pacifism and divisions, the Mussulmans for bigotry, profligacy and intolerance.

But even such generalizations do not preclude appreciation of and friendly relations between individuals. The next stage in race feeling is where the individuals of a race, as well as its specific institutions, are held to be lacking in essential virtues. Here it is that race superiority as a doctrine and not as a blind instinct first emerges. In the eighteenth century it was sometimes sanctified by an exclusive type of Christianity which assumed in Christians a virtue denied to infidels, as in the twentieth it is dignified by the pseudo-science of writers of the type of Mr. Lothrop Stoddard under the catchword of racial characteristics. It found expression in the eighteenth century—more commonly at the end than at the beginning—in the description of all Hindus as effeminate and servile, and of Mussulmans as cruel and faithless. On the other hand, Indians returned the compliment by considering all Europeans to be winebibbers, proud, unscrupulous and licentious.[94]

The last stage in the formation of a superiority complex is that which not only regards a people as inferior collectively and individually but also as one 'on whose nature Nurture can never stick'. To-day this sort of view has to seek what support it can get from science since it can get none from religion, but it has always been widely held under the name of 'practical experience'. It is the worst as it is the most subtle of these forms; it breeds a hopeless tolerance which is perhaps worse than the frank crudity of the colour maniac, it paralyzes and discourages all effort in the victims.

All these forms were present in varying degrees in India in the eighteenth century, but until the latter half never in so strong a form as to segregate completely the two races. Then what Cornwallis had unwittingly sown Wellesley and Lord Hastings reaped, and the separation which was already a fact became a dogma. Broadly speaking, race prejudice at the beginning of the century was instinctive and disappeared with time and better acquaintance; at the end it was doctrinal and precluded the acquaintance which might have removed it. India settled down to a period of social segregation and it was left for Ram Mohan Roy with his advocacy of western reforms and Bentinck with his greater sympathy towards India to lay the foundation of a new and better spirit.

Chapter IX

CONCLUSION

We have now traced the social life of the English settlements from the tumultuous common tables of Calcutta and Madras and the 'old, unhappy far-off days' of Bombay to the magnificence of Lord Wellesley, maintaining by 'means approaching to severity' a splendid isolation amidst his 'vulgar, ignorant, rude, familiar and stupid' subjects. We have watched a condition of isolation from Indian society give place to the cosmopolitanism of the middle century, which in turn hardened at the end into a new separation based on an official policy of racial discrimination, a missionary and religiose repugnance to the 'abominations of heathenism', and the growth of a herd-psychology among the settlers as their numbers increased. The simple fact, that a man will behave in one way as an isolated individual, and in quite another as part of a crowd, explains by itself much of the widening racial gulf at the end of the century. We have noted that the very factors which improved the tone of English life widened the racial gulf. Nowhere is better illustrated the principle that 'to make progress in one direction is to give things up in another'. The days of corrupt Company officials, of ill-gotten fortunes, of oppression of ryots, of zenanas and of illicit sexual connexions, were also the days when Englishmen were interested in Indian culture, wrote Persian verses, and foregathered with Pandits and Maulvis and Nawabs on terms of social equality and personal friendship. The tragedy of Cornwallis, in our view, was that in uprooting the acknowledged evils of corruption he upset the social balance without which mutual understanding was impossible, a tragedy which was only heightened by the loftiness of his character and the sincerity of his intentions. Again, the increasing number of English women in India, while it certainly improved the moral tone of the settlement, by replacing the zenana, removed one of the most potent of Indianizing influences. The tragedy, here again, lay not in the abolition of the zenana, a rotten system based neither on justice nor on mutual self-respect, but in the growth of a herd-psychology and an intenser race-consciousness. An isolated individual cannot afford, even if he wishes it, to be aggressively race-conscious, but a group of individuals, as soon as they become conscious of themselves as a group, tend to glorify themselves, if only as a defence of self-respect against other and larger groups.

It is interesting to consider to what extent the two races influenced each other during this period. Intellectually, it must be admitted, there was little or no influence ; the nascent interest in oriental things shown by Forbes and Hastings died away to be replaced by the Macaulayesque view that they were no more than curious relics of a barbarous past, and even in the study of Sanskrit literature the lead soon passed from the English pioneers Wilkins, Jones and Colebrooke to the more enthusiastic Germans. English intellectual influence on India was similarly slight. Apart from Serfaji of Tanjore (who was educated by Swartz) there is little sign of the spread of English ideas before the time of Ram Mohan Roy in the early nineteenth century, and of Hare and Duff in Calcutta in the 'forties.

In social customs, however, more influence is discernible. Apart from the Indian customs which the English in India actually adopted, a number took root and spread to England itself. First should be mentioned the cult of cleanliness. The English cult of cleanliness is quite modern ; in the eighteenth century an Anglo-Indian visiting another house had to give good notice if he wanted a bath. The Hindu love of washing is one of the things which most struck observers in the eighteenth century, and we know that the English at first adopted the Indian method of ablution, that of throwing pots of water over the body instead of stepping into a bath.[1] Another habit which contact with India probably encouraged was cigar smoking. In India the cigar replaced the hookah in the early nineteenth century, and though the cigar did not become an established fashion until King Edward popularized it as Prince of Wales, the body of retired Anglo-Indians must have formed a powerful nucleus of cigar smokers. There is also, of course, the bungalow, borrowed direct from India, and in the less probable sphere of clothes, the banyan, originally a loose muslin shirt worn in Bengal which became a kind of vest, and pyjamas, which descend from the Anglo-Indian ' long drawers '. In games, England owes to India polo, whose technical terms have been taken over entire.

What was the character of the English in India ? Were they better or worse than their contemporaries in England ? The wholesale condemnation of the Anglo-Indian in the eighteenth century will be greatly mitigated by a study of contemporary fashionable life in England. The more the two are compared, the more it will be seen that the one is only an exaggerated and vulgarized edition of the other, modified by climatic conditions, and lacking the tradition and continuity of English society. Alongside Hickey's

Memoirs and descriptions of military dinners must be set the coarseness of the Georges, the drunkenness of the upper classes, and the taste which allowed a relative of Sir Walter Scott to read aloud to fashionable assemblies in her youth books which at the age of eighty she could not read alone without shame.[2] There was never a Medmenham Brotherhood in India.

In fact the English in India were much like their fashionable contemporaries with local differences. They had not, as in England, the solid background of an old and stable society on which to rest; they were adventurers, passing phantoms and shadows in a land which they only desired to get away from. Their wealth rested not on the inalienable land, but on the shifting fortunes of despised and often doubtful commercial transactions. They possessed the restraints neither of traditional manners nor of taste. They combined aristocratic manners with a commercial atmosphere; they introduced fashion into the counting-house and commerce into the ball-room. It was this combination of commerce with aristocratic pretension which accounts for much of the unpopularity of the Nabobs in England.

The Indian life, with its absence of conventional restraints, probably led more frequently to disaster and early deaths than in England. But its opportunities also caused more, as Prof. Dodwell says, to realize to the full their possibilities; both the percentages of distinction and of complete failure were probably higher than in England. The English were neither heroes, to be placed on pedestals and worshipped, nor reprobates to be excommunicated and ceremonially committed to literary flames. They were for the most part ordinary men placed in unusual and unprecedented circumstances. Many by the opportunities given to them became great, more by their folly found in early graves 'a blank in the great Indian lottery'.

NOTES

NOTES

CHAPTER I

[1] Founded 1620 by the Danish Company.

[2] Founded 1755 and sold to the British 1845.

[3] The Ostend Company was founded by Charles VI in 1722 and suspended in 1727. Their settlement was at Bankipur on the Hugli with a station at Covelong on the Coromandel coast. Its special privileges were withdrawn by Charles VI by the treaty of Seville 1729. Its settlement in Bengal was destroyed by the Nawab in 1744. The company was revived in 1775, became bankrupt in 1784, and was finally dissolved in 1793. A journal of the Imperial Agent to India 1782-5 is preserved in Brit. Mus. Add. MSS., 32, 165. It contains little of interest. See Hassall, *The Balance of Power*, pp. 70, 83, 87; *Cambridge History of India*, V, pp. 115-16.

[4] On 5 Sept. 1698 the Company promoted by the Whig rivals of the old monopolists was incorporated as 'the English Company Trading to the East Indies'. Under government pressure, the two companies agreed to unite in 1702, the fusion being completed in 1709. See *Cambridge History of India*, V, pp. 98-100.

[5] Capt. Alex. Hamilton, 1688-1723. Ovington (in Bombay and Surat) 1690-2. C. Lockyer, 1702-10.

[6] Hamilton, *A New Account of the East Indies*, II, 12.

[7] Hamilton, op. cit., II, 7-14.

[8] C. Lockyer, *An Account of the Trade in India*, 1711, p. 4 seq.

[9] T. Ovington, *A Voyage to Surat* (ed. H. G. Rawlinson), 1689, pp. 89-90.

[10] Hamilton, op. cit., I, p. 181.

[11] Ovington, op. cit., p. 87.

[12] Hamilton, op. cit., I, p. 237.

[13] Its name was changed to Georgetown in 1911.

[14] Lockyer, op. cit., p. 24.

[15] See H. D. Love, *Vestiges of Old Madras*, II, pp. 516-19.

[16] See Ananda Ranga Pillai, *Private Diary*, 10 vols., and *Public Consultations* volumes in the India Office.

[17] The Mayor's Court, set up by the Charter of 1687, had the power of condemning to death in the case of Indians, with a right of appeal to the Council. This power was not exercised in the case of Brahmins sentenced for other than capital crimes (Love, *Vestiges of Old Madras*, I, p. 497). With regard to Europeans, Salmon (Love, op. cit., I), in 1704 writes that capital offenders were kept in dungeons until they could be sent home, and this is confirmed by Lockyer (p. 6). In 1712, President Harrison asked for powers to deal with European criminals 'who dayly make their brags [*sic*] that we have not a power to put them to death'. He interpreted the Charter, however, to authorize the execution of pirates. In 1718, President Collet refused to execute a sailor convicted of murder on the ground that 'he had not yet receiv'd any Commission for trying any persons accus'd of Murther, Piracy, and Robbery on the High Seas' (*Public Consultations*, 50, 23 June 1718).

In 1719 a Commission for the trial of pirates was received, and Roger Bullmore was hanged in the same year for deserting from the 'George' (Love, op. cit., II, p. 175).

A Mayor's Court for Calcutta was established in 1727.

[18] J. T. Wheeler, *Madras in the Olden Time*, II, pp. 225-7.

19 P. Anderson, *The English in Western India*, p. 328.

20 C. R. Wilson, *Early Annals of the English in Bengal*, I, section 131.

21 Ibid., section 177, p. 275.

22 Ibid., section 178 (24 Sept. 1708).

23 Ibid., section 87, p. 150.

24 Love, op. cit., I, 697. The Mayor's office was established by the Charter of 1687.

25 Love, op. cit., I, 499. See also W. A. J. Archbold, *Outlines of Indian Constitutional History*.

26 Love, op. cit., II, 31. *Public Consultations*, 9 July 1702.

27 Lockyer, op. cit., p. 22.

28 Wheeler, op. cit., III, 320.

29 Lockyer, op. cit., p. 20.

30 Hamilton, op. cit., I, p. 361.

31 Wheeler, op. cit., I, p. 380.

32 *Home Misc. Series*, 257 (Davenport to Woolley, 14 Oct. 1709).

33 Ibid., 68, pp. 45-7 (Frankland to the Directors, Jan. 28, 1726-7).

34 *Bengal Despatches*, No. 1, 23 Jan. 1754, paras. 80, 86.

35 The name was borrowed from the Portuguese word 'tope' or gun, because they were often employed in the capacity of gunners (*Hobson-Jobson*).

36 Lockyer, op. cit., pp. 14-15.

37 Lockyer, op. cit., p. 21.

38 Wheeler, op. cit., III, p. 253.

39 Ovington, op. cit., p. 234.

40 Wilson, op. cit., I, p. 262.

41 Ovington, op. cit., p. 235.

42 Hamilton, op. cit., I, p. 237; II, p. 7.

43 Wheeler, op. cit., III, p. 35.

44 H. H. Dodwell, *Nabobs of Madras*, p. 112.

45 H. B. Hyde, *Parochial Annals of Bengal*, p. 19.

46 Love, op. cit., II, p. 25.

47 Lockyer, op. cit., p. 13 (1710). Estimates varied a great deal; e.g., in 1691-2 the population was estimated at 400,000 (Love, op. cit., I, p. 547, *Letter Book*, vol. 9, 22 Jan. 1691-2). 1744.—It was reckoned at 250,000 in the Company's territory (Forrest, *Life of Lord Clive*). 1750.—The *Madras Dialogues* speak of 8,700 houses in Black Town. See also Love, op. cit., III, p. 557, for a series of varying estimates.

48 Hamilton, op. cit., II, p. 18.

49 Love, op. cit., II, p. 64.

50 This estimate is given in Wheeler, *Madras in the Olden time*, I.

51 Hamilton, op. cit, I, p. 237; II, p. 7.

52 Anderson, op. cit., I, p. 349.

53 Love, op. cit., II, p. 171. The Common Table was abolished in 1722.

54 Ibid., pp. 43-4. Quoted from *The Vindication of General R. Smith* (1783).

55 Ibid., II, p. 170.

56 Ovington, op. cit., pp. 230-2. A specimen dietary of the poorer class is given in the *Madras Dialogues* (1750).

57 Love, op. cit., II, p. 171.

58 Ibid., II, p. 11.

59 Lockyer, op. cit., p. 23.

60 Love, II, p. 171.

[61] Shiraz wine.

[62] *Madras Consultations*, April and May 1719 (Penny, *Church in Madras*, I, p. 234) 'which practice we apprehended to be of very dangerous consequence; many of the young gentlemen in the company's service being of good families in England, who would be very much scandalized at such marriages.'

[63] Wheeler, op. cit., I, p. 54.

[64] Ibid., I. See also *European Inhabitants* (Madras), III.A.

[65] A Castee was a person of pure Portuguese descent.

[66] A Mustee was a person of mixed Indian and Portuguese descent.

[67] They formed a company of the Madras garrison.

[68] See Baillie Fraser, *Military Memoirs of Col. James Skinner*, II, p. 159.

[69] Wilson, op. cit.; *Public Consultations* (Calcutta), 4 Mar. 1706.

[70] Lockyer, op. cit., p. 22.

[71] Ibid.

[72] Ibid.

[73] Ovington, op. cit., p. 233.

[74] Ibid., p. 229-30.

[75] Hamilton, op. cit., II, pp. 11-12.

[76] Wheeler, op. cit., III, pp. 252-4.

[77] Ibid., p. 353 (*Public Consultations*).

[78] Wilson, *Madras Army*, I, p. 8.

[79] Ovington, op. cit., pp. 232-5.

[80] Lockyer, op. cit., p. 19.

[81] Ibid., pp. 27-8.

[82] Lockyer, op. cit., p. 16.

[83] See Forrest, *Life of Clive*.

[84] Clive's first letter home well illustrates this feeling.

[85] Lockyer, p. 28. The new arrival, later called 'a griffin', was then known as an 'Orambarros'.

[86] By A. de Mandelslo in 1638.

[87] Lockyer, op. cit., p. 23.

[88] See the inventories in *Public Consultations*, 1700-25.

[89] Lockyer, op. cit., p. 23.

[90] Love, *Vestiges of Old Madras*, I, p. 235. See also Capt. Seton's case, ibid., pp. 125-6.

[91] General Letter from the Court to Bengal, Feb. 1728 (quoted by C. R. Wilson, *Old Fort William*, I, pp. 125-6).

[92] Despatch to the Court, 25 Feb. 1750 (Long, *Selections*, p. 23).

[93] See Section on Medicine, pp. 100-104 above.

[94] Manucci, *Storia do Mogor* (W. W. Irvine), I, p. 140.

[95] According to Williamson (*East India Vade Mecum*, II, p. 128) whisky was still considered 'vulgar and nauseous' in 1800.

[96] Lockyer, op. cit., p. 267.

[97] Capt. W. Symson, *A New Voyage to the East Indies* (2nd edition, 1720), p. 34; Lockyer, op. cit., pp. 266-7, and Ovington, op. cit., pp. 142-3. *Hobson-Jobson*, under 'arrack', says the term was used for spirit distilled from palm sap in the south, and from cane molasses and rice in the east and north.

[98] Symson, op. cit., p. 35.

[99] A. de Mandelslo, *Journey to Persia and the Indies*, p. 13. Punch comes from 'panj' (Persian for 'five'). See *Hobson-Jobson* (ed. 1903), Bernier's *Travels* (ed. Constable, p. 441) and Evelyn's *Diary*, 16 Jan. 1662.

100 Ovington, op. cit. p. 230.

101 Love, op. cit., II, p. 135. The Directors sent 100 pipes for the second time, 'finding how acceptable the Madeira wine by the King William was.'

Bengal Despatches, I, 1753-9, p. 13 (Long, p. 50), 300 pipes, 150 each for Madras and Calcutta, were sent. The former was allowed to retain fifty more if required. The Court on 23 Dec. 1762 (Long, p. 254) threatened to discontinue the despatch unless all the wine was sold at reasonable rates, to the company's servants.

Calcutta Proceedings, 29 Sept. 1766 (Long, p. 446): 125 pipes of Madeira were received. Of these thirteen were deducted for leakage and four were sent to the west coast. The rest were distributed as follows:—

The Governor	5 pipes
The Second	2 ,,
Gen. Carnac	2 ,,
The Councillors	1 each
2 Colonels	1 ,,
The Residents of Malda, Midnapore and Burdwan	1 ,,
3 Lieut.-Colonels	2 pipes
2 Chaplains, 11 Majors, 15 Senior Merchants and one Chief Engineer	½ each
60 Captains, 8 Factors, 5 Surgeons	⅓ each
80 Writers and 200 Subalterns	⅙ ,,

(The excess was taken from the previous year's surplus.)

102 Sieur Luillier, *A Voyage to the East Indies*, p. 337.

103 Dodwell, *Nabobs of Madras*.

104 *Madras Dialogues*, xxviii.

105 Ibid., iv.

106 Ibid., xxviii.

107 Wheeler, *Madras in the Olden Time*, I, pp. 63-7 (Letter of the Rev W. P. Warner to the Directors, 31 Jan. 1676).

108 Love, op. cit., II, p. 159 (*Public Consultations* (Madras), 1719).

109 Ananda Ranga Pillai, *Private Diary*, I, p. 243.

110 Long, *Selections*, p. 158 (Letter to the Court, 31 Dec. 1758).

111 A. de Mandelslo, op. cit., p. 13.

112 Ovington, op. cit., pp. 180-2.

113 *Madras Dialogues*, p. 29.

114 J. Macdonald, *Travels in various Parts*, p. 233.

115 Brit. Mus. Add. MSS., 29, 172, p. 26.

116 G. Elers, *Memoirs* (1797-1803), p. 157.

117 *India Office Records*. *Letter Book* 16, Dispatch to Bencoolen 6 Feb. 1717. Also ibid., Dispatch to Bencoolen 14 Mar. 1718 (quoted by P. E. Roberts, *History of British India*, pp. 79-80).

118 Love, op. cit., II, p. 15 (*Public Consultations*, 12-15 July 1701).

119 The Governor's Tamil secretary.

120 Love, op. cit., II, p. 110 (*Public Consultations*, 26 July 1717).

121 Ibid., p. 111.

122 Wheeler, *Old Madras*, III, pp. 23-4 (*Public Consultations*, 17 Aug. 1727).

123 Ovington, op. cit., p. 401.

124 The use of betel continued quite late, as can be seen from the *Bengal Inventories*, 1755-80. Manucci (op. cit., I, 62) found everyone eating pan and was instructed in its use by an English lady. La Farelle wrote about 1720: 'Le bétel est d'un grand usage, non seulement chez les indigènes mais encore

parmi les petits et grands, femmes et hommes.' According to him it was introduced by the Portuguese ladies, and a taste for it was necessary for polite society.

Chapter II

[1] In Bengal corruption extended to the country districts—with lucrative residentships, the exactions of gomastahs, free trade passes, etc., instead of being confined to a single city.

[2] e.g. see Manucci, op. cit., for English in the service of Aurungzeb. Also Stanhope, *Asiaticus* for service with the Nawab of Arcot. As late as 1780 desertions of officers took place to Hyder Ali (W. J. Wilson, *Madras Army*).

[3] C. R. Wilson, *Early Annals of the English in Bengal*, I.

[4] It is only barely mentioned in the Madras and Calcutta *Consultations*. Ananda Ranga Pillai, on the other hand (*Diary*, I, 93-5) gives a long and circumstantial account of it.

[5] *Diaries of Streynsham Master*, I, p. 252 (Company's General Letter to Agent in Ft. St. George, 24 Dec. 1675).

[6] Ibid., p. 251 (1675, para. 30 and 36).

[7] Ibid., p. 263 (General letter of Court to St. George, 24 Dec. 1675, para. 89).

[8] Letter to the Court, Dec. 1759, para. 147 (Long, *Selections*, p. 166). See Directors' File. 'Permit us to say that the diction of your letters is most unworthy yourselves and us in whatever relation considered, either as masters to servants, or gentlemen to gentlemen.'

[9] Wilson, op. cit., I, p. 275; *Bengal Consultations*, 24 Sept. 1708.

[10] Quoted in Dodwell, *Nabobs of Madras*, p. 178.

[11] This was provided for by the Infantry Regulations, Madras. Wilson, *Madras Army*, I, p. 52 seq.

[12] *Cornwallis Correspondence*, I, pp. 314-15 (Nov. 1787).

[13] Cornwallis called it 'the good old principle of Leadenhall St. economy, small salaries and immense perquisites' (*Cornwallis Correspondence*, II, p. 68).

[14] The powerful position of the 'Commercial Resident' is vividly described by Hunter in his *Annals of Rural Bengal*.

[15] The Sepoy army also then began as a body of regular troops.

[16] Dodwell, *Nabobs of Madras*, ch. VI. Also ch. I (above).

[17] e.g. the case of Ensign Gardner (Wheeler, *Madras in the Olden Time*, I, p. 346); also the Case of Capt. Seton (Love, op. cit., II, pp. 35-8).

[18] *Cornwallis Correspondence*, I, pp. 311, 402.

[19] Though Albuquerque (Hunter, *History of British India*) set the first precedent for drilling Indian troops, the practice had long been forgotten. In the early English settlements the only coloured troops were Topasses and Caffrees (Madagascans). The armed peons were undisciplined.

[20] *Madras Consultations*, 22 Dec. 1740 (vol. 70 *Madras Records*). *Select Madras Records*, ed. Dodwell, pp. 42-6; Officials were 51, Non-officials 118. Another list (*European Inhabitants*, Madras, vol. 3A) gives a list of 143 non-official names. The lists have a general resemblance though the numbers do not exactly tally.

[21] See ch. I, pp. 21-2.

[22] Wilson, *Madras Army*, I, gives examples of Indian officers rewarded by the Company for good service. They occasionally held independent commands.

[23] Wilson, op. cit., I, p. 48.

24 Ibid., p. 61.

25 Return of Troops, 12 Dec. 1758, Sundry Book 1758-9 (*Madras Rec.*, p. 109).

26 Wilson, op. cit., I, p. 281.

27 *Ind. Off. Rec., Madras European Inhab.*, 3A (1777).

28 S. C. Hill, *List of Europeans, etc.*, Introduction.

29 Broome, *Bengal Army*, appx. Q.

30 Wilson, op. cit., I, p. 142.

31 Innes Munro, *Narrative of Military Operations, etc.*, p. 23.

32 Wilson, op. cit., I, p. 235.

33 Innes Munro, op. cit., p. 23.

34 Wilson, op. cit., I, p. 58. *Regulations of* 1748, par. 22; Orme MSS. 288, 66, p. 203; for Clive's Contracts, 287, 106, p. 395 (Hill, *Catalogue*, II, p. 223). Also Forrest, *Life of Lord Clive*, I, p. 262, Jan. 1756.

35 Wilson, op. cit., I, p. 55. *Regulations for military at Ft. St. David*, 1747, arts. 12, 13, 15.

36 Ibid., p. 360.

37 R. Orme, *Military Transactions in Hindustan* (ed. 1803), I, pp. 98-9.

38 The 64th, 79th, 84th, 89th, 96th, 103rd.

39 Penny, *Church in Madras*, I, p. 350.

40 Wilson, op. cit., II, p. 167.

41 Wilson, op. cit., II, p. 169 (74th, 75th, 76th, 77th Regts.).

42 Elers, *Memoirs*, p. 178.

43 Namier, *Structure of Politics at the Accession of George III*.

44 J. M. Holtzmann, *The Nabobs in England*. See also William Hickey on Barwell. There was also of course, the natural tendency of the eighteenth century for the successful merchant to become a landed gentleman.

45 J. Forbes, *Oriental Memoirs*—see his life at Broach. See also Teignmouth, *Life and Correspondence of Sir John Shore*.

46 Forrest, *Clive*, II, pp. 225-8.

47 Letter of Vansittart to Johnstone, etc. at Monghyr, 15 Dec. 1762 (Long, *Selections*, 1747-67, p. 302). This practice was known as 'barja' and 'kishaunt'.

48 Dodwell, *Dupleix and Clive*, and the *Bengal Despatches*, 17 May 1764, paras. 31, 33, 36, 38. Brit. Mus. Add. MSS. 29,132, *Letters of Hastings and Vansittart*, Nov. 1764, para. 14.

49 For details of this, see Monckton Jones, *Warren Hastings in Bengal*—see also Long, op. cit., pp. 472-3 (1772-4).

50 See India Office Records, *Europeans in India* (quoted in ch. III, below).

51 *Home Miscellaneous Series*, 765, p. 153, Topham to Burrington, 22 Sept. 1765.

52 Described in chaps. III and V below.

53 *Bernier's Travels*, ed. cit., p. 260. 'On my first arrival it stunned me so as to be insupportable: but such is the power of habit that this same noise is now heard by me with pleasure; in the night particularly, when in bed and afar, on my terrace this music sounds in my ears as solemn grand and melodious.'

54 e.g. in public processions, see chap. I, above.

55 de Pagé, *Travels round the World*, II, p. 18.

56 D. Campbell, *Journey Overland to India* (1781-4), III, p. 124.

57 Major J. Blakiston, *Twelve Years Military Adventures in Hindustan*, 1802-14, I, p. 257. He considered that only one Indian song had any music in it—Chandah's song from Hyderabad—called after a dancer of that name. This

was duly harmonized by the master of the band of the 33rd Regiment. A few songs of the nautch girls did become popular ; translations of some are given in Carey, *Good Old Days of the Hon. John Company*, I.

58 Love, op. cit., II, p. 432.

59 Williamson, *East India Vade Mecum*, II, p. 122. By 1800 punch was given up except by the lowest classes. ' A certain odium attaches to all who are in the habit of drinking spirits, whether raw or diluted.'

60 Teignmouth, *Life of Lord Teignmouth*—Letter to Bury Hutchinson, 20 Nov. 1775, I, p. 58.

61 See below. The nautch continued as an occasional spectacle but not as a daily amusement.

62 D'Oyley, Williamson and Blagdon, *The European in India*, Plate XV.

63 W. H. Hart, *Old Calcutta*, p. 28.

64 See H. E. Busteed, *Echoes of Old Calcutta*, for an account of its career.

65 Thos. Daniel's *Oriental Scenery*, show this type well ; it can still be seen in surviving houses of the period in Calcutta and elsewhere.

66 T. Lecky, *History of England in the Eighteenth Century*. It is a minor irony of Indian history that just at the time when we were coming into contact with the Moghuls, the formal French style of Le Nôtre, which would have found natural affinities with the Moghul, gave way to the ideals of the ' wilderness ' and ' unrestricted nature '.

67 Hunter, *Journal*, p. 72 (1875).

68 Mrs. Fenton, *Journal* (1826).

69 Mrs. N. E. Kindersley, *Letters* (1754), p. 231.

70 Ibid.

71 Hart, *Old Calcutta*, p. 47.

72 *Memoirs of Asiaticus*, p. 39.

73 J. Cordiner, *A Voyage to India*, p. 120.

74 W. Tennant, *Indian Recreations*, I, p. 56.

75 *Private Journal of the Marquess Hastings* (1814), I, pp. 145-6.

76 Mrs. Fenton, op. cit., p. 243.

77 De Jacquemmont, *Letters from India*, I, 1830, p. 204. Ladies, though less enthusiastic than men, tolerated or attended them. See Cordiner 1794, Mrs. Graham 1810, Lady Nugent 1812.

78 D'Oyley, *The European in India*, letterpress to Plate XV.

79 Elers, *Memoirs*, p. 74 ; Hunter, *Journal* (1785), p. 72.

80 India Office Factory Miscellaneous Series, 23, pp. 24, 44, 51, 73 seq., 100.

81 Goldburne, *Hartly House*, p. 19, seq. ; *Memoirs of Asiaticus*, p. 46 seq.

82 Hickey, *Memoirs*, II, 1778, p. 136.

83 *Memoirs of Asiaticus*, pp. 46-7.

84 Williamson, *East India Vade Mecum*, I, p. 413 ; D'Oyley, *European in India*, Plate XIV.

85 Despatch of Directors to Bengal, 17 Mar. 1769, para. 44, complained that the Company's servants neglected trade ' that most honest way of making fortunes ' and made profits by contracts instead.

86 Teignmouth, *Memoirs*, I, p. 24.

87 Letters of Clive to Court, 22 Aug. 1757, Long, *Selections*, p. 113. Later this seems to have been remedied. See Rennell, *Diary*, 1765, *Home Miscellaneous Series*, 765, p. 158.

88 *Bengal Desp.*, 1753-9, 11 Feb. 1756, para. 92 (*Home Miscellaneous Series*).

89 Letter of Clive to the Court, 24 Mar. 1766, Forrest, *Clive*, II, p. 308.

90 Calcutta Proceedings, 16 May 1765, Long, *Selections*, p. 317.

91 Teignmouth, op. cit. (Letter to Bury Hutchinson, 20 Nov. 1775).

92 Col. Champion's Diary, 18 Dec. 1765 (*Home Miscellaneous Series*, 198, p. 294). The Colonel's grammar is his own. A few punctuation marks have been added to make the passage intelligible, but the spelling and the tenses are the Colonel's.

93 Rennell, *Journal*, 1 April 1762, p. 132 (*Home Miscellaneous Series*, 765).

94 Nearly all civil servants acquired £6-8,000 in six or seven years, and with favourable trade opportunities £30,000 or £40,000 was possible—ibid., p. 203.

95 Ibid., 1764, p. 138.

96 Ibid, p. 186.

97 Ibid., p. 192.

98 Ibid., p. 221.

99 Ibid., 1 July 1768, p. 186.

100 The Supreme Court, set up by the Regulating Act of 1773.

101 *Bengal Past and Present*, II, p. 475, Memoir of Col. Pearse (Letter of Pearse to Admiral Mann, 4 Apr. 1779). The points which distressed Pearse were the Court's interference to protect servants from maltreatment and their refusal of trial by jury to the European community. A deputation was sent to England in which Mrs. Fay's husband was concerned. See also Busteed, *Echoes of Old Calcutta*, chapter on *Hickey's Journal*. Another example of a new arrival's refusal to adopt Anglo-Indian fashions, which illustrates the same process, is William Hickey's attitude to the hookah. In ethics and morality the same process began with the arrival of the Evangelical chaplains.

Chapter III

1 There are many descriptions of voyages. Those of Hickey and Macdonald are among the more interesting. An authoritative account of the voyage is provided by Williamson in his *East India Vade Mecum*, I, pp. 1-50.

2 Innes Munro, *Narrative of Military Operations on the Coromandel Coast in* 1780, p. 18.

3 Ibid., p. 19.

4 Lady Nugent, *Journal of a Residence in India*, I, p. 82.

5 Mrs. Fay, *Letters from India*, pp. 163-4; T. Twining, *Travels in India*, pp. 51-3; J. Johnson, *Oriental Voyages*, p. 70.

6 Williamson, op. cit., I, p. 161 seq.; Blakiston, *Twelve Years Military Adventures in Hindustan*, I, p. 34.

7 *The Madras Courier*, 21 July 1790.

8 Williamson, in his *East India Vade Mecum*, has given the most detailed description of houses.

9 *Hobson-Jobson* (ed. cit.); the word was used by the first Portuguese traveller to India—' Roteiro de Viagem de Vasco da Gama ' (2nd edition, 1861, p. 62).

10 Williamson, op. cit., II, p. 203.

11 Ibid., p. 23.

12 Innes Munro, op. cit., p. 59; Cordiner, *A Voyage to India*, 1794, p. 96; Blakiston, op. cit., II, p. 274; Graham, *Journal of a Residence in India*, pp. 130-1.

13 Williamson, op. cit., II, pp. 110-112, gives a concise account of the change. There are many other scattered references.

[14] *Memoirs of Asiaticus*, p. 121.

[15] Love, op. cit., p. 180. A concise account of the debt is given by P. E. Roberts in his *India under Wellesley*.

[16] See, e.g. the opinion of Ives (*A Voyage to India*, 1754, pp. 70-2).

[17] *Memoirs of Asiaticus*, p. 32.

[18] See the opinions of Sir John Shore, Teignmouth, *Life of Lord Teignmouth*, I, p. 359 and Captain Elers, *Memoirs*, p. 64. (Love, op. cit., III, p. 527, contains press notices of his death.)

[19] Innes Munro, op. cit., p. 62.

[20] Hickey, *Memoirs*, II, p. 120; de Grandpré, *Voyage in the Indian Ocean and to Bengal*, pp. 136-7; Twining, op. cit., p. 73 (a good description); Elers, *Memoirs*, p. 156 (also good); etc.

[21] C. Cossigny, *Voyage au Bengalen*, 1789, p. 28.

[22] Long, *Selections*, p. 317 (Calc. Progs., 16 May 1765).

[23] Most of the details of the Calcutta houses and servants have been taken from Captain Thomas Williamson's *East India Vade Mecum* which, published in 1810 and based on over twenty years' experience of Indian life, is authoritative for this period.

[24] Williamson, op. cit., II, p. 9.

[25] Williamson, op. cit., I, p. 514; II, pp. 34-50.

[26] Graham, op. cit.

[27] Teignmouth, *Life of Lord Teignmouth*, I, p. 24. In 1769 'only two or three houses with venetian blinds' existed. Williamson (op. cit., II, p. 17) says that 'all' houses had them by 1800.

[28] W. H. Carey, *Good Old Days of the Hon. John Company*, I, p. 81. See also Busteed, *Echoes of Old Calcutta*.

[29] Hickey, op. cit., II, p. 268.

[30] H. Pearson, *Memoirs of Buchanan*, I, p. 217.

[31] Williamson, op. cit., I, pp. 264-5.

[32] Ibid., II, p. 250.

[33] *Madras Dialogues*, p. 27.

[34] Williamson, op. cit., II, p. 265.

[35] Mrs. Fay, op. cit., pp. 180-1. For complaints of servants and the habit of keeping banians, see p. 182. She mentions writers who drove four-in-hands two months after their arrival.

[36] Williamson, op. cit., I, p. 86, seq. all this section.

[37] Ibid., p. 198.

[38] Ibid., p. 195.

[39] Ibid., p. 219.

[40] Ibid., p. 212.

[41] *Hobson-Jobson* (ed. 1903, p. 273) derives the word from the Hindi 'karani'.

[42] The contemporary spelling is given to all these names.

[43] Williamson, op. cit., I, p. 274. He was also called the 'nye' or 'nappy'.

[44] See the advertisements in the Calcutta papers.

[45] Hart, *Old Calcutta*, p. 20. See also *Bengal Past and Present* (article by Syed Hussain), II, p. 270 seq., and Archbold, *Outlines of Indian Constitutional History*, pp. 103-4. The steps in the abolition of the slave trade were as follows:—

(*a*) 1789. Their export was forbidden by proclamation.
(*b*) 1811. Their import from Arabia was forbidden.
(*c*) 1824. Engaging in the slave trade was made piracy with the penalty of death (with certain exceptions).

(*d*) 1831. Crown slaves were emancipated.
(*e*) 1833. Slavery was abolished with effect from 1845.

46 Williamson, op. cit., I, p. 334.

47 Ibid., I, p. 335.

48 'The houcca is a machine from which the smoke of tobacco and aromatics is inhaled, through a tube of several feet or even yards in length, it is called a snake. To show the deference or indulgence shown by ladies to the practice of smoking, we need but transcribe a card for the Governor-General's and his lady's concert and supper—Mr. and Mrs. Hastings present their compliments to Mr.—— and request the favour of his company to a concert and supper on Thursday next, at Mrs. H'——s house in town. The concert to begin at 8 o'clock. Mr.—— is requested to bring no servants except his houcca-burdar.' (1 October 1779.)

49 Macintosh, *Travels*, 1777-1781, II, pp. 214-219. Dr. Busteed calls this 'a trumpery book of travel'. But the author was in India for some months and the book has, therefore, a *social* value. The picture is correct in the main, but allowance must be made for exaggerations in order to secure sensational and picturesque effect. It must not be imagined that all Anglo-Indians adopted this mode of life; many of the highest like Hastings, Cornwallis, Macartney and Shore were hard workers and lived simple lives. But books like Hickey's *Memoirs*, Williamson's *Vade Mecum*, and D'Oyley's *European in India*, after allowing for exaggerations, corroborate this as a general picture. The version printed by Carey, *Good Old Days of the Hon. John Company* (ed. 1906, I, pp. 90-2) is accurate except for the omission of the last sentence but one.

50 J. Kaye, *Life of Lord Metcalfe*, I, pp. 35-6.

51 At that time most parties were bachelors' parties.

52 Mrs. Fay, *Letters from India*, pp. 189-90.

53 Forrest, *Life of Clive*.

54 Rennell's MS Journal in the India Office (*Home Miscellaneous Series*, No. 76).

55 F. J. Shore, *Notes on Indian Affairs*, I, p. 106.

56 Wilson, *Madras Army* I, p. 70. On the arrival of the 39th Regt. in 1754, King's officers were given precedence over Company's officers of equal rank. This distinction continued till 1788.

57 Ibid., I, p. 233. General Orders laid down that the command of sepoys was 'a service equally honourable and essential with the command of Europeans' (Jan. 1766).

58 See Chapter V, below.

59 See, e.g. Aliph Cheem, *Lays of Ind'*, etc.

60 India Office Records, *Europeans in India* Series, XXV.

61 J. Page, *Swartz of Tanjore*, p. 51.

62 *Serampore Letters*, 15 Feb. 1794, p. 41.

63 Dubois, *Letters on the State of Christianity in India*, p. 17.

64 Page, op. cit., p. 17.

65 Ibid.

66 Ibid.

67 *Europeans in India* Series. The pages of these volumes are unnumbered.

68 Long, *Selections* (Clive to the Select Committee, 16 Jan. 1767), p. 515.

69 *Europeans in India* (J. Price to the Secretary of the Government, 23 April 1789), 25.

70 Ibid. (Case of Richard and John Johnson.)

71 Ibid. (Case of Michael Macnamara.)

72 *Europeans in India*, year 1799.

73 This was the Governor-General's comment to the Directors: 'The establishment of a number of Europeans of both sexes of the most abandoned principles and depraved manners throughout the company's territories, must necessarily affect the morals of the Lower Orders of British Subjects, diminish that respect for the National character which is of such essential importance to maintain among our Native subjects, and furnish ready and dangerous instruments for the Domestic and Foreign enemies of the British Government.'

74 In this section the word Anglo-Indian is used in its original connotation, i.e. an Englishman temporarily resident in India. The term 'Eurasian' is used as being more comprehensive, and including those of Portuguese and French as well as of English descent.

75 Mandelslo, *Journey*, p. 82. There is no medical authority for this statement.

76 Sieur Luillier, op. cit., p. 256.

77 J. Richter, *History of Missions in India*, p. 108.

78 de Grandpré, *Voyage to Bengal*, p. 167.

79 Blakiston, *Twelve Years Military Adventures in Hindustan*, I, p. 270.

80 de Grandpré, op. cit., p. 71.

81 Dubois, *Letters on the State of Christianity in India*, pp. 75-6.

82 Love, *Vestiges* (Report of Surgeon Wilson), III, p. 181.

83 Ibid., III, pp. 1-9.

84 Penny, *Church in Madras*, I, p. 507; S.P.C.K. *Report* for 1784.

85 Williams, *Serampore Letters*, 11, 1801, p. 67.

86 Dubois, op. cit., p. 78. Writers were singularly unanimous on this class of Eurasians.

87 Innes Munro, op. cit., pp. 50-51. This remark would include boys from the West Indies.

88 Brit. Mus. Add. MSS. 29,178, 6 July 1802 (Palmer to Warren Hastings).

89 Ibid.

90 Innes Munro, op. cit., p. 71.

91 *India Gazette*, 31 May 1792.

92 Williamson, op. cit., I, p. 460. The rate was :—

A Subaltern and Assistant Surgeon	Rs 3 a month.
A Captain and Surgeon	,, 6 ,, ,,
A Major	,, 9 ,, ,,

93 Williamson, op. cit., I, p. 439.

94 Blakiston, op. cit., I, p. 270. The tendency was helped by the custom of employing old soldiers as storekeepers of forts.

95 Tennant, *Indian Recreations*, I, pp. 69-73. 'Marriages with officers were unpopular because the parties were often excluded from society. But as the girls were unfitted by education for marriage with boys of their own class, they often became officers' mistresses.' Also ibid., p. 52. 'Any Asiatic blood will not suit persons of rank.' 'It is very strange the prejudice existing here against half-castes'—Mrs. Fenton, op. cit., p. 38 (1826). 'Portuguese girls, a few Moorish and Pariah women and those who have lost caste fall to European soldiers as temporary wives.' Innes Munro, op. cit., p. 49 (1780). Others were supported by civilians and officers as their mistresses. No Eurasian ladies were invited to Government assemblies. Ayahs were often Eurasians or Portuguese, of whom 'many became house-keepers to single gentlemen'—Williamson, op. cit., I, pp. 337, 454.

96 *Fifteen Years in India*, p. 75.

97 Carey, *Good Old Days of the Hon. John Company*.

98 F. J. Shore, op. cit., I, p. 164.

99 Ibid., p. 110.

100 e.g. Mrs. Graham, *Journal*, p. 128.

101 Valentia, *Travels*, I, p. 241.

102 Ibid.

103 See Hickey, *Memoirs*, II, p. 173, for a list of toasts and a description of full dress worn at one of the dinners 'malgré the heat'.

104 Ibid., II, p. 173 (1775-82).

105 Ibid., II, pp. 135-6. Also Williamson, op. cit., II, p. 127.

106 Curzon, *British Government in India*, I, p. 204. He describes the ceremonies with obvious enjoyment.

107 See S. C. Grier, *Letters of Warren Hastings to his Wife*, for his daily life.

108 Shore to Hastings, 16 Feb. 1787 (Add. MSS. 29,170, p. 374).

109 Williamson, op. cit., II, p. 127.

110 Hickey, op. cit., III, p. 306.

111 Turner to Hastings, 19 Sept. 1786 (Add. MSS. 29,170, p. 211).

112 Ibid.

113 Palmer to Hastings, 18 Feb. 1787 (ibid., p. 381).

114 *Cornwallis Correspondence*, I, p. 422.

115 Teignmouth, *Life of Lord Teignmouth*.

116 D'Oyley, *Tom Raw the Griffin*, p. 149. See also Wellesley, *Life*.

117 *Wellesley Papers*, I, pp. 83-4. See also Wellesley to Lord Grenville, 18 Nov. 1798 (Fortescue MSS. IV, p. 381). He considers Calcutta Society 'so vulgar ignorant, rude, familiar and stupid as to be disgusting and intolerable; especially the ladies, not one of whom, by-the-by is even decently good looking.'

CHAPTER IV

1 S. M. Edwardes, *Rise of Bombay*, p. 163.

2 A. Parsons, *Travels in Asia and Africa* (1774), pp. 251, 260.

3 Edwardes, op. cit., p. 169. It was estimated in 1780 at 113,000.

4 Parsons, op. cit., p. 246, said that large ships could not pass the bar without being partly unloaded. At high tide there was fifteen feet of water over the bar. See also de Pagé, *Travels Round the World* (1767-1771), II, p. 26.

5 Edwardes, op. cit., p. 118.

6 *Cambridge History of India*, V, pp. 113-14.

7 The Treaty of Salbai, May 1782.

8 Edwardes, op. cit., p. 225.

9 Captain Fryer mentions a Parsi Tower of Silence in 1675.

10 Valentia, op. cit., II, p. 187.

11 Ovington, op. cit., p. 87.

12 Niebuhr, *Journal of Travels to Arabia and the East* (French translation, 1780), p. 3.

13 The 'Buckshaw' fish which Hamilton mentions was probably the 'Bunnelo' fish, which is still used for the purpose, and which when dried, makes the famous 'Bombay Duck'. Col. Yule in *Hobson-Jobson* fails to identify 'Buckshaw fish', but suggests that it may be derived from the Hindustani and Marathi 'bachcha', the young of any creature. This conclusion is strengthened by Pyke (*Journal of a Voyage to East Indies*, 1745, Add. MSS. 24,931, p. 100) who mentions 'the pernicious custom of Buckshawing or Dunging the Trees with "Bombaloo" fish'.

14 Hamilton, op. cit., I, p. 181.

15 *Bombay Letters*, I, p. 17, Aug. 1722, para. 23.

[16] Ibid., 20 April 1708, paras. 60-62, 65, 67 (p. 217 of Bruce, *Collections of Annals. Home Misc. Series*, 46).

[17] Ibid., 13 Feb. 1709-10 (ibid., p. 340).

[18] Ibid., 17 Aug. 1722, para. 23.

[19] Ibid., 8 Nov. 1723, para. 107.

[20] Grose, *A Voyage to the East Indies*, I, p. 33.

[21] Some or all of these are given by Capt. Fryer (1675), Mandelslo (1669), Ovington (1689), Grose (1750-64), Rennell (1761), Valentia (1803), and Mrs. Graham (1809).

[22] Grose, op. cit., I, p. 33.

[23] Valentia, op. cit., II, p. 182.

[24] Ovington, op. cit., p. 204.

[25] Valentia, op. cit., II, p. 183.

[26] For the early troubles, see Firoz Malabari, *Bombay in the Making* and Sir W. Hunter, *History of British India*.

[27] Edwardes, op. cit., p. 97.

[28] Ibid., p. 120 (The Rev. R. Cobbe's estimate).

[29] Ibid., p. 140.

[30] Hamilton, op. cit., I, p. 287.

[31] *Home Misc. Series*, 332, Boone to Woolley, 22 Jan. 1718.

[32] Ibid. Papers relating to Sir N. Waite's arrest, p. 45.

[33] Aislabie was the second who eventually arrested him.

[34] Ibid., p. 129.

[35] Ibid., p. 132.

[36] P. Anderson, *The English in Western India*, p. 337.

[37] Boone's acting predecessor in office.

[38] *Home Misc. Series*, 332, p. 306. Boone to Woolley, 12 Jan. 1715.

[39] Ibid. Boone to Woolley, 5 Mar. 1715-16.

[40] Ibid., Boone to Woolley, 20 Mar. 1715-16.

[41] Ovington, op. cit., p. 87.

[42] *Home Misc. Series*, 332, p. 234. Strutt to Woolley, 13 Jan. 1715. See also *Bombay Letters Received*, I, 29 Jan. 1722-3, para. 99, and Phipps to Woolley, 31 May 1714 (*Home Misc. Series*, 332, pp. 241-2).

[43] *Home Misc. Series*, 332. Boone to Woolley, 12 Jan. 1715.

[44] Ibid., p. 571. *Representation of the Maratha Invasion of Portuguese Territory and the State of Bombay relating thereto*, para. 42.

[45] Add. MSS. 29,178, p. 279. Palmer to Hastings, 10 Oct. 1802.

[46] *Home Misc. Series*, 41, p. 62. Duncan to Ross, 2 June 1797.

[47] Niebuhr, op. cit., II, p. 3.

[48] J. Forbes, *Oriental Memoirs*, I, p. 151.

[49] Mrs. Maria Graham, *Journal of a Residence in India*, p. 23.

[50] Forbes, op. cit., I, p. 151.

[51] Niebuhr, Forbes and Valentia, who all were acquainted with Madras, noticed the contrast; Ovington, Parsons and Rennell, who were not, called them handsome, etc.

[52] Niebuhr, op. cit., I, p. 3.

[53] Valentia, op. cit., II, p. 183.

[54] Grose, op. cit., I, p. 52.

[55] Niebuhr, op. cit., p. 3.

[56] Forbes, op. cit., I, pp. 155-6; Niebuhr, op. cit., p. 37; Macdonald, *Travels*, pp. 187, 214.

[57] Edwardes, op. cit., p. 208.

58 Macdonald, op. cit., p. 271.

59 Ibid., p. 214, and Mrs. Graham, op. cit., p. 30.

60 *Home Misc. Series*, 765, p. 104, 20 Apr. 1761.

61 Le Couteur, *Letters from India* (1790), p. 103.

62 Macdonald, op. cit., pp. 188-9.

63 Ives, *Voyage to India* (1745), p. 34. In 1774 they were still used by the Chief of Surat (Parsons, *Travels*, p. 254).

64 Mrs. Graham, op. cit., p. 4.

65 Cordiner, op. cit., p. 63. In 1798 carts were drawn either by oxen or horses.

66 Except the 'Pariah' Christians who became Portuguese by putting on a 'Christian hat' or as many European clothes as they could afford.

67 Parsons, op. cit., p. 261.

68 Ibid., p. 215. Parsons was 'bred to the navy' and his opinion is therefore the more valuable.

69 Mrs. Graham, op. cit., p. 42.

70 *Bombay Despatches*, IV (Court to Bombay, 7 Apr. 1772, para. 2), p. 374.

71 Ibid., 5 Apr. 1776, para. 45, p. 936.

72 Mrs. Graham, op. cit., p. 42.

73 *Home Misc. Series*, 332, p. 571 (*Representation on the State of Bombay*, 1737, para. 47).

74 Ives, op. cit., p. 31.

75 *Home Misc. Series*, 765, p. 110 (Major Rennell's Diary, 28 Aug. 1761).

76 Parsons, op. cit., pp. 216-17.

77 Mrs. Graham, op. cit., p. 2.

78 Forbes, op. cit., I, p. 151.

79 Mrs. Graham, op. cit., p. 10.

80 Edwardes, op. cit., p. 231. The lighthouse was built in 1772.

81 Mrs. Graham, op. cit., p. 8.

82 Parsons, op. cit., p. 217.

83 Macdonald, op. cit., p. 192 seq. A letter to Hastings (8 Nov. 1786) mentions a man who applied for permission to go there from Bengal (add. MSS. 29,170).

84 Niebuhr, op. cit., p. 5.

85 Strength of forces in 1737 (Edwardes, op. cit., p. 144).

European soldiers	449	There were thus 748
,, sailors	299	Europeans, while another
Topasses	817	115 were stationed at
Sepoys	943	Mocha.

1764. Niebuhr, op. cit., II, p. 4, says there were seventeen companies of infantry and three of artillery composed of Europeans and some Topasses. Each company had 100-120 men. There were also 300 sepoys in Indian dress. The army was very cosmopolitan. In it Niebuhr found a Livonian, a Pole, some Swiss, Dutch, Swedes and Germans. The fate of the officers was various. Some were killed in the wars, some behaved as if in Europe and died quickly, some became merchants, a few returned to England with a fortune, and others disgruntled because they could not easily make one.

1767. *Bombay Despatches*, 4, p. 753, 12 Apr. 1755, para. 30 speaks of 1,639 European Infantry and 322 artillerymen.

1775. Ibid., p. 749, para 28, a reduction to 1,200 infantry and 312 artillery was ordered.

86 So called by J. Macdonald.

[87] These details are taken from the *European Inhabitants* series of records, V.

[88] Thus Innes Munro (op. cit.), says that Sir E. Hughes' fleet was largely manned by lascars and Mrs. Graham also comments on them.

[89] Given by Edwardes, op. cit., p. 144.

[90] *Bombay Despatches*, IV, 12 Apr. 1775, paras. 28 and 30.

[91] *Bombay Letters*, IV, 21 Mar. 1776, para 85.

[92] *Bombay Despatches*, 12 Apr. 1775, para. 18.

[93] Cordiner, op. cit., p. 71.

[94] Forbes, op. cit., I, pp. 156-7; IV, p. 214.

[95] The change took place in Bombay between 1783 and 1800 (see Forbes, IV, and Mrs. Graham, p. 29).

[96] Forbes, op. cit., IV, p. 214.

[97] Macdonald, op. cit., p. 190.

[98] Ibid., p. 188.

[99] *Bombay Despatches*, 28 Apr. 1773, para. 25 and *Bombay Letters*, 22 Dec. 1771, para. 120 give two cases of special pensions being given to widows of Company's servants, who not being Europeans could not benefit by the Military Fund in England.

[100] Mrs. Graham, op. cit., p. 28.

[101] Forbes, op. cit., IV, p. 239.

[102] Ovington, op. cit., p. 299.

[103] Niebuhr, op. cit., p. 24.

Chapter V

[1] India Office, *Home Miscellaneous Series*, 332, p. 261, Letter of Strutt to Thos. Woolley, 1715.

[2] Ibid., p. 293.

[3] A. Wright and W. L. Sclater, *Sterne's Eliza*, p. 161. Letter from Rajahmundry, 20 Jan. 1774.

[4] Wright and Sclater, op. cit., pp. 95-6. Letter 10 of Lord Baring's Collection, June 1769.

[5] *Cornwallis Correspondence*, II, pp. 203-4.

[6] For this work see Hunter, *Annals of Rural Bengal*.

[7] Hunter in his *Annals of Rural Bengal* gives a vivid picture of mofussil life with its twin deities of Commercial Resident and Collector.

[8] *Cornwallis Correspondence*, I, p. 282.

[9] See Chapter VII on this point.

[10] By the Treaty of Fyzabad 1775, two cantonments were established in Oudh. In 1778 one of these was moved to Cawnpore. The other was at Fatehgarh.

[11] S. C. Hill, *General Claud Martin*, p. 90.

[12] Twining, *Travels* 1794, p. 311.

[13] Ibid., pp. 312-13.

[14] Excluding the reign of the claimant Wazir Ali, 1797-8.

[15] Valentia, *Travels*, I, p. 173.

[16] *Bengal Obituary*, pp. 269-71.

[17] The details of his financial operations are all taken from Hill, op. cit., pp. 94-106.

[18] Hill, op. cit., p. 100. Dr. Blane's case (quoted by him) is mentioned in *M. Abu Taleb Khan's Travels*, p. 94. 'For two glass tazias with chandeliers and shades and other appointments, one to be green and the other red. The price was fixed at a lakh of rupees.'

[19] The finances of Moghul India were organized on a system of advances from the state to meet current expenses. These were recovered at death from the property of the deceased, which was attached with the Imperial seal.

[20] Lord Valentia disliked it; Von Orlich in 1843 was very impressed, while Erskine Perry in 1855 thought it very eccentric. The palace must in fact horrify the purist by its jumble of styles, but achieves a certain effect by its mass and proportions (Hill, op. cit., p. 120).

[21] Hill, op. cit., p. 72.

[22] Twining, *Travels*, pp. 308-9. The complete passage is too long for reproduction here. The best description, with a plate, of the Gumti house is reprinted in *Bengal Past and Present*, II, p. 277, from *The European Magazine*, XVII (Jan.-June 1790), pp. 86-7 entitled 'An Account of Col. Martin's Villa, near Lucknow in the East Indies'.

[23] *Life of Lord Teignmouth*, I, p. 409, 26 Feb. 1797.

[24] This was a well known Moghul hot weather device. The apartment was known as the 'Taikhana'.

[25] Hill, op. cit., p. 91. Martin's Will is printed in the *Calcutta Gazette* of 2 Oct. 1800. Most of the slaves were freed and the concubines provided for. His reasons for taking his concubines into his zenana are interesting as showing not only the current racialism but also his opinion of the type of European too common in the vicinity of Indian courts. He said 'he could not drive them into marriage with natives they despised, or into connections with Europeans whom he himself looked upon with contempt' (Hill, p. 134).

[26] Twining, *Travels*, p. 309.

[27] Innes Munro, *Narrative of Military Operations on the Coromandel Coast*, 1780, p. 186. Not only the families of officers but also those of sepoys often went on campaigns—op. cit., pp. 190-91.

[28] I have only seen this last statement made by one writer; he was certainly prejudiced against the Government of the day, and this statement must therefore be treated with caution.

[29] Blakiston, *Twelve Years Military Adventure in Hindustan* (1802-14), I, pp. 68-9.

[30] Ibid., p. 253-4. It is fair to add that this was reckoned an outfit for one in easy circumstances. Yet its effect on the mobility of the army would be the same (I, p. 65). Camels were first used in place of bullocks in N. India at this time.

[31] Ibid, pp. 63-5.

[32] Innes Munro, op. cit., p. 197. This applies to the south only.

[33] Monson and Gower, *Memoirs of Capt. G. Elers*, 1797-1807, p. 63. He gives the temperature of the officers' tents as from 90° to 100° in the hot weather.

[34] Innes Munro, op. cit., pp. 198-9.

[35] Blakiston, op. cit., I, p. 115.

[36] Innes Munro, op. cit., pp. 189-90.

[37] Ibid., p. 202.

[38] Monson and Gower, op. cit., pp. 73-4.

[39] Ibid., p. 61.

[40] Ibid.

[41] Blakiston, op. cit., p. 74; Innes Munro, op. cit., p. 87 (1780).

[42] Monson and Gower, op. cit., p. 60.

[43] Blakiston, op. cit., I, pp. 40-1.

[44] The author of *Fifteen Years in India* describes a dinner—much like that given above—in which the party broke up at twelve, except 'certain thirsty souls who remained enjoying their bottle and well-spiced devils till the generale beat at four o'clock' (p. 40).

[45] Hickey, *Memoirs*, II, p. 131.

[46] Pester John, *War and Sport in India* (ed. Devenish), p. 58.

[47] Ibid., pp. 121, 446.

[48] Monson and Gower, op. cit., p. 121.

[49] Tennant, *Indian Recreations*, I, pp. 322-7.

[50] Tennant, op. cit., I, p. 325. Glass was now used for all the houses, and was even affixed on the windward doors of tents.

[51] It was the same influence which was doubtless responsible for the distinctly improved tone of the descriptions of military life after 1785. Compare Innes Munro's account in 1780 with Capt. Elers' *Memoirs* (also in the south) from 1797 to 1807.

[52] Pester John, op. cit. (22 May 1803), p. 117 (Devenish).

[53] Ibid., p. 95.

[54] Ibid., p. 435.

[55] L. H. Thornton, *Light and Shade in Bygone India*, pp. 22-3, quoting Forbes, *Oriental Memoirs*, III, pp. 90-5.

[56] Sir M. Hunter, *Journal*, pp. 66-7 (1784).

[57] Hunts organized from Calcutta were of similar elaboration and destructiveness. Forbes, *Oriental Memoirs*, II, p. 489 mentions a tiger shoot with thirty elephants with a party including ladies and the painter, Zoffany. At another party near Plassey in 1785 (IV, 99) the following were shot, '1 royal tiger, 6 wild buffaloes, 156 hogdeer, 25 wild hares, 150 brace of partridges and floricans, with quails, duck, snipe and smaller birds in abundance'.

[58] Hunter, op. cit., pp. 64-5.

[59] Thornton, op. cit., p. 26.

[60] Hunter, op. cit., p. 66.

[61] Ibid., pp. 67-8. See also Wright and Sclater, *Sterne's Eliza*, pp. 117-20 (Letter 12, Lord Basing's Collection 1771)—for the same practice at Surat. This was a characteristic Moghul sport (like big game shooting with elephants and beaters). In 1798 Wellesley took over Tipu Sultan's hunting establishment including several trained leopards and cheetahs (Monson and Gower, op. cit., p. 123).

[62] Hunter, op. cit., p. 69.

[63] Williamson, *East India Vade Mecum*, II, p. 194.

[64] Pester John, op. cit. (1803), p. 24 seq.

[65] Ibid., p. 29.

[66] Ibid., p. 112.

[67] Tennant, op. cit. (1803), II, pp. 144-145.

[68] Sir G. Watt, *Dictionary of Economic Products of India*, IV, p. 393 seq.

[69] Govt. Circular, 13 July 1810 (quoted by R. C. Dutt, *Economic History of India* (1907), p. 266). Several individual cases of indigo planters are found in the series of *Low Europeans* (summarized in vol. 25) in the India Office Records.

[70] Quoted by R. C. Dutt, from Minutes of Evidence, etc. (1813), op. cit., pp. 265-6. 'I find no difference in traders, whether their habits are quiet or not when they quit this country; they are very seldom quiet when they find themselves among an unresisting people over whom they can exercise their authority, for every trader going into India is considered as some person connected with the Government. I have heard that within two or three years, I think in Bengal in 1810, private traders, indigo merchants, have put inhabitants of the country in the stocks, have assembled their followers and given battle

to each other, and that many have been wounded'.—Sir Thomas Munro's Evidence, p. 138.

71 R. C. Dutt, op. cit., pp. 279-80 (abstract of evidence before the Commons Committee of 1832 and of the Reports of 1830, 1830-31 and 1831).

72 Kaye, *Life of Lord Metcalfe*, Appendix; C. C. Grey and H. L. O. Garrett, *European Adventurers in Northern India*.

73 Hugh Pearse, *The Hearsays*, p. 53.

74 Ibid., p. 54 at Khasganj, near Agra. For details of the family, see Debrett, *Peerage*, under 'Gardner'.

75 Ibid., p. 64.

76 Twining, *Travels*, p. 275.

77 Ibid., p. 228. In 1803 he married the daughter of the Marquis d'Osmond, and retired to Chambèry in Savoy.

78 Now the seat of the Nawabs of Karnal. He died at the Shalimar Bagh, six miles from Delhi, where Aurangzeb first crowned himself. The garden is now in ruins. An application for a pension from one of his mistresses appears in the Delhi Residency Records.

79 Jacquemmont, *Letters from India*, II, p. 254. 'He is half Asiatic in his habits but in other respects a Scottish highlander and excellent man, with great originality of thought, a metaphysician to boot, and enjoying the best possible reputation of being a country bear.'

80 Blakiston, op. cit., I, p. 144.

81 e.g. soldiers taken by Hyder. Examples of this class are given by Garrett and Grey, op. cit.

Chapter VI

1 Kindersley, *Letters from the East Indies*, 1777, p. 291.

2 Williamson, *East India Vade Mecum*, I, p. 177.

3 S. C. Grier, op. cit., p. 364.

4 *Life of Lord Teignmouth*, I, p. 133 (21 Jan. 1787).

5 *Cornwallis Correspondence*, I, p. 401.

6 *Wellesley Papers*, I, p. 83 (Morrington to Grenville, 18 Nov. 1798).

7 Bernier, op. cit., p. 247.

8 Fryer, *New Account of East India and Persia*, Hakluyt Soc. 1909, I, p. 87.

9 Ovington, op. cit., p. 135.

10 Hickey, *Memoirs*, III, p. 268.

11 Mrs. Graham, *Journal of a Residence in India* (2nd ed. 1813), p. 30.

12 de Grandpré, *Voyage in the Indian Ocean and to Bengal* (Eng. trans. 1814), p. 154.

13 Maria, Lady Nugent, *Journal of a Residence in India*, 1811-15 (London, 1839), I, p. 122.

14 Williamson, op. cit., I, p. 214.

15 *Factory Miscellaneous Records*, 23, p. 24.

16 Niebuhr, *Journal of Travels to Arabia and the East* (French Trans. 1780).

17 Wright and Sclater, *Sterne's Eliza* (London, 1922), p. 24.

18 Williamson, op. cit., I, p. 226.

19 A. Parsons, *Travels in Asia and Africa* (London, 1808), p. 258.

[20] Williamson, op., cit. I, p. 227.

[21] J. S. Stavorinus, *Voyages to the East Indies*, 1768-78 (London, 1798), I, p. 145.

[22] Williamson, op. cit., I, p. 501.

[23] de Grandpré, op. cit., p. 155.

[24] Hickey, *Memoirs*, II, p. 136.

[25] Blakiston, op. cit., I, p. 43.

[26] See *Hobson-Jobson* (ed. 1903), art. on the Hookah.

[27] G. Elers, *Memoirs*, p. 106.

[28] Ibid., p. 153.

[29] Mrs. Graham, op. cit.

[30] Edwardes, *Rise of Bombay*, p. 122.

[31] Ovington, op. cit., p. 204.

[32] Symson, *A New Voyage to the East Indies*, p. 56.

[33] Ibid., p. 38-40.

[34] Sieur Luillier, *A Voyage to the East Indies* (ed. 1720), p. 245.

[35] Niebuhr, op. cit., II, p. 3.

[36] *Home Miscellaneous Series*, 765, p. 153 (Topham to Burrington 22 Sept. 1765).

[37] Innes Munro, op. cit., p. 65.

[38] Ives, op. cit., p. 448.

[39] Ibid., p. 445.

[40] J. Lind, *An Essay on Diseases* (London, 1768), p. 79-81.

[41] Ibid., p. 127-31.

[42] Ibid., p. 132.

[43] Ibid., p. 140.

[44] J. Johnson, *Oriental Voyages*, p. 93-4 (note).

[45] Castellani and Chambers, *Manual of Tropical Medicine* (ed. 1910), pp. 7-8.

[46] F. H. Garrison, *History of Medicine* (ed. 1917), p. 370.

[47] Castellani and Chambers, op. cit., p. 8.

[48] Garrison, op. cit., p. 367.

[49] Ibid., p. 362 and 364.

[50] Ibid., p. 373-6.

[51] Stavorinus, op. cit., I, p. 452.

[52] Williamson, op. cit., I, p. 470.

[53] J. Taylor, *Travels in India*, II, p. 100.

CHAPTER VII

[1] Richter, *History of Missions in India*, p. 69.

[2] Abbé Dubois, op. cit., p. 12.

[3] Anderson, *English in Western India*, p. 336.

[4] Penny, *Church in Madras*, I, p. 346.

[5] Ibid., p. 139 ; Lambeth Palace Library MSS., 141, 95.

[6] Penny, op. cit., I, p. 346.

7 Of Indian Christians there were the Jacobite Syrian Church of Travancore which had broken away from Rome with the decline of the Portuguese, the branch of the Syrian Church which continued in communion with Rome, and a body of Nestorian Christians consisting of Syrian Christians who had never submitted to Rome. There were in addition Armenian Christians who had their own churches in the settlement towns. Dutch missionary efforts were chiefly confined to Ceylon, where the chief relic of their work is the 'Burgher' or mixed community. There is to-day a Dutch Calvinist Church in Colombo; the services are in English, because the community has adopted that language since the English occupation. The Travancore Christians were isolated and stagnant; they seem to have exercised little influence on India as a whole. A description of their condition at the beginning of the nineteenth century is given by Claudius Buchanan in his *Christian Researches in Asia.*

8 £50 salary and £50 gratuity for good behaviour.

9 Yule, *Hedges' Diary*, II, p. 232.

10 H. B. Hyde, *Parochial Annals of Bengal*, pp. 75-6.

11 Penny, op. cit., I, p. 164.

12 Ibid., I, p. 359. The Junior Chaplain had a special allowance of £100 to support his school work.

13 The cases of two chaplains who were dismissed for trading illustrate the position. John Evans, dismissed in 1691-2 and later Bishop of Bangor and Meath, had mixed himself up in the intrigues of the free merchant opposition to the Company of that time, and Charles Long of Madras was first suspended in 1720 by the Madras Council for refusing to go to Fort St. David, and dismissed by the Directors in 1721 because they had private information that he was interfering in the Europe trade. Private trade with Europe was for a chaplain, as for other Company's servants, forbidden, but elsewhere it was at most an indiscretion which did not become serious unless it led to interference with his clerical duties. For the Rev. Charles Long, see Penny, *The Church in Madras*, I, pp. 140-51, and Love, op. cit., II, p. 181, for Rev. John Evans, see Penny, op. cit., I, p. 666, and Hyde, op. cit., pp. 19-21. There are references to the private trade of chaplains (as matters of routine business) in 1708 and 1710—the Rev. Benj. Adams (Hyde, op. cit., p. 53), 1717—the Rev. W. Steavenson *Public Consultations*, 48, 8 April 1717). There are other references to the practice in wills. For the legal aspect, see H. W. Cripps, *Law Relating to Church and Clergy* (7th ed. 1921), pp. 92-5.

14 Penny, op. cit., I, p. 380. A good case of this occurred in 1793, when the new regulations fixing his salary at 165 pagodas a year, which was a reduction, were interpreted by the Governor as being an addition to the old basic rate of £100 a year.

15 Lockyer, op. cit.

16 Hyde, op. cit. The Church at Calcutta was consecrated in 1709 and destroyed in 1756.

17 Forbes, op. cit., III, p. 32.

18 Dubois, op. cit., p. 17.

19 Penny, op. cit., I, p. 561.

20 The chaplains were librarians at Madras until the library was dispersed on its capture by the French (Penny, op. cit., I, p. 147). See also the books of the chaplain Staveley (1762); Hyde, op. cit., pp. 1-9.

21 Penny, op. cit., I, p. 290. They were nominated by Simeon and Grant and were the four Bengal chaplains, Brown, Corrie, Parson and Martyn, and Marmaduke Thompson at Madras. The reform in Calcutta, however, really began with Chaplain Owen.

22 Hamilton, op. cit., II, p. 10.

23 See the Rev. H. B. Hyde's defence of the Rev. John Evans (dismissed for private trading 1691-2, who was said by Salmon [1704] to have made enough

to ' purchase a bishoprick and sit in the English House of Lords on his return ') and the Rev. F. Penny's treatment of the case of the Rev. St. J. Browne, dismissed for killing his servant in a passion. He calls it ' an unfortunate error of judgement '.

24 Penny, I, pp. 400-5.

25 Ibid., p. 355.

26 Wheeler, *Madras in the Olden Time*, II, pp. 225-7.

27 Forrest, *Clive*, I, p. 82.

28 Hyde, op. cit., p. 260.

29 Forrest, op. cit., I, p. 21.

30 Penny, op. cit., I, p. 284.

31 Wheeler, op. cit., III, p. 35.

32 Penny, I, pp. 284-5.

33 Ibid., I, p. 248. *Madras Consultations*, 19 Jan. 1718. Rennell (26 Oct. 1765), *Home Misc. Series*, 198, p. 276, records hearing a sermon from Tillotson (No. 29) on the text ' Can the Ethiopian change his skin ? ' He says ' it was a very excellent sermon and was intended to reprove Col. Fletcher whose ill habits make him hated '.

34 S. Goldburne, *Hartly House Calcutta*, p. 25.

35 Seton-Kerr, *Selections from the Calcutta Gazette*, I, p. 209.

36 Hyde, op. cit., p. 194 (quoted from the *Calcutta Gazette*).

37 C. Simeon, *Memoir of Rev. D. Brown*, p. 32.

38 Simeon, op. cit., p. 32.

39 Penny, op. cit., I, p. 418. From 24 in ten years to nearly 50.

40 Penny, op. cit., I, p. 551.

41 Blakiston, op. cit., I, p. 276, illustrates this by his anecdote of the chaplain who excused himself from a rubber of whist ' because he had a d—d soldier to bury '.

42 The Company may be said to have entertained a vague idea of mission work itself in 1700. The Charter of 1698 provided that every Chaplain was to learn Portuguese in one year and the language of the country ' the better to enable them to instruct the Gentoos that should be the servants or slaves of the same Campany, or of their agents, in the Protestant religion '. The Rev. G. Lewis conducted his Portuguese School with this purpose, but no work among Indians developed.

43 Richter, op. cit., pp. 72-3, and Dubois, op. cit., p. 61.

44 Ibid., p. 60 seq. Manucci, *Storia Do Mogor*, III, p. 320 seq. gives further details and a circumstantial account of the collapse of the mission. His bias against the Pondicherry Jesuits is to a large extent supported by A. R. Pillai, who had no interest in the matter.

45 Manucci, op. cit., III, p. 231 seq. The Jesuits were called Romapuri and learned Sanskrit and Tamil in Malabar before going to Madura as Brahmins.

46 Ibid., III, pp. 343-5. He mentions the adoption of Hindu marriage customs, nocturnal processions and the use of Hindu caste marks.

47 Ibid., III, p. 334. He says the common people thought the Jesuits and the Capuchins had different gods.

48 Ibid., IV, pp. 381-2.

49 Dubois, op. cit., p. 69.

50 Penny, op. cit., I, p. 229.

51 Fryer, *A New Account of East India and Persia*, I, p. 38.

52 Penny, op. cit., I, pp. 465-6 (*Madras Consultations*, 30 Oct. 1787).

53 Dubois, op. cit., p. 75.

54 Dodwell, *Nabobs of Madras*, p. 201.

55 Letter to Fort St. George, 24 Dec. 1675, para. 73.

56 Love, op. cit., II, p. 46.

57 Despatch to Bengal, 3 March 1756, para. 46.

58 *European Inhabitants* (Madras), III, A.

59 Penny, op. cit., I, p. 79 (*Madras Consultations*, 22 March 1680).

60 Ibid., p. 228 and Wheeler, *Madras in the Olden Time*, II, p. 40-1.

61 Ibid., p. 234 (*Madras Consultations*, April and May 1719).

62 Prof. Dodwell (*Nabobs of Madras*, pp. 202-3) quotes some cases of this consent being refused, but these refusals were social in motive and indeed racial. It shows the growth of racial feelings since the regulations of 1687, which *encouraged* intermarriage and offered a gratuity for every child born. This still continued in 1740 (*Madras Records*, vol. 70). *Consultations*, 10 March 1739 (Penny, op. cit., I, p. 107).

63 e.g., in 1715 Governor Harrison formally exonerated the Capuchins from various Jesuit attacks, specially that of trading. (Love, op. cit., II, pp. 49-50.)

64 Love, op. cit., II, p. 45.

65 Hyde, op. cit., pp. 116 and 121.

66 Penny, op. cit., I, p. 337.

67 Wilson, *Madras Army*, I, p. 41 (Artillery Regulation, December 1747. Paras. 26 and 33).

68 Sargent, *Memoir of the Rev. H. Martyn*, p. 298.

69 There are a few exceptions to this. There is a reference to 'Black Canarese Priests' in Padre Milton's Letter, 26 Oct. 1712 (*Home Misc. Series*, 59). Dubois says that they were not capable of carrying on alone, which was probably because they had not been properly educated or drawn from the right class. This is confirmed by Fra. P. de San Bartolomeo (*Voyage to the East Indies*, p. 200), who said that 'Black Priests' were 'proud and ignorant and unfit for responsibility'.

70 Twining, *Travels*, pp. 178 and 204-5. The meeting was in 1793-4.

71 Richter, op. cit., p. 104 seq.

72 On the recommendation of Chaplain Stevenson of Madras, 1714-18.

73 Penny, op. cit., I, p. 193.

74 Love, op. cit., III, pp. 431-2.

75 *Bengal Obituary*, pp. 34-5.

76 Penny, op. cit., I, p. 194 (*Home Misc. Series*, 59).

77 J. Page, *Swartz of Tanjore*, pp. 75-6.

78 Martyn, *Journal*, I, p. 449 gives a good description of this.

79 Pearson, *Memoirs of C. F. Swartz*, pp. 74-5 (in a letter to the Rev. G. A. Francke, 6 Oct. 1768).

80 Ibid., p. 239 (Letter to Dr. Knapp, 27 Jan. 1771).

81 This was not typical of all missionaries.

82 Page, op. cit., p. 195. This was related to Bishop Wilson by Kohloff at a dinner and repeated in his Charge of 1839.

83 Ibid., pp. 75-6.

84 Martyn, *Journal*, I, pp. 512-13.

85 *Bengal Obituary*, pp. 34-5.

86 Richter, op. cit., p. 124. They also worked at Serampore from 1777-91.

87 Carey, *William Carey*, p. 97. See also his life by C. B. Lewis.

88 Ibid., p. 145.

89 He was joined by Fountain as a lay helper in 1797. The only other English missionary was the first arrival of the London Missionary Society.

90 Carey, op. cit., pp. 178-9 (Diary of Marshman, 1 Dec. 1799).

[91] Richter, op. cit., pp. 124-5.

[92] Fort St. George to the Court, 20 Aug. 1711, para. 172 (*Home Misc. Series*, 46, p. 517. MSS. Collections for Bruce's Annals).

[93] *Home Misc. Series*, 46, p. 331 (Despatch of 1 April 1708).

[94] Wheeler, op. cit., II, p. 177. Ziegenbalg was given a passage from Madras for this reason.

[95] Schultze, in Madras from 1728, was the first to be wholly supported by the S.P.C.K.

[96] Wheeler, op. cit., II, p. 178.

[97] *Home Misc. Series*, 59. The stores included money, books, stationery, printing requirements, beer, wine, cheeses, hour glasses, spectacles, etc.

[98] Manucci, *Storia do Mogor*, IV, p. 112.

[99] Ibid., III, p. 197.

[100] *Cornwallis Correspondence*, I, p. 398.

[101] Valentia, *Travels*, I, p. 364.

[102] Carey, op. cit., p. 143.

[103] Penny, op. cit., I, pp. 497-8 ; Coupland, *Life of Wilberforce*, p. 383.

[104] Simeon, op. cit., pp. 54-5.

[105] Sergeant, op. cit., p. 258.

[106] Martyn, *Journal*, II, p. 32 (17 March 1807).

[107] Ibid., I, p. 449 (20 May 1806).

[108] These details are taken from the introduction to his *Remains*.

[109] Pearson, op. cit., p. 145.

[110] Pearson, op. cit., I, p. 155.

[111] Ibid., p. 143.

[112] Rev. Dr. Kerr, a company's chaplain, Page, *Swartz of Tanjore*, p. 190.

[113] Pearson, op. cit., p. 314.

[114] Ibid., p. 43.

[115] Ibid., p. 264.

[116] Ibid., p. 120.

[117] Ibid., p. 113.

[118] Ibid., p. 316.

[119] Grose, *Voyage to the East Indies*, I, p. 262.

[120] Pearson, op. cit., I, p. 347 (Letters to S.P.C.K., 22 Feb. 1797).

[121] Ibid., p. 104 ; cf. e.g., Martyn, *Journal*, I, pp. 443, 448, 452.

[122] Martyn, *Journal*, II, pp. 32, 499.

[123] Pearson, op. cit., p. 142.

Chapter VIII

[1] Mrs. Graham, *Journal of a Residence in India*, p. 174.

[2] Visits of Moghul Governors to Madras like that of Da'ud Khan in Gov. Pitt's time. See chap. I.

[3] The Rev. G. Lewis, see chap. I, p. 18. He never actually went, as the embassy, proposed in 1708, did not reach Delhi until 1714, when he had left India (*Cambridge History of India*, V, p. 111).

[4] Ananda Ranga Pillai, *Diary* (ed. Dodwell and others).

[5] Ibid., X, p. 220.

6 Ibid., I, p. 26. M. Delorme 'made no distinction between rich and poor, never took a bribe, and treated the native on a footing of equality with the European'.

7 Ovington, op. cit., pp. 143-4.

8 Ibid., p. 230.

9 e.g. Ibid.; Symson, *A New Voyage to the East Indies*, 1702, p. 43; Sieur Luillier, *Voyage to East Indies*, 1720, p. 285; Grose, *Voyage to East Indies*, 1774, I, p. 105; Niebuhr, *Journal of Travels to Arabia and the East*, 2 vols., 1780, p. 13.

10 Symson, op. cit., pp. 46-7.

11 Ovington, op. cit., p. 235.

12 See chap. I, p. 18.

13 Forbes, op. cit., III, p. 32; Blakiston, op. cit., I, p. 276.

14 Fryer, op. cit., p. 38. At Masulipatam 'the English keep their fashion tho' cloth'd in white'.

15 *The Diaries of Streynsham Master.*

16 *Hobson-Jobson* (ed. 1903), p. 65. Letter from an Old Country Captain in the *India Gazette*, 24 Feb. 1781.

17 D. Dewar, *Handbook to the Records of the U.P.*, pp. 368-9 (Circulars for Superior Courts, 1826-41). This was specially directed against the Hon. F. J. Shore (see Dewar's *Bygone India*). For another instance in the Agra Records, see p. 198 in the *Handbook*.

18 Fran. Pelsaert, *Remonstrantie*.

19 Manucci, op. cit.

20 e.g. Those of Sir F. Norris to Aurangzeb's court and of Surman to Farruksiyar.

21 See chap. III, pp. 78-80.

22 Love, op. cit., III, p. 224.

23 *Memoirs of Asiaticus.*

24 Johnson, *Oriental Voyages*, p. 74. No European was allowed to enter the Palace, so that a wag wrote over the door, 'the way to Europe'.

25 Ives, *A Voyage to India*, pp. 70-1.

26 Innes Munro, op. cit., p. 62.

27 Add. MSS. 29,170, p. 15 (Grattan to Warren Hastings, 18 Mar. 1786).

28 Hill, *Catalogue of Orme MSS.*, II, p. 57 (MS. No. 28, 11 [10], pp. 217-227 Orme to Payne, 17 Nov. 1757).

29 D'Oyley, Williamson and Blagdon, *The European in India*. Letterpress to Pl. XX.

30 Elers, *Memoirs*, p. 78.

31 D'Oyley, Williamson and Blagdon, ibid.

32 Blakiston, op. cit., I, pp. 211-12.

33 Shore, *Notes on Indian Affairs*, II, p. 108.

34 Ibid., I, p. 106.

35 Hickey, *Memoirs*, pp. 236-7 (the case of Potts).

36 *Cornwallis Correspondence*, I, p. 529.

37 *Home Misc. Series*, 68, pp. 473-4 and 479-80.

38 Valentia, op. cit., I, p. 173.

39 Twining, op. cit., pp. 167-8.

40 For a fuller description of Lucknow, see supra p. 140-4.

41 Grier, *Hastings' Letters to His Wife.*

42 Valentia, op. cit., I, p. 143.

43 See chap. III.

44 Grier, op. cit., p. 262, gives one example.

[45] e.g. see the *Journals* of Lady Nugent (1811-15) and Mrs. Fenton 1826-30).

[46] Symson, op. cit., p. 63.

[47] Macdonald, op. cit., p. 204.

[48] Parsons, op. cit., p. 261. In Surat thirty large ships were owned by Parsis and manned by English captains and officers.

[49] Macintosh, op. cit., II, pp. 36 and 40.

[50] Valentia, op. cit., I, pp. 187-8.

[51] Mrs. Graham, *Journal of a Residence in India*, pp. 42-3.

[52] Macdonald, op. cit., p. 211.

[53] Blakiston, op. cit., I, p. 111.

[54] He founded the Calcutta Madrasah in 1781.

[55] Carey, op. cit., I, pp. 308-14, has printed several examples of these.

[56] Grier, op. cit., p. 276.

[57] Add. MSS. 29,178, p. 280 (Gen. Palmer to Warren Hastings, 10 Oct. 1802).

[58] Add. MSS. 29,173, p. 338 (Turner to Hastings, 24 Mar. 1795).

[59] Add. MSS. 29,171, p. 372 (Palmer to Hastings, 13 Aug. 1789).

[60] Tafazzul Husain Khan, Minister of Oudh, and Vakil in Calcutta.

[61] Add. MSS. 29,170, p. 37 (Thomson to Hastings). Here the intimacy goes far enough for joking.

[62] Add. MSS. 29,178, p. 63 (Palmer to Hastings, 10 July 1801).

[63] *Cornwallis Correspondence*, I, p. 282. On the very next page he suspects that every Collector was deeply engaged in private trade.

[64] Add. MSS. 29,170, p. 298 (Larkins to Hastings, 20 Nov. 1786), and ibid., p. 346 (Pearse to Hastings, 8 Jan. 1787).

[65] Add. MSS. 29,172 (Palmer to Hastings, p. 220, 19 Sept. 1786), p. 257 (8 Nov. 1786), p. 274 (14 Nov. 1786), and p. 276.

[66] *Cornwallis Correspondence*, I, p. 529.

[67] Ibid., II, pp. 201-2.

[68] Add. MSS. 29,170, p. 224 (Palmer to Hastings, 19 Sept. 1786).

[69] Ibid., p. 257 (Palmer to Hastings, Nov. 1786). 'Shore has many strong prejudices, and a universal one against the Natives of India.'

[70] Shore, op. cit., II, p. 500. When this was the tendency it is not surprising to find that Cornwallis had vigorously to assert the honour and importance of commissions with Indian equally with European regiments.

[71] Mirza Abu Taleb Khan in his *Travels* (ed. C. Stewart), pp. 51-2, gives a good instance of this attitude. See also the *Seir Mutaqherin*, III, pp. 161 and 170-1.

[72] Add. MSS. 29,178, p. 278 (Palmer to Hastings, 10 Oct. 1802).

[73] Williamson, op. cit., I, p. 347.

[74] Lady Nugent in her *Journal* (1809-13) gives an instance of the latter. In Devendranath Tagore's *Autobiography* (pp. 74-5) there is an instance of the former and of the jealousy it excited among the Bengalis.

[75] Mrs. Graham, op. cit., pp. 136, 139.

[76] Tennant, *Indian Recreations*, I, pp. 39-40. He adds: 'The dissipation of the Europeans is far more conspicuous than the insolence of the natives.'

[77] Williamson, op. cit., I, p. 336. The passage refers to the servant class of European women, who frequently broke their contracts in order to marry or to set up on their own.

[78] Shore, op. cit., II, p. 500. See the whole chapter for many examples of this state of things. Shore's memory reached back to the eighteenth century and his evidence is therefore that of an eye-witness.

[79] Ibid., p. 114.

[80] Ibid., p. 108.

[81] Ibid., p. 496.

[82] e.g. See Curzon, *British Government in India* for the scale and spirit of Wellesley's household. See also the Private Journals of the Marquess of Hastings.

[83] A good example is given in the *Hastings Correspondence* (Miss Peacock in Add. MSS. 29,170 and 29,171).

[84] e.g. the fashions of eating pan and smoking hookahs.

[85] For this see chap. III on the Later Settlements.

[86] For examples see Kaye, *History of the Sepoy Mutiny* and the *Life of Lord Canning*. For the soldier's attitude see E. Thompson, *The Other Side of the Medal*. Tannenbaum, *Darker Phases of the South* shows the same psychology at work in the United States.

[87] *Observations on India* (Anon.), p. 149.

[88] Mrs. Fenton, op. cit., p. 242.

[89] Martyn, *Journals*.

[90] Mrs. Fenton, op. cit., p. 82.

[91] Manucci, op. cit., III, p. 73; Hickey in his *Memoirs* gives examples of this.

[92] Grose, op. cit., I, pp. 28-74, was one of the first to notice that all Indians were not black.

[93] Macintosh, op. cit., II, p. 47, mentions a general Hindu complaint of the insolence of the common soldiers. See also the opinion of Swartz, Dubois and Cornwallis about them.

[94] See above, p. 59.

Chapter IX

[1] Williamson, *East India Vade Mecum*, I, p. 127.

[2] Lecky, *History of England in the Eighteenth Century* (ed. 1920), II, p. 155 quoted from Lockhart's *Life of Scott*, V, pp. 136, 137.

APPENDIX A

SKETCH OF THE POLITICAL HISTORY OF INDIA IN THE EIGHTEENTH CENTURY

At the opening of the eighteenth century the Moghul Empire, stretching from Madras to Kabul, administered by the tireless octogenarian Aurangzeb, seemed to the casual observer as strong as ever in its history. The kingdoms of the south had been annexed, the troublesome robbers of Maharastra were being hunted down in their hill fastnesses, the discontented Rajput chiefs did not seem to be a serious menace, and the English merchants, who had hoped to emancipate themselves from imperial control, had been firmly repressed. But the imposing façade of imperial power hid an internal decay which was sapping the empire from its foundations; like Aurangzeb himself the empire had lost the secret of renewing its youth and could only struggle on with ever increasing perplexity and decrepitude.

The Moghul Empire, as established by Akbar, had rested on three foundations—the Rajput alliance, the policy of toleration, and the willing obedience of both Hindus and Muslims. On these three pillars were raised the centralized administrative system which enabled the Emperor to hold together the vast area of India with the limited resources and communications of the time. Aurangzeb by his re-imposition of the 'jizya' tax (on non-Muslims) and the Maratha war had alienated both Rajputs and Hindus, and by his many campaigns impoverished the whole country. The empire, from being an embryo national state in which all classes could take an equal pride, reverted to the status of a military government by a minority community, which must inevitably collapse when subjected to any serious strain.

Aurangzeb was followed by no capable successor who might have restored the original conception of the empire, and the main interest of the first half of the eighteenth century is consequently the gradual break up of the empire. There follows a short period of political confusion, which ended with the emergence of four great military powers—the Maratha Confederacy, Mysore, the Sikhs and the East India Company.

The short revival of Moghul power represented by the crushing of the Sikhs in 1717 and the rule of the Sayyid brothers died away with their overthrow and the heedless incompetence of Mohammad Shah (1719-48). Unable to rule himself and unwilling to allow others to rule for him, the 'merry king' drifted from compromise to compromise until he handed the empire itself to Nadir Shah the Persian in 1739. Mohammad Shah was the Louis XVI of the Moghul Empire and he, more than any other single man, must bear the responsibility for its irredeemable ruin. In 1726 the Wazir Asaf Jah, disgusted with the Emperor's fickleness, retired to the Deccan provinces, there to become the first Nizam of Hyderabad. In 1738 the Marathas cut the empire in two by the annexation of Malwa (now the Maratha states of Gwalior and Indore) and in 1739 came the crowning blow of the invasion of Nadir Shah. Pusillanimity and treachery together lost the day at Karnal and led step by step to the humiliation of Delhi and the terror of its sack. This was the end of the empire as an effective ruling power in India; its end as a political institution was completed between 1750 and 1761 by Ghazi-ad-din Khan, whose unrestrained ambitions and tragic infatuation verified too completely the proverb 'Whom the gods doom to destruction they first deprive of reason'. In 1761 Afghans and Marathas fought over the prostrate body of the empire at Panipat while the Emperor was a fugitive in Behar.

Panipat deprived the Marathas of the succession to the empire, but the Afghans were too weak and unorganized ever to rule Hindustan themselves. They could do no more than make occasional destructive raids which increased the anarchy their first invasions had commenced. In Delhi itself the Moghuls lingered on for another twenty years as rulers of Delhi and Agra; their fortunes flared up in a last gleam of prosperity under the leadership of Mirza Najaf Khan until it was finally extinguished in blood and fire by the renegade chief Ghulam Kadir in 1788. The blinding of Shah Alam was a symbolic atrocity, for with his sight was finally extinguished the last traces of imperial power; his touching lament is the death song of the Moghul Empire. The Punjab, after being the playground of adventurers for thirty years, was at the end of the century restored to order by the genius of the Sikh chief Ranjit Singh.

The Persians struck the most fatal blow at the Moghul power, but it was the Marathas who inherited most of their power. Excluded by Panipat from the north, the Marathas advanced in the centre and south as the Moghuls retreated. By 1750 their dominions centred in Poona, stretched from the west to the Bay of Bengal, and from the banks of the Ganges to the borders of Mysore, they remained substantially united until 1772, but from that time competing claims to the Peshwaship and the rivalries of the great subordinate military chiefs, like Sindia and Holkar, gradually broke up their unity. The diplomacy of Nana Fadnavis held them together in a loose confederacy until 1800, but after his death the mutual jealousies of the five great Maratha chiefs enabled Lord Wellesley first to divide and then to defeat them in turn in the Maratha war of 1803.

In 1748, when the English and French first began to take an active part in Indian politics, India was divided between the Maratha Confederacy in the centre, the independent offshoots of the Moghul Empire represented by Oudh, Bengal, Hyderabad and the Carnatic, and the independent state of Mysore in the south, shortly to become formidable under the Muslim adventurer Hyder Ali and his son Tipu Sultan. There was a multiplicity of states but no balance of power, a fictitious legal unity centred in Delhi, but no recognized rights and duties as between the possessors of actual power. Behind all this was the old Indian tradition of unity and the tendency always to seek through a period of confusion and strife a new synthesis with the emergence of a new paramount power.

During the second half of the century the two centres of interest in Indian history are, first, the struggle for supremacy in the north or Hindustan, and secondly, the gradual growth of British power from the coast, at the expense successively of the French, the Nawab of Bengal, Mysore and the Marathas.. To take the north first, Panipat was not a decisive battle in that it gave Hindustan to the Afghans, for it only ordained that the Marathas should not control it. Panipat postponed the ultimate fate of Hindustan for forty years until the third Maratha war gave Delhi and Agra to the British, and the Treaty of Amritsar in 1809 made the Sutlej the boundary between the British and Sikhs.

During these years the British power grew step by step in a series of wars which began as defensive measures against the French, were continued for the security of trade, and completed from imperialistic motives by Wellesley. The Anglo-French wars ended in 1761 with the capture of Pondicherry and its dismantlement; henceforward the English had no serious European rivals. There followed the conquest of Bengal, inaugurated by Clive at Plassey and completed in 1764 by Munro's victory over the Emperor Shah Alam, Shuja-ad-daula of Oudh, and Mir Kasim of Bengal at the hard fought battle of Baksar. The next wars were against the Marathas and the new military power of Hyder Ali in Mysore between 1775 and 1782; it was the achievement of Warren Hastings that he faced a coalition of the Nizam, Hyder Ali and the Marathas at a time when no reinforcements could reach him from Europe on account of the American War of Independence, and maintained his possessions intact. His successor Cornwallis did not try to extend English influence, but busied himself with purging the government of corruption, and reorganizing the administration and the services on lines which largely subsist to-day.

But it was significant that no gain previously made was given up, and even Cornwallis drifted into a war with Tipu Sultan of Mysore which resulted in large annexations in the south. The final period commences with the governorship of Wellesley, who by his policy of subsidiary alliances deliberately set himself to establish the East India Company as the new paramount power of India. He virtually achieved this by the Maratha war of 1803-5 and his work was completed by Lord Hastings in 1818.

APPENDIX B

A SELECTION OF INVENTORIES CONTAINED IN THE FACTORY MISCELLANEOUS RECORDS, THE PUBLIC DESPATCHES, AND THE BENGAL INVENTORIES

Unless otherwise stated, each inventory is given in full. Some of these lists are Account Sales of those who died intestate. In these cases the prices obtained and the buyers are omitted.

I. Selections from the goods of Mr. Vincent Broom, sold on 2 Jan. 1701-2 (*Factory Miscellaneous Records*, 23, p. 44).

Dram bottle and snuff box.
A byonett and two medalls.
A Cotton bed and Curtains.
A black Coat.
Cannary 38 bottles.
A Cask of tobacco.
Shoes six pair, Slippers two pairs.
Three pairs of Briches and night gown.
A long old wigg.
A pallaqueen.

II. Selections from the Account Sale of Mrs. Eliz. Arwaker of Bombay, 18 Oct. 1701 (*Factory Miscellaneous Records*, 23, p. 44).

1 Caraboy of Arrack.
2 Old Landskipps.
A Box of Pipes.
Gowns, Petticoats and Fanns.
A parcel of Pewter Dishes and Plates.
10 Goa Hogsheads.
1 Do. of Limejuice.
55 Napkins and 44 pillow beers.
12 Sneakers.
A Cott with bedding and Laceing.
Do. with curtains, etc.
A Slave man and Woman.
2 Amber neckclothes.
An Old Mosquetta Bag.
2 Sett of Curtaines.
A box of pipes.
3 pallumpores.
A slave boy.
A Carraboy of Limewater.

III. Selections from the Account Sale of Ambrose Thompson, at Bombay Castle, 27 Sept. 1701 (*Factory Miscellaneous Records*, 23, p. 44).

A Black Coat, Wastcoat and breeches.
A Chest of Limbeck bottles.
A Bible, paper, etc.
A Pallaqueen and furniture.
3 Wiggs.
28 Neckcloths.

1 Microscope.
A Carraboy of Portugall wine.
A Slave boy.
48 gallons of Clarett.

IV. Inventory of Goods and Merchandise belonging to Mr. E. Hanslopp, of Bombay, taken Sept. 1710.

Various snuff boxes, 1 gold, 1 silver, and 2 gilt.
A Bundle of China Pictures.
One Black Damask Waste Coat and Breeches with Linnen not made up.
One Old Hoboy.
A Box with a Dead Scorpion.
6 Banian Wastecote & Drawes.
1 Buckshaw.
4 Images.
1 Old Quilt, 1 Musketta Bagg.
1 China Tobaco pipe and purce.
1 Box of Pipps.
19 Pair of Velvet Slippers.
1 China Purse.
3 China Wenches.
74 prs. pelongs sundry sorts.
3 pieces black Taffetee.
150 ffanns.
44 Rice Boxes.
15 Tea Pots.
888 Brown Cups.
2 Rosewater Bottles.

V. List of things found in Mrs. Browne's house (widow of Samuel Browne a bankrupt), 1 Sept. 1720 (*Bengal Public Despatches*, 1720, p. 197).

12 Madras Chairs.
1 Couch.
2 Tables.
A Writing Desk.
4 Old Pictures.
A Pallenkeen Shell and Bamboo with 4 Silver feet.
A Crown Compass.
A Glass Lanthorn.
A Board for Armes on which a Doll.
A pair files.
An old cloth fann.
An old cott.
An Ebony Table.
A Writing Escrutore and Table.
A Wigg box.
A great empty chest.
3 Lances.
An empty case.
A Claps cott.
A Copper frame and kittchen
A Carpett.
A small table.
A Chest of Draws.
A brasswork chest.
A Glass and dressing table.
A small dram case.
A large black press.
A small chest and parcell of books.

A Child's cott.
2 silver spoons.
A knife and fork with silver ferrels.
A Quilt.
A small looking glass.
A small box.
14 Chairs and a Couch.
2 pr. Stands and 2 Stools Ebony.
A Standing Cott and Curtains.
A small Cabinett.
A flower peice.
A few China Begers.
A Pallenkeen with brasswork.
A pair Glass sconces.
Cookroom utensils: a spitt, boiler, dish, ladle, Copper pott and cover, saucepan and 4 seerpooses, 6 Dishes and plates.

Wearing Apparell

2 Gowns and Petticoats.
2 pr. Shoes.
2 quilted pettycoats.
A parcel of White Lennen.
A new black silk pettycoat.
A parcell of foul Linning in a Black press, and 2 coats.
4 Sticht Wastecoats and 6 pr. of Briches.
3 Gyngham Wastecoats and 6 prs. of Briches.
10 pair White draws and 30 new Shirts.

VI. Inventory and Sale of the Effects of Mr. George Shelton, deceased, at four months' credit. 4 May 1725. A Selection (*Factory Miscellaneous Records*, 23, p. 100).

A Crucifix and Beads.
1 Lace and 1 plain Hat.
1 Gold headed Cane.
1 Brass mounted Sword.
4 Canes, one Silver headed.
1 Wigg, a hat and 2 Combs.
1 China Hand Escritoire.
A Slate, a few belts with one Silver Buckle.
A Cot, Curtains, Pillows, etc.
A Parcell of Sheets and Tablecloths.
3 Palampores.
4 Wastecoats and 4 Breeches Stitch'd.
6 Wastecoats and 6 do. Gingham.
5 flowered Wastecoats and 1 pair Breeches.
5 Thick Caps, etc.
A parcell of Men and Women's Gloves.
29 Shirts.
23 pair of Caswar stockings.
5 Banyan Coats.
A parcell of Pictures.
A pair of Pistolls.
1 Coat trimmed with Silver.
A Parcell of Handkerchiefs.
A large Escrewtore.
Some China Ware Guglets, etc.
A Flask of Oyl and a Sims Tinder Box.
2 Musick Books.
3 Flutes and a Hautboy.

A Lock and Hammer.
A Parcell of Candles.
A pair of Stretchers and Lasts.
A Suit of Livery Cloathes.
A Parcell of Tobacco and Pipes.
2 old Gunns.
A Pleasure Boat.

VII. Inventory of the Effects of Nicholas Clarembault, Esquire, deceased, begun the 18 November 1755 (*Bengal Inventories*, I, pp. 30-4, 2nd section).

Household Effects, etc.
1 Gold Repeating Watch with a Shagreen Case.
1 ring Emerald set with Sparks.
2 Family Rings.
4 old broken Watches.
1 new pinchbeck'd Do. in a shagreen case.
1 set of Silver Buckles.
1 Seal with his Arms.
2 Boxes containing 2 Watch Glasses.
3 Buttons and a Smelling Bottle.

In the Hall and Outer Rooms
6 Teak and Oil Wood Tables.
1 Beaufet with Glass Doors.
4 Couches.
4 Great Chairs.
2 Jackwood Chairs.
11 Ebony Arm Chairs.
1 Glass Lanthorn.
4 Japan Stands.
1 Writing Desk.
20 Old Pictures in Wooden Frames.
4 Brass Pigdannies.
2 Brass Astabarreys.
2 Jars containing Tobacco and Kishmisses.
1 Box with two Looking Glasses without Frames.
2 Jars Damag'd Pickles.
1 Almira.
1 Backgammon Table.
1 Almira with Books.

In the Bed Chamber
1 Writing Desk.
1 Almeira with a Glass Front.
2 Paper ditto.
11 Small Chairs.
2 Escrutoirs with Papers.
4 Arm Chairs.
4 Card Tables.
2 Small Scrutores.
1 Bed and Curtains.
6 Glass Shades.
A Set of Prints representing the Passions.
32 Ordinary Pictures.
A Brass Chellumchee.
A Brass Teakettle.
1 Backgammon Table.
2 Mahogany Tea Chests.

1 ditto. Knife Case.
1 Broken old Clock.
10 Baskets containing China and Glassware.
4 Cattys of Tea.
1 Armoury Board containing 5 Musquets
1 Blunderbuss.
A Parcel of damag'd Stationery.
2 Chests of Glass ware.
2 Boxes and 1 chest of ditto.
2 Small Looking Glasses.
1 Basket of Rubbish.

First Chest

2 New Goldlac'd Hatts.
1 Plain ditto.
2 Sword Belts.
2 Silver kilted Swords.
2 do. Hangers.
2 Gold headed Canes.
1 Chubdar stick silver mounted.
1 do. half-mounted.
3 Table Rings (Silver).
1 Silver Kettle with a Lamp.
2 do. Sugar dishes with Coverlids.
1 do. Soup Spoon.
2 do. Rose Water Bottles and Stands.
1 do. Small Mug.
1 Orange Strainer.
1 Otta Box with a Silver Salver.
2 Shells set in Silver.
1 Persian Callioon Silver.
17 Table Spoons Silver.
2 Hooker Glasses with their Nutte.
Silver Cruets and Pepper Box.
19 Silver Tea Spoons.
2 Small Silver Salvers.
1 Large ditto.
2 Guglets Silver-mounted.
1 Silver Coffee Pot.
1 do. Saucepan.
1 do. Tea Pot.
1 do. small Coffee Pot.
2 do. Muggs.
1 Pair of Silver Cullusses.
1 Silver Tiger's Head.
18 do. Tassels.
2 Goa Stones.
1 Murchall Silver Handle.
1 Piece of Virgin Camphire.
Old Cloathes and Linen.

Second Chest

1 Otter Dannie, Old Cloathes and Linen.

Third Chest

1 Large Silver Tobacco Box.
17 Old Snuff Boxes.
2 Judah Stones.
1 Small Padlock.
9 Remnants of Gold and Silver Lace.

12 Papers of Silver and Gold Thread Buttons.
2 New Hatts.
A Remnant of China Velvet.
3 Pieces of Nankeen,
1 do. Scarlet Camblet.
3 do. Cunor Dute (?).
2 do. Cossimbazaaar Taffaties.
5 Remnants of Europe Silk.
1 Piece Cossimbazaar Silk.
1 do. China Silk.
1 do. Black Padusoy.
1 do. Greenflower'd Gauze.
6 Remnants of Broadcloth.
3 Canes.
2 Pairs Scarlet Knit Breeches.
1 Gold Point de Espagne.
2 Pairs Handkerchiefs.
1 Box of Rubbish.
2 Smelling Bottles.
1 Corkscrew.
4 Japan Counter Boxes.
2 Pairs Cambrick.
3 do. Madras Handkerchiefs.
1 Rosewood Counter Box.
5 Pieces of Long Cloth.
1 Pair Cussordule Curtains.
Linnen and Rubbish.
1 Remnant of Camblet.
1 Pipe Case.
3 Bundles of Sealing Wax.
14 Small Pictures.
8 Pairs of Bristol Stone Buttons.

Mahogany Beauroe
1 Silver Buckle.
14 Pieces fine Black Ribbon.
9 do. Damag'd Cloth.
1 Pair of Gloves.
1 Japan Cord Box with Counters.
1 Bundle of Cards.
1 do. of Rubbish and old Linen.

Fourth Chest
1 Piece of Longcloth.
2 do. Handkerchiefs.
Linnen Cloths.

First Godown
1 Chest Sower Claret.
1 Pipe Madeira Wine.
1 do. Lisbon Wine.
2 Hogsheads of Beer.
1 Case of Cordial.
1 Chest with some Claret.
2 do. with some Madeira.
5 Bottles Brandy.
150 do. damag'd Wine.

Second Godown
3 Small Cases Brandy.
1 Chest containing Hock and Brandy.

Fourth Godown

75 Wine Glasses and Tumblers.
6 Baskets of China Ware.
1 Pipe of Sherry.
2 Hogsheads of Beer.
1 Smoothing Iron.
1 Tea Kettle.
1 Fire Stove, Shovel, etc.
1 Small Parcel Cookroom Furniture.
130 Bottles Sower Wines.
1 Quarter Cask of Brandy.
1 Large Ramsingy.
1 Musquet.

Fifth Godown

55 Pieces Dacca Cloth.
2 Tubes Sugar Candy.
3 Pieces Damag'd Camblets.
1 Chest of Lumber from Tergony.
14 Mahogany Chairs.
2 Small Looking Glasses.
19 Small Pictures.
4 Baskets of Glass and China Wares.
13 Bottles Madeira Wine.
2 Baskets of Pipes.
4 Purdars.
63 Pieces of Linnen from the Washerman.
1 Iron Treasure Chest.
22 Table Cloths and Sheets.
1 Bed Palankeen.
1 Chair do. with Silver Nails.
1 Old Chair Palankeen.
2 Horses.
1 Deer, 15 Hogs and 4 Oxen.
1 Pair false Earrings.
1 Pair Pistols.
1 Box of Tobacco.
3 Chests containing Wine.

Books (see Appendix C.)

VIII. Selection from the Inventory of Major James Kilpatrick, 8 Nov. 1757 (*Bengal Inventories*, I, p. 90, 2nd section).

4 pair scarlet breeches.
4 pair black breeches.
4 Hats (with gold and silver lace).
47 pairs Breeches (Gingham).
97 pairs stockings.
58 Old Shirts.
161 New Shirts.
37 Neckcloths.
3 pair long Drawers.
79 Wastcoats.
3 Quilted Banyan Coats.
42 Handkerchiefs.
A Suit of Musketo. Curtains.
12 Sneakers.
15 Curry Plates.
Many Gold and Silver Joys.

Liquors, etc.

A Chest containing 97 bottles Madeira wine.
Do. do. 116 bottles Orange Shrub.
Do. do. 13 dozen brown Arrack.
Do. do. 8 dozen white Arrack.
28 bottles Goa Arrack.
48 bottles Mango Shrub.
A Leaguer containing 115½ gallons Batavia Arrack.
A Hogshead English Beer.
925 Empty Bottles.
A Dried Salmon.

IX. Selection from the Inventory of Capt. David Graham, deceased, 4 Sept. 1756 (*Bengal Inventories*, I).

A Gold Watch.
A Gold headed Cane.
10 White Banyan Shirts.
6 Striped ditto.
10 pair of coarse Stockings.
A Silver Toothpick Case.
7 Caps.
6 Pairs of Short Drawers.
2 Pairs of Silk Stockings.
4 Pairs of Miltons.
1 Quilted Soucie Waistcoat.
4 White Wastcoats.
12 Stocks.
A Blue Broad Cloth Coat.
4 Quilted Caps.
4 Black Silk Wastcoats.
1 Catty of Haysan Tea.
A Free Mason's Apron.
A Coarse Surat Palimpore.
A Banyan Coat.
A Silk Coat.
Silver Breeches Buckles.
A Silver Twizer Case.
A Pair of Gold Sleeve Buttons.

X Selection from the Inventory of Capt. Thos. Holmes, deceased, 28 Nov. 1758 (*Bengal Inventories*, I).

Two Pairs Long Drawers.
1 Punch Strainer.
1 Punch Ladle.
A Tonguescraper.
1 Beetle Box inlaid with Tortoizeshell and Silver, mounted with three Silver Cups and Chunam Spoon.
1 Peruke.
1 Slave Boy named Kent.
1 Slave Girl named Johanna.
3 Brick Houses and one Garden.

XI. Selection from the Inventory of Lieut. J. Peter Mustel, deceased, 2 Oct. 1773 (*Bengal Inventories*, XIV, no. 43).

1 Bathing Tub, 1 Water Stand.
2 Wooden Stools, 2 rat traps.
Folding Blackwood Card Table.
Rattaned Cot and Curtains.
2 Cases Arrack, 2 empty Cases.
2 Pigdannies and Chillumchie.
A House and Garden.

XII. Selection from the Inventory of James Bonwhich, deceased, 30 Aug. 1774 (*Bengal Inventories*, XIV).

1 Pair Silk Mosquito Curtains.
1 Pair Muslin ditto.
1 small Thermomiter.
1 Quilted Looce Banyan Coat.
6 pairs Long Drawers.
1 Red Silk Coat with Wastcoat.
2 Blue Silk Coats with Wastcoats.
A Cow and a Calf.
His Wines included :—
22 dozen Port.
11 dozen Madeira.
1 dozen Claret, 21 Bottles of Hock, 9 Bottles Shrub, 6 Bottles Arrack, 4 Bottles Brandy, 1 dozen Bottles Cape Wine, 2 Bottles Vinegar, 1 Cask of Rum.
1 Philtering Stone.

XIII. Selection from the Inventory of James Brenner, deceased, 1775 (*Bengal Inventories*, XIV, no. 80).

1 New Pennace unfinished.
1 Old Budgerow.
3 new Wellock Boats.
Banyan Coats and Long Drawers.

XIV. Selection from the Inventory of Thomas Sheeles, deceased, 4 May 1775 (*Bengal Inventories*, XIV, no. 82).

Tonguescrapers.
Silver Milk Pot.
Punch Strainer.
A Lady's Fan.
Silk Long Drawers.
10 dozen, 3 Bottles Cyder in a Chest.
A pair of French Horns.
A Billiard Table.
A Bathing Tub.

XV. Selection from the Inventory of Nicholas Weller. Public Auction, 18 Feb. 1775 (*Bengal Inventories*, XIV).

8 Night Capps.
1 Chintz Banyan Coat.
2 pair of Ruff Worsted Breeches.
3 Striped Silk Long Drawers.
1 Free Mason's Medol.
Gold Buttons.
1 Pocket Chess Board.
2 Teapoys.
1 Buggy and Horse with Harness.
3 Turkeys, 2 Cocks, 1 Hen.
3 Geese.
4 Ducks.
1 Garden Bungelow.

XVI. Selection from the Inventory of George Wood, filed 13 Oct. 1775 (*Bengal Inventories*, XIV, no. 63).

5 Blue and 2 Red Cloth Coats.
8 Silk Wastcoats.
5 Pairs old Sattin Breeches.

2 pairs new Cloth do.
15 pairs Silk do.
20 Banian Shirts.
22 Wastcoats.
20 pairs Breeches.
4 pairs Long Drawers.
1 Banian Coat.
21 Caps.
3 pairs Gloves.
1 Shawl Wastcoat.
2 old ditto.
33 pairs Stockings.
6 Pairs Silk Stockings.
3 Pairs Black ditto.
1 Pair Knee and Shoe Buckles.
1 Pinchback Watch.

XVII. Selection from the Inventory of Mrs. Anne Nowlan, taken 26 Oct. 1775 (*Bengal Inventories*, vol. XIV, no. 128).

11 Bombay Blackwood Armchairs.
2 Blackwood Couches.
1 Mahogany Bereau and Glass Bookcase.
1 Small Blackwood Cott with Curtain Posts.
1 Beetle Box Silver mounted.
1 Dressing Glass without a Glass, and a Board to Tye Shawls.
2 Large Brass Cuspidores. (Spittoons)
1 Chillemchy and a Gooty.
1 Chafing Dish and a Tea Kettle.
1 Massaul and a Teldanny.
1 Pistoll and Mortar.
32 Bottles Brandy.
20 do. Madeira.
33 Plates.
5 Sneakers.
9 Enamell China Copper Saucers and 1 Cuspidore.
2 China Teapotts.
3 do. Milk Potts and Caucers.
3 Brown Teapotts.
2 Rose Water Bottles.
1 Iron Snuffer and Stand.
2 Persia Rosewater Bottles with Some Rose water.
1 Chair Palankeen.
1 Pegue Jarr with Some Sugar Candy.
1 Silver Teapott.
1 Small Salver.

Jewels (complete list)

1 Small Diamond Ring with 2 Sparkes.
2 Small Ruby Rings.
1 Chrystall Ring.
15 large and small Gold Rings.
4 Tamback Rings.
3 false Hoop Rings.
5 false Stone Rings.
1 Pearl Necklace of 4 Strings.
1 do. smaller and do. with Garnetts.
1 pair Bracelets mounted on Gold.
1 pair do. do. with Mallabar Stones.
1 Pair Gold Chain Bracelets each containing 4 Strings.
1 pair Gold Braceletts containing 22 Beads.

1 Gold Necklace containing 6 Strings with a Solitore.
1 do. do. Chain do. 4 Strings.
1 do. do. Chain for Neck, 3 do.
1 do. Rosario.
1 Sett containing 8 Gold Buttons for Choly and Sleeves.
1 do. do. 10 do. with Mallabar Stones.
1 Large Gold Sprigg with Small Pearl.
1 Small do. workt.
1 Smaller do.
3 pairs Gold Earrings mounted with Pearl.
1 Small Gold Solitore.
4 Paste Pinns.
1 pair Paste Earrings.
1 Sett Silver Patte Buttons for Wastcoat and Silver Chain.
1 Ivory Scrutore.

Clothes (complete list)

1 Red Embroidered Silk Petticoat.
1 Red Satin Laced Petticoat.
1 Light Blue Silk Petticoat.
1 Crimson Cassimbuzaar do.
3 Black Petticoats.
3 old and 3 new Shawls.
8 Marchoys, Gingham, Silk and Patna, Chintz, Old and New Petticoats.
4 White Petticoats.
24 Bajues, flower'd, Plain and Dooreas.
1 Gauze Bajue.
1 Bodlaw do.
18 Cholies flower'd, Plain and Dooreas.
17 Madrass Red flower'd Old and New Handkerchiefs.
19 White Bordered, Blue, flowered and Silk Handkerchiefs.
19 Half Handkerchiefs for Head.
9 pairs Stockings Old and New.
16 White and Gingham pellocases.
4 Sheets, 2 Towells.
3 Sarrys.
1 Curtain, 2 Pallampores Surat, and 3 Madrass do. old and new.
2 pairs Red flower'd Damasks.
1 do. Crimson Sattin.
1 do. Blue do.
3 pairs Slippers.
1 Slave Girl.

APPENDIX C

SELECT BOOK LISTS OF THE EIGHTEENTH CENTURY

A selection from book lists found in the *Home Miscellaneous Series* of the India Office, the *Bengal Public Despatches*, the India Office *Series of Inventories*, and printed sources, is here given in order to provide some illustration of the mind of the eighteenth century Englishman in India.

I. Selection from the 'Catalogue of Books in the Library of Fort St. George, with the letters and numbers of their places'. Sept. 1719. (India Office, *Home Miscellaneous Series*, 260)

(i) *Hebrew and Arabic Books, etc.*

23 Books including a Polyglot Bible and various Lexicons.

(ii) *Greek Books*

75 books, including :—

The New Testament (1632).
The Greek and Latin Works of Stobai (1609).
Aristotle's Opera Philosophia (1590).
Select Dialogues of Plato.
Tragedies of Sophocles.
Eusebius' Ecclesiastical History.
Some Early Greek Fathers, as
  Justin's Apologia (1703).
  Ignatius' Epistles (1680).
4 Works of Chrysostom.
Clement of Alexandria (1556).

(iii) *Latin Books.* 357 books.

These were chiefly theological, and included :—

St. Augustine's Works.
Luther's Opera in 7 vols.
Boem's Encherideon precum.
Tertullian's Opera.
Th. Beza's New Testament (Cambridge, 1642).
Calvin's Opera Omnia, and 16 separate works, including the 'Institutiones' (Geneva, 1568).
Three Works of Erasmus.

The following were included among the general Latin books :—

'Antiquitas Academiae Cantabrigiensis.'
Bacon's Novum Organum, Sermones Ethici, Politici, Oconomici Amstel, and Historia Regni Henrici VII.
Descartes' Opera Philosophica.
Grotius' De Jure Belli et Pacis.
Two Universal Histories.
Justinian's Institutes.
Livy's History.
Martial's Epigrams and Vergil.

(iv) *English Books.* 698 books.

A very large number were theological, of which the following are a selection :—

Bishop Andrews' Sermons, etc.
Anabaptists, several sorts described.

Bishop Atterbury's Sermons.
Bishop Burnet—6 vols., but not the 'History of His Own Times.'
Baxter's Call to the Unconverted.
Bp. Cosin's History of Transubstantiation.
3 English Bibles and 1 Welsh with the Book of Common Prayer.
Bishop Offspring Blackhall. 3 works.
The Icon Basilike.
Calamy's Sermons.
The Catechumen or the Young Person instructed for the Holy Sacrament.
Bp. Wilson's Christ's Sufferings and Descent into Hell.
Culverwell's Light of Nature, etc.
Cudworth's Intellectual System of the Universe.
The Cure for Enthusiasm.
Fuller's Holy War.
Bishop Hall's Works.
Hooker's Ecclesiastical Polity.
Bishop Ken's Exposition of the Catechism.
Luther on Galatians.
Laud's Life.
Andrew Marvell's Growth of Popery, etc.
The Romish Horsleech or Popery's intolerable Charge to the Nation, and several anti-papalist works.
The Religio Medici.
Bishop Pearson on the Creed.
Bishop Stillingfleet's Sermons and Works.
Seven works of Dr. Sherlock.
Thomas à Kempis (translated).
Dr. South's Sermons.
Strype's Memorials of Archbishop Cranmer.
Archbishop Tillotson. 5 works.

The following is a selection of the secular works in English :—

Bacon's Advancement of Learning.
Brathwaite's Nursery for Gentry (3 copies).
Boethius' Consolation of Philosophy.
Six Scientific Tracts of Boyle.
Bayle's Defence of Descartes' 'De Anima Brutorum.'
Caesar's Commentaries.
Mr. Collier's Immorality of the Stage (With an Answer).
Customs of Tonnage and Poundage, etc.
Education, specially for Young Gentlemen.
Sir R. Filmer on Usury.
Hobbes' Leviathan.
Hakluyt's Voyages.
The Right Way to Preserve Life and Health.
Parliamentary Journals of Queen Elizabeth.
Sir Matthew Hale's Discourses.
Lucian's Dialogues, vols. 2 and 4.
Locke's Essay in the Human Understanding.
The Anatomy of Melancholy.
Malebranche's Search after Truth.
Bernier's Revolution in the Moghul Empire.
Machiavelli's Works.
Milton's History of Britain (but no Paradise Lost).
Purchas' Voyages.
Plutarch's Lives.

Peacham's Complete Gentleman, with the Order of an Army in Battle.
Sir Walter Raleigh's History of the World.
Shakespeare's Plays.
Thevenot's Travels.
Whiston's Josephus.
The Young Man's Guide (bound up with 'A Word to Saints').

(v) *French and Dutch Books*, etc. 48 books.
They included :—
La Vie do Borromeo.
Nouvelles de Bocace.
A Spanish Bible.
A Book of Devotions in High Dutch.
An English Liturgy (trans. into Portuguese).
The Psalms in Portuguese.
The Life of Turenne.
La Véritié de la Religion Catholique.

(vi) 'Books translated into ye Tamilie (or Malabars) and into ye Gentou Languages.' (Complete List)
The Bible and New Testament in Tamil.
The Bible in Gentou.
The Catechism (In Malabar and Portuguese).
The Cathecism and Christian Doctrine explained.
Sancta Caena Institutio ante arca et post receptionem.
Ad Gentiles omnes epistola.
Grammatica Malabaria.
Gentilismi Abominatio.
Mores sive Ethici Christiani.
Psalmi Davidi in lingua Tamilia.
Salvatio per Christum.
Theologica Thetica sive dogmata ad Satulem necessaria.
Hymnalogia Tamilica.

II. Selection from the books of the Rev. Thomas Consett in the Fort St. George Library, Oct. 1729 (*Home Miscellaneous Records*, 260).

(i) *Hebrew Books, etc.* 25 vols.

(ii) *Greek Books.* 57 vols.
They included seven works of Aristotle, Chrysostom, Epictetus, and the Orthodoxa Confessio Ecclesiae Ruthenicae.

(iii) *Latin Books.* 231 vols.
Classical and theological authors were well mixed, amongst them being the following :—
The Works of Vergil, Suetonius, Terence, Sallust, Plautus, Pliny and Plutarch.
Milton's Life of Cromwell.
Martial's Epigrams.
Thomas Aquinas' Summa Theologiae.

(iv) *English Books.* 283 vols.
Theological works are again very prominent and include all shades of thought. They included works by Calamy, Baxter, Calvin, the Caroline divines, and the Latitudinarians (Burnet, Stillingfleet, Hoadly and Sherlock). Also 'The Present State of the Church in Russia, with a Collection of Several Russian Tracts'.

Among the general books were the following :—Milton's Paradise Lost, The Clergyman's Companion in Visiting the Sick, and The Polite Gentleman.

(v) *French, Highe and Low Dutch Books.* 21 vols.

III. Among the items of expenditure at Calcutta between April 1755 and June 1756, were the following :—

Law Books. Rs. 242-13-3.
Divinity Books. Rs. 175-2-3.
(J. Long, *Selections from the Unpublished Records of the Government*, etc., p. 186, *Calcutta Proceedings*, 20 Sept. 1759)

IV. Books bequeathed by Eliz. Thomlinson, widow of Chaplain Thomlinson, in 1720 (*Bengal Consultations*, IV, pp. 214-15).
The books included :—

3 vols. of Sherlock's Works.
6 vols. of Dr. Offspring Blackhall's Works.
2 vols. of Dr. Tillotson's Works.
The Whole Duty of Man.
6 vols. of Clarendon's History.
Her Latin, Greek and Hebrew books were bequeathed to the Church of Calcutta.

V. Selection from the Books of Nicholas Clarembault, Esq., died 18 Nov. 1755 (*India Office Inventories*, I, pp. 30-4, Second Series).

(i) *Books in Foreign Languages*

Memoires de la Bourdonnaye.
Histoire de Jean de Bourbon.
5 vols. of de Thevenot's Travels.
8 vols. of Molière.
1 vol. of Racine.
Histoire des Grands Maîtres de Rhodes.
5 Occurres de Rabelais.
Voltaire's Henriade.
La Mothe's Iliade.
Contes de la Fontaine.
Télémarque.
3 Nouvelles Saintes Bibles.
8 odd Italian volumes.
In all there were over 40 French and one Dutch book.

(ii) *English Books*

They included—
Harris' Collection of Voyages.
Thucydides by Hobbes.
Dr. Taylor's Life of Christ.
2 vols. of Sir William Temple.
4 different European Dictionaries.
8 vols. of Plutarch.
2 vols. of Dion Cassius.
4 vols. of Hebrew Antiquities.
3 vols. of the History of China.
Locke's Essay in the Human Understanding.
Dampier's Voyages.
Hamilton's Voyages.
The Danish Missionaries at Tranquebar.
Shaftesbury's Characteristics.
A Treatise on Music and Happiness.

8 vols. of the Spectator.
Addison's Travels in Italy.
3 vols. of the Freethinker.
The Guardian.
Shakespeare (2 sets).
6 vols. Dryden's Plays.
Gay's, Pope's and Thompson's Works.
Clarke's Boyle Lectures.
One Large Bible.

In all there were seventy separate entries of English books, in addition to a large number of pamphlets and broken sets, all however, ' much Damag'd by Worms and Ratts '.

VI. Selection from the Books of William Belcher, died 9 May 1757, at Fort St. George (*Inventories*, I, 2nd section, pp. 26-7).

Boyle's Works.
Tillotson's Works.
Anson's Voyage.
2 vols. of the Spectator.
Whiston's Philosophy.
Newton's Opticks.
Horace's Epistles.
The Busy Body.
Naphet on Foods.
Shaftesbury's Works.
24 Books of Music.

In all there were 31 items.

VII. Selection from the Books of James Bonwich, 30 August 1774 (*Bengal Inventories*, XIV).

15 vols. of the London Magazine.
Military Transactions of Hindustan.
Sterne's Sentimental Journey.
Belisarius.

VIII. Selection from the Books of James Brenner. 1775 (*Bengal Inventories*, XIV, no. 80).

Bach's Periodical Overtures.
Abel's Six Symphonies.
Pugnani's Six Overtures.
Handel's Overtures in 4 Books.
Correlli's 12 Sonatas in 3 Books.
Handel's Sampson and Esther.
Handel's 12 Grand Concertos.
Herschel's Six Sonatas.

Other music books filled about two pages in the *Inventory Books*. There were about 200 other books, which included :—

Tristram Shandy.
Montesquieu's Esprit des Lois.
Rousseau's Emile.
Télémarque.
Butler's Hudibras.
Milton's Works.
Jones' Persian Grammar.

IX. Selection of Books on Sale in Calcutta, 7 Oct. 1784 (Seton-Kerr : *Selections from the Calcutta Gazettes*, 1784-1823, ed. 1864).

Orme's History of the late War in Hindustan.
Burleigh's State Papers.

Richardson's Persian Dictionary.
Blackstone's Commentary.
Phillidore on Chess.
Chesterfield's Letters.
Dr. Johnson's Dictionary.
Abbé Raynal's Revolution in America.
Voltaire's Age of Louis XIV and XV.
Voltaire's Memoirs.
Arabian Nights Entertainment.
Whiston's Josephus.

X. Selection of books advertised for sale from the Library in Calcutta, 1785 (The *India Gazette*, 31 Jan. 1785).

Richardson's Persian Dictionary.
Chippendale's Designs of Household Furniture.
Boyle's Works.
Hawkins History of Music.
Raynal's Histoire des Indes.
Hume's History of England.
Locke's Works.
Priestley's Works.
Johnson's Poets. (68 vols).
Annual Register, 1758-82.

XI. Sir John Shore, who was an Evangelical, mentions in a letter to Charles Grant (9 March 1796), that his reading consisted of the following :—

The New Testament.
Warburton's Divine Legation.
Jortin's Ecclesiastical History.
Paley's Evidences.
Jortin's Sermons 'over and over'
And other like books.

APPENDIX D

SELECTION OF EUROPEAN CRIMES IN BENGAL, 1766-1800

These are taken from the series of Records in the India Office labelled *Europeans in India*. Volumes I-XXIV are detailed accounts of the cases, and volume XXV contains concise summaries. They are very valuable as throwing further light on the problem of the 'Low Europeans'. The cases given below will all be found summarized in volume XXV.

I. 1776. Case of Vernon Duffield, a dismissed officer.
Edward Deake.
James McKee.

These men were apprehended by the Faujdar of Chaperal while trying to enter Oudh dressed as Moors. They threatened him with violence, and then defied the Patna Chief, Le Sage, at Bankipore. The matter was debated in Council, where (it is interesting to note) Hastings and Francis were outvoted by Barwell, Clavering and Monson. The majority released them on their expressing contrition and engaging never to enter Oudh.

II. 1787. Case of John Thomas.

This man came out to India as the servant of a Captain. He left his service and stayed on in Calcutta without leave. There he set up an arrack shop inside the Maratha ditch, where he corrupted soldiers 'in every kind of drunkenness and debauchery'. He was ordered to be sent home by the next ship due to sail, the 'Oxford'.

III. 1788. Case of A Mason,
Two Carpenters,
Two Tailors,
A Horsedealer.

They were sent down from Patna to Calcutta, having proved very troublesome on account of their belief that the judges had no power to touch them. They had been involved in frequent disputes with the local inhabitants, and as they possessed no licence of residence they were ordered to be sent home.

IV. 1789. Case of Allen.

He posed as a merchant. He was sent to Calcutta by the Collector of Chittagong on the complaint of Ensign Sherrock, whose Indian mistress he had seduced, robbed and turned adrift. He was ordered to be detained by the Town Major as an unlicensed vagabond European.

V. 1794. Case of John Adams.

He was a 'young, good-looking man' who spoke English, French, Italian, Spanish and Portuguese well. In 1789 he was taken for murder at Cox's Bungalow, but was sent ashore at Culpee (outside the Company's dominions). He reappeared in Calcutta but was released on giving security to leave by a Portuguese ship. He then joined the ship of Captain Wilson as a carpenter and when the fraud was discovered he threatened the Captain with murder. He was sent back to Calcutta at the end of

1792, when he was ordered to go home on the packet 'Tartar' (Capt. Wilson). The crew refused to sail with a murderer, however, and he was then sent on to the 'Lansdowne', from which he again escaped. In Oct. 1794 he was again charged with fraud by Capt. Wilson and was ordered to be sent home by the next ship.

VI. 1795. Case of Burglary.

Three men were convicted of burglary by the Nizamat Adalat. They were sentenced to death, but the sentence was commuted to transportation to England with a threat of execution if they returned.

VII. 1796. Case of Richard and John Johnson.

These men were indigo planters who were accused of ill-treatment of ryots on the strength of evidence which had been tendered *for the prosecution* in the course of a trial of three of them for theft. The Court's report, sent through Mr. James Stuart, Deputy Regis of the Nizamat Adalat of Tirhut, accused them of the following :—'illegal exertion of magisterial authority by putting the prisoners Bholah and Mussumant Bussee (Bholah's wife) in irons, confining them on the stocks, flogging Bholah, putting them in fear of their lives, and finally publicly exposing the said Bholah and his wife Busseiah by beat of Dowl (drum) on asses with their faces towards the animals' tails, through the division of the neighbouring villages'.

The villagers refused to proceed against the Johnsons, but at the trial the prosecution witnesses corroborated the story. The local court was unable to deal with this case, and the only remedy lay before the Court of Circuit or the Criminal Court at Calcutta, neither of which was practicable for a villager. The two Johnsons were ordered to Calcutta within seven days, and were forbidden to return to their estate. Richard Johnson was convicted of an 'assault on natives' at the Supreme Court in January 1797.

VIII. 1796. Case of William Orby Hunter.

This man was an indigo-planter in Tirhut (village Mirzaffapur) and was accused of cruelty against three girls of low caste in the service of 'Bhangwannah Kowar, with whom Mr. Hunter cohabited as his Bibbee.'

The charge against Hunter is thus stated in the official summary. The three girls 'had had their noses, ears and hair cut off, and one of them her tongue cut out. That they had fetters put on their feet, that they were wounded in their private parts, and were affected with the venereal disease (of which disease Mussammant Kinojee, who was brought to the magistrate in a litter, afterwards died in Tirhoot), and that they had been otherwise treated with great cruelty. It was alleged by all the females that they had been forcibly violated by Mr. Hunter, and one of them stated that she had, under a sense of the dishonour, attempted to drown herself in a well'.

This statement was made before a magistrate, and the facts do not seem to have been disputed. Hunter, however, placed the blame on the bibbee, while the bibbee maintained that the cruelties had been carried out by Hunter's express orders. The Governor-General, not believing all the evidence, ordered a trial in Calcutta. In December 1796, true bills were found against both. On 10 Jan. 1797, they were convicted in the case of the first girl. On 16 Jan. Hunter put in an affidavit pleading ruinous expense of the prosecution, and the Court finally allowed a settlement to be made with the prosecutrix. Sicca Rs. 1,000 were to be paid to each of the girls, which were to be invested and paid out to them at their marriage. Hunter was found guilty of all the counts of the indictment, and the bibbee of all but one. Hunter was given a fine of Rs. 100, and the bibbee six months imprisonment (of which five months had already expired) and a fine of one rupee.

IX. 1797. Case of a Punch House Keeper.

A man, his wife and two sons, after serving a sentence of transportation in Botany Bay, arrived in Calcutta and set up a Punch House. Besides acting as a crimp, he arranged with the merchant captains for the impressment of men, and after delivering them, arranged for their desertion again. The whole family was deported.

X. 1798. Case of a Journalist.

A young man in the office of the *Telegraph*, who had printed a libel on Wellesley signed ' Mentor ' without the permission of the paper, was sent back to England.

XI. 1798. Case of Ramsay, alias Ramsden, alias Kelly.

This man was sent to Calcutta from Serampore by the Danish Government, where he had taken refuge for debt. They reported that he was frequently absent at Patna, engaged in the liquor trade, but that as he always left Serampore with very little and returned with a fully laden boat, ' in a battered condition ' and ' very much bruised and wounded ', he was suspected of irregularities.

The Town Adjutant reported that he had escaped from the Town Prison by undermining the walls, and had later escaped from a ship to which he had been sent by Sir John Shore. He was ordered to be sent to Europe, and ' to be put in irons if necessary '.

XII. 1798. Case of a Punch House Keeper.

This man, with a confederate, seized men belonging to one ship and transferred them to another in order to get impress money. On discovery he was sent home, but his confederate, who had a post in the Sheriff's office, was allowed to stay on furnishing security.

XIII. 1799. Case of Two Journalists.

They were the editors of the *Asiatic Mirror* and the *Relator*; they were sent home as their policy was displeasing to the Governor-General (Lord Wellesley).

XIV. 1799. Case of William and Ann Smith.

The couple kept a disorderly Punch House. On being ordered home Smith barricaded himself in his house and shot a sepoy, who died. In January 1800 he was convicted of murder and executed.

APPENDIX E

EUROPEAN AND INDIAN MUTUAL OPINIONS

I. EUROPEAN OPINIONS

A. *General*

1. Manucci. *Storia do Mogor*, II, p. 452.

'Never are they (Indians) ready to listen to reason; they are very troublesome, high and low, without shame, neither having the fear of God. The Hindus who turn Mohammedan are the worst of all; these are ordinarily the most insolent, the greatest talkers, and held in no consideration. As for Europeans who come to India, they must arm themselves with great patience and prudence, for not a soul will speak to them, this being the general attitude of India. Although they are deceivers, selfish, contumacious and unworthy of belief, we are abhorred by the lower classes, who hold us to be impure, being themselves worse than pigs.'

2. Sieur Luillier. *A Voyage to the East Indies* (1702), p. 285.

'Indians are a very sober People and effeminate, yet strict Observers of their Religion. They are extremely covetous of Money, which is not over plentiful in India; and so predominate is this Avarice, that there is nothing they will not do, nor any Torments they will refuse to endure for it; so that we need not admire if they suffer what has been said on that Account.'

3. Letter of the Court to Madras, 4 Feb. 1708, par. 35 (*Home Misc. Series*, 46, p. 233).

'It is too sad a truth that the Natives who first admired the Europeans for their innocency, should now by their examples have grown so crafty.'

4. Dr. Ives. *A Voyage to India* (1754), p. 48.

He said that Indians were 'very quiet inoffensive people'. They were honest inland but on the coast their dishonesty was the fault of tricky Europeans. He specially noted the washing of the Hindus, and said of Indian servants—'They are an artful cunning people, and very ready at inventing an answer'.

5. Clive. Forrest, *Life of Clive*, II, p. 120 (Letter of 30 Dec. 1758).

'This rich and flourishing kingdom may be totally subdued by so small a force as two thousand Europeans, and the possession thereof maintain'd and confirmed by the Great Mogul upon paying the Sum of 50 Lacks per annum paid by former soldiers.'

6. J. Z. Holwell (Quoted by Forbes, *Oriental Memoirs*, II, p. 457).

'Gentoos in general are as degenerate, crafty, superstitious and wicked a people as any race in the known world, if not eminently more so, especially the common run of Brahmins.'

7. Mrs. N. E. Kindersley. *Letters from the East Indies*, p. 132.

'They are gentle, patient, temperate, regular in their lives, charitable and strict observers of their religious customs. They are superstitious, effeminate, avaricious, and crafty, deceitful and dishonest in their dealings and void of every principle of honour, generosity and gratitude.'

'They are the most tedious people in the world . they have a method of putting everything off till to-morrow; when it is found out, as it often is, that they have told an untruth, they have no shame for it, but immediately tell another and another. Nothing can hurry them; nothing can discompose them or put them out of count, nothing can make them angry; provided their gains are sure, the master may fret to find his business go on slowly, may abuse them for want of honesty, may argue with them for their ingratitude, may convict them of falsehood and double dealing; it signifies nothing; the same mild and placid countenance remains, without the least symptoms of fear, anger or shame.' (pp. 129-130)

8. 1764. Niebuhr. *Journal of Travels to Arabia and the East*, p. 13.

Niebuhr found the Hindus 'doux, vertueux, et laborieux', who 'are among men those who least seek to do wrong to their neighbour'. They were 'the most tolerant nation in the world', but 'no nation was less sociable than these Hindus'.

9. 1768. Major Rennell. *Diary, Home Misc. Series*, 765, p. 182 (20 Jan. 1768).

''Tis a mistake to conclude that the natives of Hindustan want courage . . . With respect to passive courage the Inhabitants of these Countries are perhaps possessed of a much larger share of it than those of our own. To see them under Misfortune you would conclude that they had no passions . . . The Bengall People certainly suffer Pain and misfortune with much greater Philosophy than Europeans do. 'Tis remark'd that among an equal number of wounded Persons of both Countreys, the blacks recover in a proportion of six to one.'

10. 1769. Eliza Sterne. Letter from Tellicherry, June 1769 (*Sterne's Eliza*, p. 98).

'The Brahmins are very easy, plain, unaffected sons of simple nature —there's a something in their Conversation and Manners that exceedingly touches me; the Nairs are a proud, Indolent, Cowardly but very handsome people and the Tivies excellent soldiers in the Field, at Storming or entering a Breach, the latter seems as easy to them as stepping into a closet.'

11. 1770. de Pagé. *Travels round the World*, II, p. 41.

The Brahmins were 'of unaffected simple manners, gentle, regular and temperate in the whole conduct of their lives'.

12. 1770. John Macdonald. *Travels in various parts of Europe, Asia and Africa*, p. 230.

'If God excused the Rechabites, how much more shall he excuse Gentoos, who had no Bible?'

13. Robert Orme. *History of Military Transactions in Hindustan*, pp. 5-6.

'An abhorrence to the shedding of blood, derived from his religion, and seconded by the great temperance of a life which is passed by most of them in a very sparing use of animal food, and a total abstinence of intoxicating liquors; the influence of the most regular of climates, in which the great heat of the sun and the great fertility of the soil lessen most of the wants to which the human species is subject in austerer regions, and supply the rest without the exertion of much labour; these causes, with various consequences from them, have all together contributed to make the Indian the most enervated inhabitant of the globe.

'He shudders at the sight of blood, and is of a pusillanimity only to be excused and accounted for by the great delicacy of his configuration.

This is so slight as to give him no chance of opposing with success the onset of an inhabitant of more northern regions.'

14. Mrs. Fay. 1780. *Letters from India*, pp. 162-3.

'I wish these people would not vex me with their tricks; for there is something in the mild countenances and gentle manners of the Hindoos that interests me exceedingly.'

15. 1780. Innes Munro. *Narrative of Military Operations*, etc., 1780, pp. 67 and 100.

He considered that Indians were extremely lazy. Ease was their chief luxury; they could not understand the European love of exercise. He quotes the maxim 'It is better to walk than to run; to sit than to stand; but lying is best of all'. On p. 100 he speaks of 'the pusillanimous disposition of these unfortunate natives'.

16. 1782. Hodges. *Travels in India*, p. 34.

He comments very favourably on the simplicity, cleanliness and courtesy of the Hindus, and on the grand manners of the Mussulman gentlemen.

17. 1790. The Commissioner of Police (in a report). Love, *Vestiges of Old Madras*, III, p. 484.

'We may venture to say that the inhabitants of Madras, down to the lowest orders, are not to be surpassed in Acuteness at any call of interest.'

18. 1790. Le Couteur. *Letters from India*, p. 336.

'Indians are in general effeminate, lazy and cowardly; but their vices have with no great reason been attributed to the effects of the climate in which they live . . .'

19. David Brown. Simeon, *Memoir of the Rev. D. Brown*, p. 55.

'Utter disgust, intermingled with the greatest pity, seemed to be the result in Mr. Brown's mind, of the knowledge he had acquired, in his investigation of the filthy and sanguinary frivolity of the debased religion and of its baneful influence on the principles and morals of its votaries.'

20. William Carey. *Serampore Letters*, p. 62, 1794.

The Hindus were 'literally sunk into the dregs of vice. 'Tis true that they have not the ferocity of American Indians, but this is abundantly supplied with a dreadful stock of low cunning and deceit. Moral rectitude makes no part of their religious system, and therefore no wonder they are sunk, nay wholly immersed, in all manner of impurity'.

21. 1799. Claudius Buchanan. *Memoir by the Rev. H. Pearson*, I, p. 176.

He says of Indians 'their general character is imbecility of body and imbecility of mind'.

Forbes, *Oriental Memoirs*, IV, p. 309, thus quotes Dr. Buchanan. 'Hindoos are destitute of those principles of honesty, truth and justice, which respond to the spirit of British administration and have not a disposition which is in accordance with the tenor of Christian principles.'.

22. 1800. Major Blakiston. *Twelve Years Military Adventures in Hindustan*, II, pp. 110-111.

He says of the Hindus in general (from which he excepts the Rajputs but not the Brahmins) that they have the 'constitutional timidity' of warm climates, and in addition many vices and few virtues which are the result of their system of government. Their virtues are sobriety, patience and fortitude; their vices sensuality, avarice, cunning, duplicity and falsehood. 'There is no part of the world,' he says, 'where less atrocious crimes are committed.' He also regrets the paucity of the opportunities for meeting any but subordinate Indians.

23. 1806. Henry Martyn. *Journal*, I, p. 449 (20 May).

On going to see a temple he says: 'The cymbals sounded and never did sounds go through my heart with such horror in my life. . . . I shivered at being in the neighbourhood of hell, my heart was ready to burst at the dreadful state to which the Devil had brought my poor fellow creatures.'

24. 1809. Mrs. Graham. *Journal of a Residence in India*, p. 72.

'These people, if they have the virtues of slaves, patience, meekness, forbearance and gentleness, have their vices also. They are cunning and incapable of truth; they disregard the imputation of lying and perjury, and would consider it folly not to practise them for their own interest.'

She also speaks of 'traces of the manners and simplicity of the antique ages'.

25. 1813. Lord Hastings. *Private Journal*, I, p. 30.

'The Hindoo appears a being nearly limited to mere animal functions and even in them indifferent. Their proficiency and skill in the several lines of occupation to which they are restricted, are little more than the dexterity which any animal with similar conformation but with no higher intellect than a dog, an elephant, or a monkey, might be supposed to be capable of attaining. It is enough to see this in order to have full conviction that such a people can at no period have been more advanced in civil polity.'

'In Bengal at least they are infantine in everything. Neat and dexterous in making any toy or ornament for which they have a pattern, they do not show a particle of invention.' (p. 66)

26. 1876. H. G. Keene. *The Fall of the Moghuls*, pp. 21-2.

'All Asiatics are unscrupulous and unforgiving. The natives of Hindustan are peculiarly so; but they are also unsympathetic and unobservant in a manner that is altogether their own. From the languor induced by the climate, and from the selfishness induced by centuries of misgovernment, they have derived a weakness of will, an absence of resolute energy, and an occasional audacity of meanness almost unintelligible in a people so free from the fear of death.'

B. *Mussulmans*

1. Dupleix. 1742. Ananda Ranga Pillai, *Private Diary*, II, p. 307.

In conversation with Pillai he spoke disparagingly of Mohammad, using expressions like 'look at these Mohammedan dogs', etc.

2. 1758. Clive. Forrest's *Life of Clive*, II, p. 120. Letter dated 30 Dec. 1758.

'The Moors as well as the Gentoos, are indolent, luxurious, ignorant and cowardly beyond all conception.'

'These Mussulmans, gratitude they have none, base men of very narrow conceptions, and have adopted a system of Politics more peculiar to this Country than any other; viz. to attempt everything by treachery rather than force.'

3. 1763. Col. Adams, and General Carnac. Letter of Adams and Carnac to Gentil offering him Rs. 50,000 to come over. *Calcutta Proceedings.* 3 Oct. 1763. Long, *Selections from unpublished Records*, p. 362.

In the course of the letter they say 'only necessity could have engaged you in so dishonourable a service to a Christian as that of the Moors, who always treat with the grossest cruelty those of our religion and Europeans when it is in their power to do so with impunity'.

4. 1770. de Pagé. *Travels round the World*, II, p. 41.

The Mussulmans 'with all their simplicity, are proud and haughty, and ever prone to consider themselves in a position superior to other men'.

5. 1772. Hodges. *Travels in India*, p. 34.

The low class Mussulmans were 'haughty not to say insolent; irritable and ferocious'. However a 'Moorish gentleman may be considered as a perfect model of a well bred man'.

6. 1800. Major Blakiston. *Twelve Years Military Adventures.* II, pp. 110-11.

He says that the Mussulmans have the same vices and virtues as the Hindus—sobriety, patience, fortitude, sensuality, avarice, cunning, duplicity and falsehood—with the addition of pride.

7. Swartz. *Remains and Journals*, p. 120 (1768).

'The young Nabob, or the Nabob's second son, who is a genuine disciple of Mahomet (that is, inclined to cruelty) watches narrowly the lives of Europeans.'

8. Henry Martyn. *Journal*, II, p. 32. (17 March 1807.)

'This is Mahometanism, to murder as infidels the children of God, and to live without prayer. I have never felt so excited as by this dispute (on the lawfulness of putting people to death for blasphemy), nor felt such terror at this damnable delusion of the devil; and it followed me all night in my dreams. Now that I am more cool, I still think that human nature in its worst appearance is a Mahommedan. Yet, oh may I so realise the day of judgement that I may now pity and pray for those whom I shall then see overwhelmed with consternation and ruin.'

II. INDIAN OPINIONS OF EUROPEANS

1. Sultan Abdullah Qutb Shah. A story reported by Manucci, *Storia do Mogor*, IV, p. 93.

'He (the Sultan) sent word for the slaughter of a stag, and it was divided into joints. He then ordered the distribution of the pieces, one to each nation. The Englishman, without waiting until they handed it to him, laid hold on the biggest piece there was and carried it off. From this the King said that this nation loves to take things at its own risk. The Dutchman held out his hand humbly and accepted the share offered to him. From this it was inferred that this nation was one of merchants who through their humility have become rich.

'The Portuguese refused his portion, telling his servant he might take it. At this the King said that this nation was overbearing and would rather die of hunger than abandon its dignity. The Frenchman, without waiting for orders, laid hold of his sword, struck it in two pieces, and throwing out his chest, marched away. Judging from this, the King said that this nation was a valorous one, most generous and fond of good living.'

2. Manucci, *Storia do Mogor*, III, p. 73.

The Hindus called the Europeans Farangis and believed 'that they have no polite manners, that they are ignorant, wanting in ordered life, and very dirty'.

p. 315. He says that new arrivals in Pondicherry 'hold the Farangis in most singular aversion, trembling at their approach, more especially the women'.

p. 320. The Hindus have 'considerable contempt' for Europeans—'even greater than that of persons of quality in France for night-soil workers and scavengers'.

3. Ananda Ranga Pillai. *Diary*, I, p. 26 (1740).

He describes as an exception M. Delorme, who 'made no distinction between rich and poor, never took a bribe, and treated the native on a footing of equality with the European'.

On the other hand, in II, p. 395, occurs the following :—

'One cannot understand what M. de la Bourdonnais means by writing one thing one day to the Council at Pondicherry and the next another as if he was joking. Knowing that there is generally concord and good understanding amongst Europeans, and that they never disagree, we cannot see what he means by saying at one time that he has restored Madras, and at another that he has not, and thereby disgracing others. The ways of Europeans, who used always to act in union, have apparently become like those of natives and Mohammedans.'

4. Omichand. Long, *Selections*, p. 87 (*Select Committee's Proceedings*, 25 Feb. 1757).

Mr. Watts reported from Murshidabad Omichand's opinion of the English. He said that after living under English protection for forty years he had never known them break their word, and that if a lie was proved against them in England 'they were spit upon and never trusted'.

5. 1771. John Macdonald. *Travels in various parts of Europe, Asia and Africa*, p. 267.

The Mussulmans said to him, 'Mr. John, we like you, because God has given you a temper like a girl; we can do everything that we see you do . . .'

6. Sayed Ghulam Hussain Khan. *Seir Mutaqherin*, III, pp. 170-1.

He complains that the English are aloof and absorbed in their own concerns, and that they surround themselves with sycophants.

He speaks of 'the aversion which the English openly show for the company of the natives, and such is the disdain that they betray for them that no love and no coalition . . . can take root between conquerors and conquered'. (p. 161)

7. 1794. M. Williams, *Serampore Letters*, 15 Feb. 1794.

At Debarta in Bengal the villagers 'have kept from others because they think Englishmen worse than tigers'.

8. 1798. Mirza Abu Taleb Khan. *Travels*, ed. by C. Stewart, I, pp. 51-2.

'During this scene (a storm at sea) Mr. Grand, who was of enormous size, and whose cabin was separated from mine only by a canvas partition, fell with all his weight upon my breast, and hurt me excessively. What rendered this circumstance more provoking was, that if, by any accident, the smallest noise was made in my apartment, he would call out, with all the overbearing insolence which characterizes the vulgar part of the English in their conduct to Orientals, "What are you about? You don't let me get a wink of sleep!" and other such rude expressions.'

APPENDIX F

LIST OF RECORDS, MANUSCRIPTS AND PRINTED BOOKS CONSULTED

I. MANUSCRIPT LETTERS AND PRIVATE PAPERS

In the India Office Library

Bengal Despatches.
Bengal Public Consultations.
Bombay Despatches.
Bombay Letters Received.
Madras Letters Received.
Home Miscellaneous Series. (765 vols.)
Factory Miscellaneous Series. (26 vols.)
European Inhabitants in India.
Europeans in India. (25 vols.)
Bengal Inventories. (1755-80)
Bengal Mayor's Court Proceedings (For Wills).
Orme Papers, 28.
Letters of Major J. Rennell to the Rev. A. Burrington 1761-78. *Home Miscellaneous Series.*
Letters of C. Martin and J. Duncan to Col. A. Ross 1786-1811. *Home Miscellaneous Series*, 741.
Diary of Col. Champion 1764-66. *Home Miscellaneous Series*, 198.
Lord Macartney's Correspondence. *Home Miscellaneous Series*, 246.
Letters to Lee Harcourt at Tellicherry. *Factory Miscellaneous Records*, vol. 26.

In the Imperial Record Office, Calcutta

Original Law Consultations (Legislative Dept.), 1794-1810.
Home Miscellaneous Series.

In the British Museum

Warren Hastings General Correspondence—Brit. Museum Additional Manuscripts.
Journal of Col. Upton 1775-6—Brit. Museum Additional Manuscripts.
Journal of a Voyage to the East Indies 1704-5—Brit. Museum Additional Manuscripts.

II. PRINTED RECORDS, COMPILATIONS OF AND SELECTIONS FROM RECORDS

Sundry Book of 1680-1. Hughli Letters sent. Ed. H. Dodwell (*Records of Fort St. George*) 1913.
Sundry Book of 1686. Affairs in Bengal. (*Records of Fort St. George*) Madras, 1913.
Sundry Book of 1758-9. The Siege of Madras. (*Records of Fort St. George*) Madras, 1915.

Selections from the Public Consultations, and Letters from Fort St. David and St. George, 1740. (*Records of Fort St. George*) Madras, 1916.

S. C. Hill. *List of Europeans and others in Bengal in 1756 at the time of the Siege of Calcutta.* Calcutta, 1902.

C. R. Wilson, *Old Fort William in Bengal*, 2 vols. *Indian Record Series*, 1906.

C. R. Wilson, *Early Annals of the English in Bengal*, 4 vols. London, 1895.

J. Long, *Selections from the Unpublished Records of the Government*, etc., Calcutta, 1869.

H. D. Love, *Vestiges of Old Madras*, 3 vols.

J. T. Wheeler, *Madras in the Olden Time*, 3 vols.

III. TRAVELS, VOYAGES AND DESCRIPTIONS

Fra. P. de San Bartolomeo, *Voyage to the East Indies* 1776-89. 1792.

F. Bernier, *Travels in the Mogul Empire*, 1656-1668. Oxford, 1891.

C. Biron, *Curiositez de la Nature et de l'art*, etc. Paris, 1703.

D. Campbell, *Journey Overland to India* (1781-84). 1796.

J. Capper, *Observations on the Passage to India.* London, 1784.

Rev. J. Cordiner, *A Voyage to India.* 1820.

Capt. H. Cornwall, *Observations on several Voyages.* London, 1720.

C. Cossigny, *Voyage au Bengal, etc., en* 1789. 2 vols. Paris, 1799.

D'Oyley, Williamson and Blagdon. *The European in India.* 1813.

C. Duquesne, *New Voyage to the East Indies*, 1690-1. London, 1696.

W. Francklin, *Observations made on a Tour from Bengal to Persia*, 1786-7. London, 1790.

J. Fryer, *A New Account of East India and Persia.* 3 vols. Hakluyt Society. London, 1909.

M. L. J. O'Hier de Grandpré, *Voyage in the Indian Ocean and to Bengal.* (Eng. trans.) 1814.

T. Grose, *Voyage to the East Indies*, 2 vols. 1774.

Alex. Hamilton, *A New Account of the East Indies*, 2 vols. British Museum copy.

W. Hodges, R.A., *Travels in India*, 1782-5.

Eyles Irwin, *Voyage up the Red Sea, etc.* London, 1780.

E. Ives, *A Voyage to India.* 1754.

J. Johnson, *Oriental Voyages.* London, 1807.

Journal d'un Voyage aux Indes Orientales (1691-2). 3 vols. Rouen, 1721.

C. Lockyer, *An Account of the Trade in India.* 1711.

Sieur Luillier, *A Voyage to the East Indies.* London, 1720.

John Macdonald, *Travels in various Parts of Europe, Asia and Africa.* London, 1790.

James Macintosh, *Travels in Europe, Asia and Africa*, 1777-81, 2 vols. London, 1783.

Madras Dialogues—'The large and renouned town of Madras, etc.'. Halle, Saxony, 1750.

A. de Mandelslo, *Journey to Persia and the Indies.* 1669.

Mirza Abu Taleb Khan's Travels, 1799-1803, 3 vols. Edited by C. Stewart. London, 1814.

C. Niebuhr, *Journal of Travels to Arabia and the East.* French trans. Amsterdam and Utrecht.

C. Noble, *A Voyage to the East Indies*, 1747-8. London, 1762.

P. Oliver, *Voyage of F. Leguat* (Hakluyt Society). London, 1891.

Rev. T. Ovington, *A Voyage to Surat*, 1689. 1696. (References given are to the edition of H. G. Rawlinson. O.U.P., 1929.)

de Pagé, *Travels Round the World*, 1767-71, 3 vols. London, 1791.

A. Parsons, *Travels in Asia and Africa*. 1808.

Francisco Pelsaert, *Remonstrantie*. (Trans. by W. H. Moreland and P. Geyl as *Jehangir's India*.) Cambridge, 1925.

Bar. Plaisted, *Journal from Calcutta to Busserah*. London, 1757.

Sketches of India by an Officer. London, 1821.

M. Sonnerat, *A Voyage to the East Indies and China*, 1774-81, 3 vols. Calcutta, 1788.

J. S. Stavorinus, *Voyages to the East Indies*, 1768-78. Trans. by J. H. Wilcocke, 3 vols. London, 1798.

Capt. W. Symson, *A New Voyage to the East Indies*. 2nd edition, London, 1720.

Major J. Taylor, *Travels in India*, 1789, 2 vols. London, 1799.

Rev. E. Terry, *A Voyage to East India* (1616). London, 1777.

T. Twining, *Travels in India a Hundred Years Ago*. 1893.

Lord Valentia, *Travels in India*, 3 vols. 1806.

The Editor of the *Windham Papers*. *The Wellesley Papers*. 2 vols. London, 1914.

Thos. Williamson, *The East India Vade Mecum*, 2 vols. London, 1810.

Thos. Williamson, *Oriental Field Sports*, 2 vols. London, 1819.

IV. LETTERS, DIARIES, JOURNALS, NARRATIVES AND MEMOIRS

Major J. Blakiston, *Twelve Years Military Adventures in Hindustan* (1802-14). 1829.

The Cornwallis Correspondence, 3 vols.

Abbé Dubois, *Letters on the State of Christianity in India*. 1823.

Capt. G. Elers, *Memoirs*, edited by Lord Monson and G. Leveson-Gower (1797-1807). 1903.

Mrs. Fay, *Letters from India*.

Journal of Mrs. Fenton, 1826-30. 1901.

Fifteen Years in India, by an Officer (R. G. Wallace). 1819.

J. Forbes, *Oriental Memoirs*, 4 vols.

J. B. J. Gentil, *Memoires sur l'Hindustan*. 1822.

Seid Gholam Hossain Khan, *Seir Mutaqherin*, 4 vols. Calcutta, 1903.

Sophia Goldburne, *Hartley House, Calcutta*. 1789.

Maria Graham, *Journal of a Residence in India* (1809-1811). 2nd edition. London, 1813.

S. C. Grier, *Letters of Warren Hastings to his Wife*.

Private Journal of the Marquess Hastings, ed. by the Marchioness of Bute, 2 vols. London, 1858.

William Hickey, *Memoirs*, 4 vols.

J. Hough, *Reply to the Abbé Dubois' Letters on the State of Christianity in India*. 1824.

Journal of Gen. Sir Martin and Lady Hunter (1802-14). Ed. by Miss A. Hunter. 1894.

Victor de Jacquemmont, *Letters from India*, 2 vols. (1828-31). London, 1834.

Mrs. N. E. Kindersley, *Letters from the East Indies*. 1777.

La Farelle, *Memoires et Correspondence*. (Brit. Museum copy)

Le Couteur, *Letters from India*. 1790.
W. C. Macpherson, *Soldiering in India*, 1764-87. 1928.
N. Manucci, *Storia do Mogor*, ed. W. Irvine, 4 vols. 1908.
Henry Martyn, *Journals and Letters*, 2 vols. 1837.
Innes Munro, *Narrative of Military Operations on the Coromandel Coast in 1780*. 1789.
Maria, Lady Nugent, *Journal of a Residence in India*, 1811-15, 2 vols. London, 1839.
Observations on India (Anonymous). 1853.
Pester John, *War and Sport in India*, 1802-6. Ed. by J. A. Devenish. 1913.
Ananda Ranga Pillai, *Private Diary*, ed. by H. Dodwell, 10 vols. 1922-5.
P. D. Stanhope, *Genuine Memoirs of Asiaticus*.
Diaries of Streynsham Master, ed. by Sir R. Temple. *Indian Record Series*, 2 vols. 1911.
C. F. Swartz, *Remains and Journals*. 1826.
J. Taylor, *Letters on India*. (Camb. Univ. Library)
Rev. W. Tennant, *Indian Recreations*, 2 vols. Edinburgh, 1803.
A. Townley, *Reply to the Abbé Dubois' Letters on the State of Christianity in India*. 1824.
Mornay Williams, *Serampore Letters*. 1892.

V. BIOGRAPHIES

S. Pearce Carey, *Life of William Carey*. London, 1924.
Coupland, *Life of Wilberforce*. 1923.
T. Fisher, *Life of Charles Grant*. London, 1833.
Sir G. Forrest, *Life of Lord Clive*, 2 vols. London, 1918.
W. Francklin, *Military Memoirs of George Thomas*. London, 1805.
Baillie Fraser, *Military Memoirs of Col. James Skinner*. London, 1851.
S. C. Hill, *Life of Claud Martin*. Calcutta, 1901.
J. Kaye, *Life of Lord Metcalfe*, 3 vols.
C. B. Lewis, *Life of John Thomas*. 1873.
R. J. Mackintosh, *Memoirs of Sir J. Mackintosh* (1804-10), 2 vols. London, 1835.
J. Page, *Swartz of Tanjore*. London, 1921.
Col. H. Pearse, *The Hearsays*.
Rev. H. Pearson, *Memoirs of the Rev. C. Buchanan*, 2 vols. Oxford, 1817.
Rev. H. Pearson, *Memoirs of C. F. Swartz*. 1834.
Charles Simeon, *Memoir of the Rev. D. Brown*.
J. Sargent, *Memoir of the Rev. H. Martyn*. 1819.
Teignmouth, *Memoirs of the Life and Correspondence of Lord Teignmouth*, 2 vols. London. 1843.

VI. SECONDARY AUTHORITIES AND GENERAL WORKS

Allen and Maclure, *History of the S.P.C.K.*, 2 vols, 1908.
P. Anderson, *The English in Western India*. 1856.
W. A. J. Archbold, *Outlines of Indian Constitutional History*. London, 1925.
B. Bannerje, *Begam Samru*. (Sarkar & Sons) Calcutta, 1925.
A. Broome, *History of the Bengal Army*, I. 1851.

H. E. Busteed, *Echoes of Old Calcutta.* London, 1908.
W. H. Carey, *Good Old Days of the Hon. John Company.* Calcutta, 1906.
J. J. A. Campos, *History of the Portuguese in Bengal.* Calcutta, 1919.
Eyre Chatterton, *History of the Church of England in India.* London.
H. Compton, *Hindustan under the Freelances.* 1907.
Description of the Port and Island of Bombay. 1724.
D. Dewar, *Bygone India.* 1922.
H. H. Dodwell (ed.) *Cambridge History of India,* V.
H. H. Dodwell, *Nabobs of Madras.* 1926.
J. Douglas, *Bombay and Western India,* I. 1893.
S. M. Edwardes, *The Rise of Bombay.* 1902.
Elliott and Dowson, *History of India as told by its Own Historians,* VI London, 1872.
C. C. Grey and H. L. O. Garrett, *European Adventurers in Northern India.* Lahore, 1929.
Rev. W. H. Hart, *Old Calcutta.* Calcutta, 1895.
J. M. Holtzman, *The Nabobs in England,* 1760-5. New York, 1926.
Sir W. W. Hunter, *Annals of Rural Bengal.*
H. B. Hyde, *The Parish of Bengal.* Calcutta, 1899.
H. B. Hyde, *Parochial Annals of Bengal.* Calcutta, 1901.
The Indo Briton. Bombay, 1849.
H. G. Keene, *The Fall of the Moghul Empire.* 1876.
N. N. Law, *Promotion of Learning in India by Europeans till* 1800. London, 1915.
Dr. J. Lind, *An Essay on Diseases, etc.* London, 1768.
Firoz Malabari, *Bombay in the Making.* 1910.
M. E. Monckton Jones, *Warren Hastings in Bengal* 1772-5. 1918.
L. S. S. O'Malley, *The Indian Civil Service,* 1601-1930. London, 1931.
R. Orme, *History of the Military Transactions of the British Nation in Hindustan,* 2 vols. 1780.
Rev. F. Penny, *The Church in Madras,* 3 vols. 1904.
J. Richter, *History of Missions in India.* 1908.
E. T. Sandys, 145 *Years at the Old Mission Church, Calcutta.* (In *Bengal Past and Present,* VIII)
Hon. F. J. Shore, *Notes on Indian Affairs,* 2 vols. 1857.
A. Stark, *Hostages to India.* Calcutta, 1926.
L. H. Thornton, *Light and Shade in Bygone India,* 1927.
Col. W. J. Wilson, *History of the Madras Army,* 4 vols. 1882.
A. Wright, *Early English Adventurers in the East.* 1917.
A. Wright and W. L. Sclater, *Sterne's Eliza* (1757-74). London, 1922.

VII. REFERENCE BOOKS

The Bengal Obituary. 1848.
Castellani and Chambers, *Manual of Tropical Medicine.* London, 1910.
D. Dewar, *Handbook of the Records of the United Provinces.* 1919.
F. H. Garrison, *History of Medicine.* London, 1917.
Handbook of the Bombay Government Records, by A. F. Kindersley Bombay, 1921.
Handbook to the Records of the Government of India, 1748-55. Calcutta 1925.

S. C. Hill, *Catalogue of MSS. in European Languages*, II. (*The Orme Papers*) Oxford, 1916.

Hobson-Jobson, by Col. Yule and A. C. Burnell, Ed. by W. Crooke. London, 1903.

Indian Monumental Inscriptions, II. Lahore, 1910.

Madras Monuments, etc., compiled by J. J. Cotton. Madras, 1905.

Dictionary of National Biography.

Sir G. Watt, *Dictionary of Economic Products of India*. London, 1890.

VIII. NEWSPAPERS

Seton-Kerr, *Selections from the Calcutta Gazettes*, 1784-1823, 5 vols. 1864.

The Madras Courier, 1790-2. (British Museum)

The India Gazette, 1782-5. (British Museum)

Hickey's Journal, 1780-2. (British Museum)

IX. PRINTS, DRAWINGS, etc.

Calcutta and its Environs—lithos from Sir C. D'Oyley's Drawings (1800 30). London, 1848.

D'Oyley, Williamson and Blagdon, *The European in India*. 1813.

Thos. Daniels, *Oriental Scenery*, two series. London, 1795 and 1797.

Fraser's *Views of Calcutta*. 1824-5.

Capt. R. M. Grindlay, *Views in Bombay and Ceylon* (1810-20). London, 1826.

Salt's *Views in Egypt, Abyssinia, India, etc.* London, 1809.

Island of Bombay and the Vicinity, Twelve Views (1791-2). J. Wales. London, 1803.

Punjab Notes and Queries.

Bengal Past and Present.

INDEX

[Important topics discussed in the text are printed in small capitals.]